Operating System

Operating System

Concepts and Techniques

"First edition"

M. Naghibzadeh

Professor of Computer Engineering

iUniverse, Inc.

New York Lincoln Shanghai

OPERATING SYSTEM
CONCEPTS AND TECHNIQUES

iUniverse books may be ordered through booksellers or by contacting:

iUniverse
1663 Liberty Drive
Bloomington, IN 47403
www.iuniverse.com
1-800-Authors (1-800-288-4677)

ISBN: 978-0-5953-7597-4 (sc)
ISBN: 978-0-5958-1992-8 (ebk)

Printed in the United States of America

iUniverse rev. date: 10/13/2011

Contents

Preface

Computers are widely employed in almost all the activities of today's modern man. They are used by people of all ages in a variety of environments. We recognize the computer as a set of devices, such as the main case, monitor, keyboard, mouse, etc., collectively called the hardware. In one session's work with the computer, we turn it on, wait a few seconds until it is ready for use, and then start asking the operating system to run our program of choice. Therefore, it is correct to assume that every computer has an operating system.

The Operating System (OS) is the most essential program of all without which it becomes absolutely cumbersome to work with a computer. It is the interface between the hardware and us (i.e., the computer users), making it much easier and more pleasant to use the hardware. Familiarizing ourselves with the operating system and its services helps us to utilize the computer in a more effective manner and to do our jobs well. With this in mind, we need to know the operating system's services and how to make use of them. The operating system itself has to be written so that it can exploit the hardware in the most efficient way possible. Much effort has been put into this matter. Since the computer was invented in the 1940s, many scientists have strived to make this software user-friendly and efficient for the operation of the hardware. The net result is truly a masterpiece that utilizes a multitude of innovations and the fruit of much hard work.

There are tens of operating systems of different sizes and brands, and hundreds of books instructing us how to use them. Also, many innovators and authors have written books on explaining the design concepts of the operating system. The expected readers of the latter are operating system professionals and university students that are taking courses about similar subjects.

In this book, we first discuss a less clarified aspect of the operating system, namely the way the operating system takes over the hardware and becomes the real internal owner of the computer. This knowledge, plus a macro view of what the operating system does and how it does it, provides an insight and advantage to make better use of the overall facilities of the computer. It also provides the basis for a more comprehensive understanding of the complex aspects of the operating system. Then, we elaborate on concepts, methods, and techniques that are employed in the design of operating systems.

This book is for everyone who is using a computer but is still not at ease with the way the operating system manages programs and available resources in order to perform requests correctly and speedily. High school and university students will benefit the most as they are the ones who turn to computers for all sorts of activities, including email, Internet, chat, education, programming, research, playing games etc. Students would like to know more about the program that helps out (in the background) to making everything flow naturally. It is especially beneficial for university students of Information Technology, Computer Science and Computer Engineering. In my opinion, this book must definitely be read by students taking an operating systems course. It gives a clear description on how advanced concepts were first invented and how they are now implemented in modern operating systems. Compared to other university text books on similar subjects, this book is downsized by eliminating lengthy discussions on subjects that only have historical value.

In Chapter One, a simplified model of computer hardware is presented. We refrained from including any detail that is not directly related to our goals. The fetch-execute cycle of performing instructions is described in this chapter.

In Chapter Two, the role of Basic Input Output System (BIOS) in initial system checking and the operating system boot process is explained. The layered view of the operating system is elaborated on. Kernel (the essential part or the seed of the operating system) and its role in helping fulfill the needs of other layers of the operating system and computer users are talked about. Another important issue called computer security and protection is briefly explained.

Chapter Three describes the reasons behind multiprogramming, multitasking, multiprocessing, and multithreading. The most fundamental requirements for facilitating these techniques are also discussed in this chapter. A brief discussion on process states, the state transition diagram, and direct memory access is provided. The basic foundations of multithreading methodology and its similarities and dissimilarities to multiprogramming are highlighted.

Chapter Four is about processes. Important questions are answered in this chapter, such as: What is a process? Why and how is a process created? What information do we need to keep for the management of every process? How is a process terminated? What is the relationship between a child process and its parent process? When is a process terminated? A short discussion is included on the properties of process-based operating systems. The real-life scenarios of this chapter are based on the UNIX operating system which is a process-based operating system. This chapter emphasizes the process as the only living entity of process-based operating systems. Possible state transitions of processes are discussed and the role of the operating system in each transition is explained.

Chapter Five focuses on threads. Despite the existence of processes, the reason for using threads is explained along with its relation to processes. Some operating systems are thread-based. Kernel functions of this kind of operating system are performed by a set of threads. In addition, a primary thread is generated as soon as a process is created. Other questions are studied in this chapter, like: What is a thread? Why and how is a thread created? What information do we need to manage every thread? How is a thread terminated? What is the relationship between a child thread and its parent? When is a thread terminated? Examples are taken from the Windows Operating System. Possible state transitions of threads are discussed and the role of the operating system in each transition is explained.

Scheduling is the subject of Chapter Six. It is one of the most influential concepts in the design of efficient operating systems. First, related terms: request time, processing time, priority, deadline, wait time, preemptability are defined here. Next, scheduling objectives are discussed: maximizing throughput, meeting deadlines, reducing average turnaround time, reducing average response time, respecting priorities, maximizing process utilization, balancing system, and being fair. Four categories of scheduling, namely high level, medium level, low level, and I/O scheduling, are distinguished. Many algorithms used in scheduling processes in single processor environments are investigated. They include: first come first served, shortest job next, shortest remaining time next, highest response ratio next, fair-share, and round robin. Most of these scheduling algorithms are also usable in multiprocessor environments. Gang-scheduling is also examined for multiprocessor systems. Intelligent rate-monotonic and earliest deadline first algorithms are widely utilized algorithms in the scheduling of real-time systems. These schedulers are introduced in this chapter. The case studies presented in this chapter are based on the Linux operating system.

Chapter Seven investigates memory management policies. It briefly introduces older policies like single contiguous partition, static partition, dynamic partition, and segmentation memory management. Other non-virtual memory management policies are discussed next. Relocatable partition memory management and page memory management are the two subjects covered in this subsection. The emphasis of the chapter is on virtual memory management policies. Above all is the page-based virtual memory management policy that is followed by almost all modern operating systems. A good portion of this section is devoted to page removal algorithms. The page table of large programs takes a great deal of memory space. We have presented multi-level page table organization as a method for making the application of virtual memory techniques to page tables possible. Windows uses a two-level page table and this model is investigated in detail, as a case study of the multi-level page table policy. We carefully studied address translation techniques that are an essential part of any page memory management as well as demand-page memory management policies. Both internal and external fragmentations are looked into. At the end of the chapter, a complementary section on cache memory management is featured. Real-life techniques presented in this chapter are based on the UNIX operating system.

Processes that run concurrently compete for computer resources. Every process likes to grab its resources at the earliest possible time. A mediator has to intervene to resolve conflicts. This mediator is the interprocess communication/synchronization subsystem of the operating system. Race condition, critical region, and mutual exclusion concepts are first defined. It has been found that by guaranteeing mutual exclusion, conflict-free resource sharing becomes possible. Methods to achieve this are categorized into five classes, namely disabling interrupt, busy-wait-based, semaphore-based, monitor-based, and message-based methods. We have covered these approaches to process communication/synchronization in Chapter Eight.

Deadlock is an undesirable side effect of guaranteeing mutual exclusion. This concept is explained and the ways of dealing with deadlock are discussed. Ignoring deadlock, deadlock prevention, deadlock avoidance, and deadlock detection and recovery are four approaches discussed in Chapter Nine. Another less important side effect is starvation. The dinning philosophers' dilemma, as a classic example of interprocess communication problem, is defined. It is shown that straightforward solutions may cause deadlock and starvation. We have provided an acceptable deadlock and starvation-free solution to this problem. In this context, the concept of starvation is elucidated.

Student enthusiasm was the motivation behind adding a new chapter to this version of the book. Chapter Ten discusses management policies for persistent information or what is usually called file systems. The efficient organization of information on disks plays a critical role in every operating system. For this purpose, numerous file systems have been designed and implemented. In this chapter, the fundamental issues on these topics are presented. Two very popular file systems, the UNIX file system and the Windows new technology file system, are studied. The Linux File System which is based on the Berkeley Fast File System, an improved version of the UNIX File System, is also briefly explored.

Chapter Eleven is dedicated to operating system categorization and an introduction to new methodologies in operating system design. With the advances in software technology, operating system design and implementation have advanced, too. In this respect, monolithic operating systems, structured operating systems, object-oriented operating systems, and agent-based operating systems are distinguished. Based on the acting entities, operating systems are categorized as process-based, thread-based and agent-based. The differences of these categories are highlighted in this chapter. The kernel is an important part of every operating system. We have differentiated among macro-kernel, microkernel, and extensible kernels. Extensible kernel design is a new research subject and much effort is going into producing commercial extensible kernels. One more categorization parameter is the hardware structure on which an operating system sits. The platform could be single-processor, multiprocessor, distributed system, or the Internet. Properties of the corresponding operating systems are described. Real-time systems require special operating systems in order to provide the quality of service necessary for these environments. Real-time and non-real-time operating systems are the last topics that are investigated in this chapter.

I would like to express my gratitude to my wife, son, and daughter for their encouragement and patience. Their support made the writing of this book a pleasant task for me. In addition, I would like to thank Victoria Balderrama for her assistance in proofreading the text.

M. Naghibzadeh
Winter 2011

Chapter 1

Computer Hardware Organization

A computer is composed of a set of hardware modules properly connected together to interact in such a way that the total system is reliable and performs its duty in a correct manner. The operating system sits on top of the computer hardware. It uses hardware facilities to provide an efficient platform for running programs and managing resources and users. To understand the operating system, it is very helpful if a simplified view of the hardware is described first. Going into the details of modules and circuits is not necessary and doing so will divert our attention from our main purposes.

A computer is a device that runs programs. A **program** is a set of instructions that is prepared to do a specific job. Different programs are written to do different jobs. This makes a computer able to do different things for us. A program is normally stored on a disk. This may be a Hard Disk (HD), Compact Disc (CD), flash memory, etc., but it has to be in the computer's Main Memory (MM) in order to run. The main memory of a computer is usually called **Random Access Memory** (RAM)- see side textbox. As soon as a program is ready for running it is no longer called program, rather, it is called a **process**. We, however, will not be choosy and, in this chapter, will use program and process interchangeably.

> Main memory is called *random access* because the access time of all locations is the same. It does not matter whether the location in the memory is at the beginning, at the end, or anywhere in between.

What brings the program to the main memory? Of course, another program called the *loader*, with the help of the Operating System (OS). Using a computer language, programs are written by human programmers. These programs have to be translated to a computer friendly language that is usually called **machine language**. What performs the translation? Once again, a program called the *translator*, with the help of the operating system, does this. Therefore, the operating system is the focal point of all activities within every computer.

1.1 The Fetch-Execute Cycle

As soon as the computer is turned on, it reads an instruction from the RAM and moves it to a temporary place called the **Instruction Register** (IR) in the **Central Processing Unit** (CPU). The computer then finds out what has to be done with respect to this instruction and performs the actions. It repeats this cycle of moving an instruction from the main memory to the CPU and executing it over and over again until it is turned off. A more detailed course of action for a computer is shown in Figure 1.1.

In Figure 1.1, the PC is the register that keeps track of what instruction has to be executed next. The PC is automatically filled with an initial value when the computer is started and thereafter it is updated as shown in the figure. Instructions come from a program that is currently being executed. Within a program, when an instruction is executed, the next instruction to be **fetched** is most likely the one immediately following. However, this is not always the case. Look at the piece of program below that is written in a **pseudo code** format.

> In some texts, the PC is called the *Location counter* (LC), but when distinction is necessary, we will use LC when talking about a pointer that points to the next instruction of the current program and PC when we mean the *register* within the CPU that holds the current program's LC. A *register* is a temporary small memory within the CPU.

> A *pseudo-code* is an algorithm (or piece of algorithm) expressed in a simplified language similar to that of a programming language, but is not an actual *program*.

```
1.   If   A > B
2.      then   print A
3.         else    print B
4.   endif
```

Here, we would like the computer to either execute instruction 2 or instruction 3, but not both. There must be a way to jump over instruction 2 when we do not want to execute it. This is actually done by a jump instruction. The execution of a jump instruction is to change the content of the PC to the **address** of the next instruction that has to be executed. The action is needed when the physical instruction order cannot be followed for this time's running the program.

To *fetch* an instruction is to bring the instruction from the main memory to the CPU's *instruction register* and performing some preliminary actions like *adjusting* PC and *decoding* the instruction (i.e., finding out what operation it is.) Fetch may also be used for bringing a datum from main memory to one of the CPU's registers.

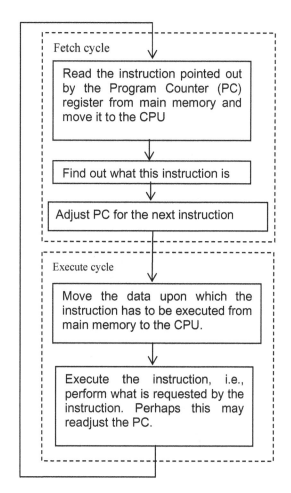

Figure 1.1: A simplified functional model of a computer hardware

The model presented in Figure 1.1 is for a sequential computer, that is, roughly speaking, a computer with one general processing unit called the CPU. There are other computers called multiprocessor computers that are much faster than sequential computers and can execute more than one instruction simultaneously. Most of the computers that we are currently using, such as personal and laptop computers, are of the multiprocessor type. However, each processor executes the same fetch-execute cycle shown in Figure 1.1.

The fetch-execute cycle of the simplified model of a computer hardware is completed after the possibility of interrupting the cycle and switching to execute another task is considered. This will be explained in Chapter 3.

During the execution of a program, instructions and data are taken from main memory; therefore, it is necessary to have these ready beforehand. This technique is called **stored-program concept** and was first documented by John Von Neumann. According to this concept, programs, data, and results are stored in the same memory, as opposed to separate memories. The innovation of stored-program concept was a giant step forward in advancing the field of computer science and technology from punched cards to fast reusable memories.

The central processing unit of a computer is composed of the **Arithmetic Logic Unit** (ALU), the **Control Unit** (CU), special registers, and temporary memories. The ALU is the collection of all circuitry that performs arithmetic and logic operations such as addition, multiplication, comparison, and logical "AND." The CU is responsible for the interpretation of every instruction, the designation of little steps that have to be taken to carry out the instruction, and the actual activation of circuitries to do each step. We have already used special registers. Two of which are the instruction register and the program counter. There are other registers for holding current instruction's results, program status, and so on. There are also one or more sets of registers that are reserved to be used by the program that is **running**, (or being executed). Data that is needed frequently, or will be needed in the near future, can be kept in these registers. This way, we save time by not sending them back and forth to the main memory. **Cache memory** is also an essential part of current computers. It is a relatively large temporary memory that can store a good portion of a program's data and instructions that are actually copies of the same data and instructions that reside in the main memory. This is a faster memory than the main memory but usually slower than CPU registers.

1.2 Computer Hardware Organization

Within every computer there are many hardware devices. The control unit, arithmetic-logic unit, cache memory, and main memory are basic internal devices. Other devices are either installed internally or as external devices. All of the latter devices collectively form the Input/Output Unit (IOU) of the computer. Figure 1.2 illustrates a hardware model of a **general-purpose computer**. Only essential connections are shown in this figure. Dark connections are for data or address transfer and light connections are for control purposes.

A general-purpose computer is able to run different programs. Therefore, it can perform variety of tasks and it is not restricted to doing one (or very few) tasks. On the other hand, we can think of **special-purpose computers**. A special-purpose computer is designed and built to be used in a specific environment and do one or a few specific tasks, efficiently. In this kind of computer, the program that it runs does not change very often.

In reality, all modules of a computer are connected via an internal bus. The bus can be viewed as a three-lane highway, with each lane assigned to a specific use. One lane is for transferring data, another for transferring addresses and the third for control signals.

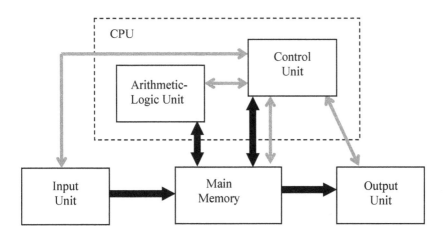

Figure 1.2: Computer organization model

We all know what data is. 123 is a datum, "John" is a datum, etc. If a datum/instruction is needed from the main memory, the requesting device must supply the address in the main memory. The same is true for storing a datum/instruction in the main memory.

Addresses travel via the address bus. An address is the identity of a location in the main memory. To access the main memory we must supply the location to be accessed. This is the essential property of contemporary main memories.

In a computer every single micro-activity is performed under the control and supervision of the control unit. The control unit commands are sent through the control bus. For its decision-making, the control unit collects information

> Every *byte (collection of cells)* in the main memory is given an *address* that facilitates referring to that byte. Addressing starts from zero, which is assigned to the first byte of the memory. By giving consecutive integers to consecutive locations, addressing continues up to the last location of main memory.

from almost all devices that are connected to the computer. For example, a command should not be sent to a device that is not turned on. The control unit must make sure the device is ready to accept the command. Such information is collected from the device itself.

The majority of computer devices are not directly connected to the computer's internal bus. A device is inserted in a **port** that is connected to the bus. There are mechanisms for possessing the address bus and data bus, otherwise data and addresses from different devices could become mixed up. A model of the bus-based computer organization is shown in Figure 1.3.

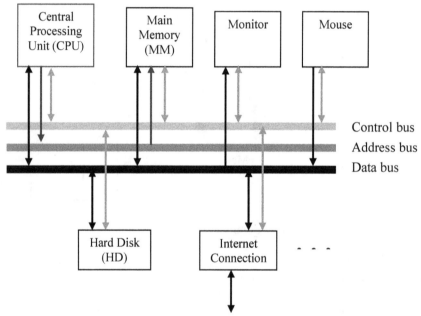

Figure 1.3: Bus-based computer organization

Some devices are placed on the mainboard of the computer, others, have to be installed before use. The mouse, diskette device, light pen, etc. are some of the latter devices. Installing a device involves registering the device with the operating system and providing a **device driver** for communication between the device and other parts of the computer. The installation process is started either automatically by the operating system itself or manually by the user. Today's operating systems are intelligent; and once the computer is turned on, the OS recognizes almost all types of newly connected hardware devices and immediately begins the installation process. Therefore, a device for which the installation process starts automatically by the operating system and which usually does not require any human intervention, is called a **plug-and-play device**. Few hardware devices have the user manually initiate the installation process. If this is the case, then the OS will interact with the user to complete the process.

> A *driver* is a piece of software (program) that is used as an interface between a hardware device and its external world. It is usually designed by the device manufacturer in such a way that the device is used in a highly efficient and appropriate way. This is a good reason for using the manufacturer's provided driver. Operating systems have drivers for almost all devices however, due to these driver's generality, they may not work as efficiently and as fast as the manufacturer's provided drivers.

Without any software, the computer is called a bare machine, having the potential to perform many functions but no ability to do so in its present state. We will add other features, in a layered fashion, to make our computer handy and user friendly. The current view of our abstracted computer is shown in Figure 1.3.

```
┌─────────────────┐
│    Computer     │
│    Hardware     │
│  (Bare Machine) │
└─────────────────┘
```

Figure 1.3: A bare machine

1.3 Summary

From the hardware point of view, a computer is composed of a set of devices, each intended to perform a specific program. The modular design of computer systems has made the task of constructing it much easier and more reliable compared with the monolithic design method. Nevertheless, the design of a computer system is so complex that understanding it requires a certain background including many university courses. In any case, knowledge of all hardware details is not needed to comprehend how an operating system is designed and how it uses hardware facilities to help run programs correctly and efficiently. A simple understanding of computer hardware is absolutely necessary to cover topics in the coming chapters. The fetch-execute cycle explains the microinstructions involved in executing each machine instruction and the many devices and circuits involved in the execution of instructions. This knowledge is immensely helpful for comprehending how programs are executed and how program switching is done. A global organization for computer hardware provides a basis for all kinds of communication among the essential modules of the system.

1.4 Problems

1. The processor checks for an interrupt at the start of each fetch cycle (or at the end of each execute cycle). If there is an unmasked interrupt, the processor has to handle the interrupt(s) first, before fetching the next instruction. Modify the first part of Figure 1.1 so that it reflects this notion.

2. In the fetch-execute cycle, in order to adjust the PC for the next instruction, the length of current instruction, expressed in bytes, is added to the PC. Categorize your computer's processor instructions based on their length.

3. What are the benefits of adjusting the PC register during the fetch cycle even though we have to readjust it during the execute cycle for some instructions?

4. For a processor that uses two different segments, i.e., the code segment and data segment for instructions and data, respectively, how would you explain the stored-program concept?

5. Explain the advantages and disadvantages of bus-based organization versus point to point connection.

6. Suppose you have just bought a new personal computer. No operating system is installed on it and you are supposed to do this. Is it presently a bare machine? If not, what software does it have and for what purposes?

7. Suppose that your computer is a 32-bit one. Some instructions have no operand and some have one operand field. The operand field is 24 bits long and it can have an immediate value such as 2958 or an address of a datum in main memory.

a. What is the maximum memory size that your computer can directly address (without using a base register)?

b. Now suppose from these 24 bits, one bit is used for a base register. If the content of this bit is zero, the base register is not used. On the other hand, if it is one a base register is used. The base register is 32 bits long. An effective address in this case is the contents of the base register plus the contents of the remaining 23 bits of the address field. Now, if the address bus is 32 bits wide, what is the maximum memory size that your computer's processor can directly address?

Recommended References

The concept of stored program was developed by J. Von Neumann, J. Presper Eckert, John Mauchly, Arthur Burks, and others following the design of the ENIAC computer [Bur63]. There are many resources about computer organizations and architecture, among which John P. Hayes [Hay02], William Stalling [Sta05], and H. A. Farhat [Far03] have written excellent books on the subjects covered in this chapter.

Chapter 2

The BIOS and Boot Process

The main memory, cache memory, and internal registers of the CPU are supposed to be volatile. The information that is stored in these devices is lost when the computer's power is turned off. From the previous chapter, we learned that a computer is a device that fetches the instruction from main memory which the PC register points to. The computer then executes the instruction. This cycle is repeated over and over again until the computer is turned off. However, if we have only **volatile** memories, there is no instruction in the main memory when the computer is turned on. To overcome this problem, a program is designed and stored in a special memory called the **Read Only Memory** (ROM) and it is installed into the computer's motherboard (sometimes called the main-board). This program is called the **Basic Input Output System** (BIOS). When the computer is turned on, an address is automatically loaded into the PC register. This is done by hardware circuitry. The address given is the location of a jump instruction to the BIOS POST. For a four giga bytes memory this hexadecimal address is usually fffffff0 but the hardware will provide a proper address for memories of size less than 4 giga bytes. The

Volatile is a term for a storage device whose contents are lost when its power is turned off. Volatile storage can be made non-volatile by connecting it to a battery. However, this is not an assumption during the computer's design. Devices like magnetic disks and compact discs, on the other hand, are *non-volatile*.

The *Motherboard* is a platform ready for insertion of all the internal devices of the computer. It has many ports which are necessary for connecting external devices to the computer. In simplified terms, we can think of it as the computer bus.

A *read-only memory (ROM)* is a non-volatile memory which, for our interest, is filled with the BIOS program by the manufacturer. There are many varieties of ROMs with similar functionality.

journey starts from there. Although BIOSs are produced by many factories, but they all perform the same basic functions.

2.1 BIOS Actions

The following is a list of actions that are partially done automatically and partially by the computer user, right after the computer is turned on:
- Power-On Self Test
- BIOS manufacturer's logo display
- CMOS and setup modifications

2.1.1 Power-On Self Test

The **Power-On Self Test** (POST) is an important part of any BIOS. After the computer is turned on, the POST takes over controlling the system. Before the computer can proceed to execute any normal program, the POST checks to make sure every immediately required devices are connected and functional. In this stage, the main memory, monitor, keyboard, the first floppy drive, the first hard disk drive, the first Compact Disc (CD), and any other device from which the OS can be *booted* are checked. A beeping sound will inform the user if something is wrong. A speaker does not have to be connected to the computer in order to hear this sound. As this sound occurs before any audio system could have been installed. The beep comes from an internal primitive speaker within the computer.

2.1.2 BIOS Manufacturer's Logo

At the earliest possible moment after the POST process, the BIOS manufactures' logo will be displayed on the monitor. There are many factories that produce BIOSs: Compaq, Phoenix, Intel, IBM, and Award plus a long list of others. Depending on the brand of BIOS that is installed on your computer's motherboard, different logos and manufacturer information will appear on the display.

CMOS and Setup Modifications

The date and time that we may see on our monitor comes from a part of the BIOS called the CMOS BIOS. The CMOS stands for **Complementary Metal Oxide Semiconductor** memory. This is one of the technologies used to make the CPU, Dynamic RAM and other chips of the computer. It is a **Read/Write** (RW) **memory** as opposed to a read only memory. The possibility of a setup/modify

CMOS is required in order to be able to change things such as date and time in the BIOS. Remember that there are many reasons why we might need to change these data, e.g., using local date and time in different parts of the world. CMOS BIOS is connected to a small durable battery that works for many years.

At this stage, the system will let you define and/or change CMOS settings. There are many possibilities and options that are categorized below. As seen, the list is reasonably long indicating we can store a large amount of information within CMOS. One interesting aspect of CMOS is that a checksum of all the information within CMOS is also stored in CMOS. Checksum

> Despite the large amount of information that can be stored in the *CMOS BIOS*, its size is small, usually around 64 bytes. CMOS technology is an energy efficient technology, i.e., it uses very little electric energy. CMOS is, therefore, a Non-Volatile Random Access Memory (NVRAM).

is a summarization of all the information in CMOS. If an error occurs and some data is corrupted, the system will recognize this from the checksum. When we make changes to CMOS during the setup, the checksum is recalculated to represent the new state and then restored within CMOS. The following is a brief list of setup/modifications possible with the CMOS:

- Setup/modify date, time and floppy and hard drive properties
- Setup/modify the order in which non-volatile devices (floppy, hard, CD, etc.) can be used for bringing the OS to main memory
- Setup/modify power management allowing the monitor and disk drives to be turned off when they are not in use for a long time. This is to conserve energy. These devices will automatically turn back on with the first activity of a user that needs the device
- Setup/modify on-board serial and parallel ports, which are used for connecting peripheral devices
- Setup/modify the user password. One user may be assigned as the administrator of the computer. He/she has a password to setup/modify CMOS data. Other users are prevented from entering the CMOS setup/modify program.

We now have a computer with BIOS that can start, check itself, permit the setup/modify of essential properties, etc. Therefore, our view of the overall system must be modified, accordingly. Figure 2.1 illustrates the current view.

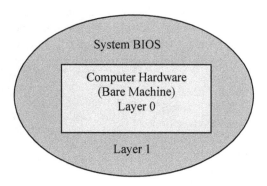

Figure 2.1: A two-layer machine with system BIOS

Figure 2.1 shows the first step of a layered operating system design. This concept is defined in the first multiprogramming operating system called "THE". THE" is the basis of most modern operating systems e.g., UNIX and Windows. The "THE" operating system utilized two very important concepts, namely the hierarchical operating system design and the concept of multiprogramming. The designer of "THE" operating system is Edsger W. Dijkstra who was one of the operating system design pioneers.

2.2 The Operating System Boot Process

One of the functions of the BIOS is to start the process of loading the operating system. The OS is a giant program that cannot be stored in a small ROM memory. Despite this, we would like our computer to be flexible so that we are able to run any operating system we like. Therefore, the OS has to be installed after the computer is purchased. The operating system is usually stored on one or more CDs and must be transferred to

> To *Load* is to bring a program to the main memory and prepare it for execution. In other contexts, it may also mean filling a register with a data, instruction, or address.
>
> *Compaction* is the process of transforming a file into a format that requires less space, while preserving the integrity of the information. The file must be expanded before being used by the corresponding software.

main memory in order to become functional. Hard disk drives are much faster than CD drives, so we prefer to first permanently transfer the OS from the CD to the hard disk. This will save a tremendous amount of time in future OS usage. The process of transferring the entire OS from a CD to a hard disk while expanding compressed files and initializing the whole system for use is called **OS installation**. Under some circumstances, for example, when we have already installed an OS and want to install a second one, it is possible to load the OS source from a CD to a hard disk and then start the proper program to do the installation. As seen, either the OS performs the self-installation process or a previously installed OS helps to install a new one.

For a moment, let's examine an ordinary automobile. It is manufactured to carry a driver and other passengers from one location to another. It has four wheels, one engine, one chassis, two or more seats, etc. However, all ordinary automobiles are not the same. Some are small, large, safe, dangerous, expensive, or cheap. Some are designed well and yet others are poorly designed. Similarly, not all operating systems are designed the same and there are variety of operating systems. BIOS does not know all the properties and details of the operating system that is to be loaded. Therefore, BIOS only starts the process of loading the OS and then transfers control to the OS itself which completes the process. This sounds reasonable. BIOS must at least know where the operating system is located. Is it on one or more floppy disks, on a hard disk, on one or more CDs, etc.?

An **Initial Program Load** (IPL) device is a device that may have an operating system, like CD or hard disk. A device that contains the operating system, and from which the OS can be loaded, is called a **bootable device**. If you remember, the order in which non-volatile bootable devices are used to load the OS can be defined or modified by the user during BIOS setup. There is an IPL table and an IPL priority vector for this purpose in the BIOS CMOS. The table lists all recognized bootable devices and the vector states the order in which they have to be checked during the boot process.

Suppose that a CD drive is defined as the first *bootable device*. If there is a bootable in the designated CD drive the OS will be booted from this CD. Otherwise, the next bootable device from the ordered list is checked. This process continues until either the OS can be booted or there is no other device to check. In the latter case, an error message will be displayed by BIOS.

The BIOS will load only one block of data from the first valid bootable device to the main memory. This block of data is taken from a specific and fixed place of the bootable device and is put in a specific and fixed place of main memory (usually address 0x7c00). The size of the data is usually 512 bytes and is usually taken from block zero of track zero of the bootable device. This is the first block of the device. The block contains, among other information, a small program that is sometimes called **bootstrap**. After loading the bootstrap, control is then transferred to this little program. By doing so, BIOS disqualifies itself from being the internal owner of the computer. This does not mean that we will not need BIOS anymore. We will

Every *hard disk* is organized into a collection of coaxial plates. Every plate has two surfaces. On every surface there are many concentric rings called *tracks* upon which information is stored. These tracks may or may not be visible to us, depending on the type of medium.

Every track is further divided into an integer number of sections called *sectors*. The number of sectors is the same for all tracks, disrespectful of their distances from the center and/or the circumference of the track.

A *block* is a collection of either one or more sectors. It is the smallest unit of data that can be read or written during one access to the disk.

continue to use the BIOS facilities, but under the control of the operating system. BIOS contains many other useful procedures (little programs), especially for interacting with input/output devices.

We now have a small temporary part of the operating system loaded and running, in main memory. It is important to know that this little program (or bootstrap) is different for Windows, UNIX, Mac, etc. and is tailor-made to fulfill the requirements of a specific operating system. This program has the responsibility of loading the next big chunk of the operating system and usually loads the whole kernel of respective operating system.

A **Kernel** is the essential part, or the inner part, of the seed of an operating system. On the other hand, kernel is a program that is composed of a many routines for doing activities that are not performed by any single operation of the computer hardware. Every routine is built using machine instructions and/or BIOS functions. In addition, kernel is composed of many essential processes (threads or agents) each designed to carry out a responsibility of the operating system.

The booting process may stop here or it may perform one more step. If it is to do one more step, it will transfer control to a program within the kernel that will bring another chunk of the operating system to the main memory. With the kernel being loaded, our hierarchical model of the operating system will resemble what is shown in Figure 2.2.

A **kernel primitive** consists of very few instructions and/or BIOS functions. A kernel primitive performs only one little task and it is allowed to access hardware devices directly. In other words, the hierarchical structure that is depicted in Figure 2.2 is not strict.

The kernel can bypass BIOS and directly access the hardware. As a matter of fact, nothing is safe from the kernel. Remember that, the kernel is an essential part of the operating system and is designed with the highest accuracy and precision. The concepts used in the kernel are presumably theoretically proven to work well and do not produce any undesirable side effects.

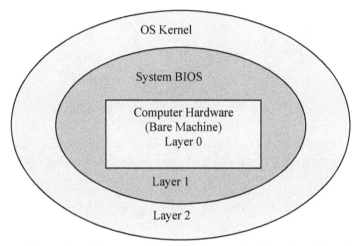

Figure 2.2: A three-layer machine with system BIOS and OS kernel

There are one or more other layers of the operating system that sit on top of the kernel. The number of layers varies from one operating system to another. The exact number of layers is not important for us for we are more interested in the global structure and the way the operating system is brought into main memory.

Not all parts of the OS are always resident in the main memory. During one session working with the computer, some parts of the operating system may never be used. Therefore, there is no need to bring them into main memory. By not loading them, users will have more space in the main memory for their own programs. Since the system does not know which part of the OS will be used or not used, non-essential parts are brought into main memory on request and are removed when no longer needed. Our complete hierarchical model of a modern computer is revealed in Figure 2.3.

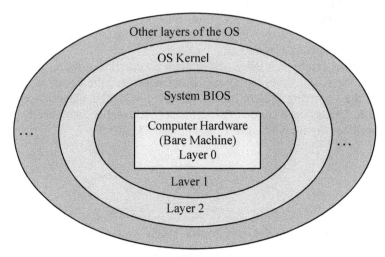

Figure 2.3: A complete layered operating system

The structure of some Windows versions is presented in Figure 2.4 as a sample existing layered operating system. In the forthcoming chapters, we will study some of its parts in detail as a general operating system.

As it can be seen in Figure 2.4, device drivers are in the same level as kernel routines. Hence device operations need not go through kernel in order to access the hardware. By doing so, input/output efficiency is improved. It is the operating system which lets and provides means to install all kinds of drives.

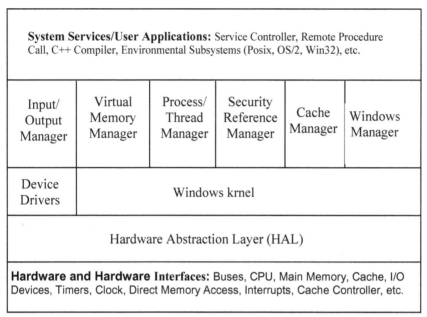

Figure 2.4: The structure of Windows

2.3 Protection Mechanisms

Our application programs sit on top of the operating system. They use the facilities provided by all layers of the system in a systematic and secure way, to do what these application programs are made to do. It is worth mentioning again that, with the existing operating systems, programs cannot directly and freely use the facilities within the lower layers. It is the operating system that monitors the activities of every running program. In the absence of any **protection** mechanism, strange things could happen and the system could, in

A *virus* is program or a piece of code (not a complete program) that is written to do something damaging. It is transferred to our computers without our knowledge and permission. A virus can replicate itself and can attach itself to our files, contaminating them. Under certain circumstances, a virus can activate itself and do what is made to do.

A *worm* is also a destructive program that can replicate itself. Within a network, it can autonomously move from one computer to another. A worm does not need a host program to attach itself to. When specified conditions are met and the predetermined time arrives, the worm becomes active and performs its malicious action.

short, become unreliable. In a multi-user system, one person's process (program) can change somebody else's process, making it do something it shouldn't. A process can even modify the operating system itself, hence, making it useless and even harmful to other programs. The existence and propagation of

> A *hacker* is a person who tries to pass the security and protection mechanisms of a computer in order to steal information.
> A *cracker* is a person that wishes to break the security and protection systems of computers and networks for the purpose of showing off and/or stealing information.

viruses, worms, Trojan horses, etc. in computers is directly related to the existence of weak security points within the operating system. The existence of these dangerous programs must not have us believing that there are no protection mechanisms within the computer. Rather, it should convince us that protecting the system from crackers and hackers is a tough job. Many operating system and network researchers are exclusively working to make our systems less vulnerable.

Protection is currently applied to all layers of the system. Deep in the core of computer hardware, there are circuitries for performing machine instructions. Every computer usually supports 256 (two to the power eight) machine instructions. These instructions could be categorized into a small number of classes. For example, in the "add" class we might have: add two small integers, two medium integers, two large integers, two medium real numbers, two large real numbers, two extra large real numbers, contents of two registers, and add with carry, etc.

Not all machine instructions are available to computer users and even to higher levels of the operating system. Every machine instruction belongs to either **non-privileged** or **privileged** classes. In a reliable operating system, any program can use a non-privileged instruction. However, the operating system kernel (or core) is the only program that can use a privileged instruction. For example, in Pentium 4, the machine instruction HLT is a privileged instruction which stops instruction execution and places the processor in a halt state. An enable

> We computer specialists really like powers of the number two. A memory cell (called a *bit*) has two states: "zero" and "one". A *byte* is 8 bits, which is two to the power 3. A word is 32 (or 64) bits, or two to the power 5 (or 6). One *K* (*kilo*) byte is 1024 bytes, or two to the power 10 bytes. One *Meg* (*Mega*) byte is 1,048,576 bytes, or two to the power 20. One *Giga* byte is 1,073,741,824 bytes, or two to the power 30, One *Tera* byte is 1,099,511,627,776 bytes, or two to the power 40. Almost everything within a computer is made a power of two long. A *register,* or a *word,* of memory, is 32 (or 64) bits. There are usually 256 machine instructions.   RAM   memory contains a power of two bytes, etc.

interrupt instruction (we will talk about interrupts in the forthcoming chapter) or a computer reset by the user can resume the execution. Imagine if, in a **multiprogramming** environment, one program decides to execute a HLT operation and put the computer to sleep. Then, all other programs will also be halted. By resetting the computer, we will lose all that was done by the previously running programs.

> Kernel routines that are made available to application programs are called *system calls* (or *kernel services*). There are numerous system calls in each operating system. Through system calls application programs are able to directly use kernel and BIOS routines, without observing the hierarchy of operating systems layers. However, the operating system guarantees that there will be no harm made to the operating system or other processes running concurrently with this application program.

One other protection mechanism is to forbid one program from writing something in a location of main memory that is occupied by another program or even by the operating system, itself. Memory protection is also realized through joint effort of the hardware and operating systems. In any reliable operating system, the appropriate protection mechanisms are enforced so that every program is protected from other programs that may try to change something within its address space.

The kernel program is protected from other parts of the operating system, too. However, kernel routines can be used by other parts of the operating system through a specific procedure. Every computer has at least two modes of operation. One, in **Kernel mode**, or **supervisor mode**, all machine instructions, whether privileged or non-privileged, are useable. Two, in **user mode,** privileged instructions are not usable. One of the most remarkable features of any operating system is the way mode transfer is made possible. While running an application program, e.g., a simple accounting system written in say C++, we are able to use some kernel routines. It is obvious that the program is running in user mode. It is also clear that the procedure called for is within the kernel and therefore, could only be used while in kernel mode. This mode transformation is done automatically by the operating system, in such a way that while the user program is inside the kernel, it cannot do anything except execute the specified kernel routine. As soon as the execution of the routine is finished, the operating system will change the operation mode to user mode.

2.4 Think of Making Your Own Operating System

It is a good initiative to think of making your own little operating system. By doing so, lots of questions will be raised, some of which we will talk about in the following chapters. It should be clarified that with the knowledge that we have gathered so far, it is impossible to write an actual operating system. However, by writing and installing a small operating system you will learn a great deal of professional materials that could not have been learned by just reading books. This section is actually a review of what we have talked so far about. I would suggest the following steps in writing your own little and do nothing useful, operating system.

1. Using a running computer, write a mini program to do something over and over again. I would prefer this program to display the word "Hello" on the computer monitor. The size of the program is important and its actual machine language size must be less than 512 bytes. This program will be your operating system. To write this program you have to know at least one programming language. Assembly language is preferred, but C or C++ is acceptable. Let's suppose you will choose to write the program with C. After writing the program, compile it and produce an executable file.

2. An executable file has two sections: (1) the file header and (2) the actual machine language instructions. The header contains information about the file, e.g., size of the file. Suppose the file header is 512 bytes (it depends on the operating system and the language being used). Write a mini program to change your executable file into a file without a header by removing the first 512 bytes of the executable file. Let's assume this file is called a "com" file.

3. Write a program to transfer the "com" file to the first sector of track zero of a diskette or any other bootable media.

4. Prepare a diskette.

5. Transfer the "com" file to the first sector of track zero of the diskette. You have successfully stored your operating system on the diskette.

6. Reset the computer and enter the BIOS setup/modify program. Make the first floppy drive be the first bootable device.

7. Insert your own operating system diskette into the first floppy drive of the computer and reset the computer again. Wait until your operating system comes up.

You have your own operating system running. Can it run any program? Does it have any protection mechanism? Does it have any facilities like formatting disks

An *executable* file is a ready to run program. By double clicking on its icon (or by using other means of activating it), an executable file starts running. In such a file, the file's attributes are stored in its beginning sectors.

A *command* file is a pure machine instruction program without any attribute sector.

There are numerous file formats and every application program works with certain file formats. For example, MS-Word produces and works with document (doc) files, among and copying files? No, but your operating system owns the computer facilities and you know what it does exactly and how it is set up.

2.5 Summary

In following complex concepts and design issues of the operating system, a good knowledge of how the operating system is loaded into main memory and the process of overtaking the general management of systems is very constructive. In addition, a brief introduction of its major responsibilities is helpful. The layered structure of the OS provides a platform to study each layer and its responsibilities, separately. Although, some computer vendors preinstall the operating system on their computers, BIOS is the only piece of software that is for sure provided with any computer hardware. It has the ability to boot a small program from a bootable media that supposedly has a small part of the operating system. This new program will load another part of the operating system and so on, until the essential parts of the operating system are completely loaded. Some parts of the operating system are loaded upon request and may or may not be loaded in one session's work with the computer. The layered superstructure also provides the basis for protection related issues. These issues can be discussed separately for hardware, kernel, and the other upper layers of the operating system.

2.6 Problems

1. Your personal computer definitely has a BIOS. Find out what company has made it. Also, see whether or not its source is available for study. If the source is available, list all procedures and their possible usages.

2. In your opinion, is BIOS part of the operating system or is it part of the platform on top of which the operating system sits?

3. What are the disadvantages of storing all parts of the operating system in a read only memory (if we utilize a large ROM), instead of storing the BIOS only?

4. Are there BIOS routines that are useable after the operating system is installed? If yes, name a few of these routines and their applications.

5. Is the operating system kernel allowed to directly use hardware facilities or must it obey a strict hierarchical structure and use the facilities via BIOS?

6. List all the privileged instructions of one of the modern processors with which you are familiar. For each of these instructions, explain why it must be privileged.

7. During the system startup process (i.e., IPL process), is the system in user mode or kernel mode? Why? What about right after the IPL process?

8. By searching the Internet, find the source of a very small operating system. Try to compile it, store it on a bootable device, and make it work.

9. What does a device driver do?

10. In software engineering, a system is broken down into subsystems and this process continues until the final subsystems are easy to implement. In this chapter, an operating system, as a large piece of software, was divided into layers. Compare these two approaches and discuss whether or not they complement each other in the analysis, design and implementation of operating systems.

Recommended References

The concept of a layered operating system design is defined by Edsger W. Dijkstra [Dij68a]. It was used in the first multiprogramming operating system called "THE" operating system. Prabhat K. Andleigh has covered the layered structure of the UNIX operating system [And89].

Protection and security issues are discussed by Silberschatz et al. [Sil08] and Tanenbaum [Tan07] in their operating system concepts and modern operating system books, respectively. Specific and detailed treatment of the subjects are given by Graham and Denning [Gra72], Loscocco and Smalley [Los01], Bishop [Bis04], Hsiao, et al. [Hsi79], and Pfleeger [Pfl06].

Chapter 3

Multiprogramming and Multithreading

Within a computer there are many devices with different speeds and different capabilities. The trend is to make computer modules faster than ever. With future advances, today's speed will seem obsolete tomorrow. It is not advisable to quote actual device speeds in a textbook because they may appear out of date by publication. On the other hand, giving vague information, or none at all, will not help in understanding the reason for switching from **single-programming** operating systems to **multiprogramming** ones. We will try to mention real speed values when possible, but it must be understood that the numbers may not be valid in all contexts.

Hertz, or Hz, is a unit of computer clock frequency equal to one cycle per second. It is named after Heinrich Rudolf Hertz. One Giga Hz is 2^{30} cycles per second.
One *Millisecond* is 10^{-3} of a second.
One *Microsecond* is 10^{-6} of a second.
One *Nanosecond* is 10^{-9} of a second.

The CPU of a personal computer runs at the speed of around ten Giga *hertz*. Roughly speaking, on the average, the CPU executes one Giga machine instruction every second. A human being will take around 20 seconds to add together two ten-decimal digit numbers. This better done twice to make sure the result is correct. Compared to a CPU, a human is much slower in computations. The cache memory access time, i.e., the time that it takes to store a datum in cache or to read a datum from cache, is approximately 20 nanoseconds. In other words, for a personal computer, the number of cache memory accesses per second reaches $5*10^7$ times. The access time for a **dynamic RAM memory** is around 50 nanoseconds. Hard disk access time is a few milliseconds. Access time increases as we go down the list of **Digital Video Discs** (DVD), compact disks, and floppy disks. The printing speed is much lower, due to the mechanical movements involved. At the end of the speed spectrum is the computer user, who may take seconds to enter a datum, provided that he/she is available at the computer when the data is needed and does not need to think about what to enter. In a single-programming environment, most of the time the dominating speed for the whole system belongs to the slowest device. It is clear that this is not an efficient way of using a powerful computer.

3.1 Process States in Single-Programming

In a single-programming environment, only one process can be live at any given time. This process is born when a program is chosen for execution and brought into main memory (perhaps partially) with its preliminary requirements fulfilled. Right after its birth, the system starts executing its instruction. The instruction execution continues until the process needs to read some data from an input device or wants to write some results on an output device. There are special purpose processors called Input/Output (I/O) processors for transferring data from input devices to main memory and from main memory to output devices. Different input/output device classes have different I/O processors.

An I/O processor is a special-purpose processor that is made to do a specific task efficiently. It is understandable that such a processor will perform the specific task better than a general-purpose processor, or CPU. While an I/O operation is in progress, the CPU has to wait and do nothing. After the I/O operation is completed, the CPU will resume execution of the instructions. This cycle, of going through **process states** of running and input/output, may be repeated over and over, until the job is completed or, for some reason, the process is aborted.

The life cycle of a process in a single-programming environment is shown in Figure 3.1.

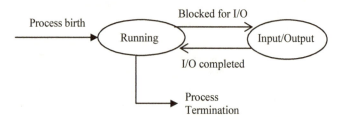

Figure 3.1: The life cycle of processes in single-programming environments

If the average CPU time of a program in a single-programming environment is equal to e and the average I/O time, i.e., the average total time spent on input/output operations of the program, is b, then the ratio $\dfrac{b}{e+b}$ is called the **CPU wait fraction** and is represented by:

$$w = \frac{b}{e+b} \qquad (3.1)$$

This value, w, is actually the fraction of the time the CPU is idle. For example, if the average execution time of programs is 10 seconds, of which, on the average, 9 seconds is spent on I/O operations, then $w = 9/10 = 0.9$. This means, in a single-programming environment, on the average, 90% of the CPU time is wasted. It is not only the CPU's time that is wasted, but also when the CPU is not used efficiency, that of other devices, e.g., the memory, cache, and/or hard disk, will not be utilized well. This occurs while the computer user's time may be wasted by not being able to run other programs simultaneously.

The fraction $1-w$, which is equal to $\dfrac{e}{e+b}$ is called the **CPU busy fraction**.

How much is efficiency increased when we switch from single-programming to multiprogramming? We will answer this question in terms of CPU utilization in the next section.

3.2 The Multiprogramming Concept

Multiprogramming is the solution to the following two undesired situations:

I. Suppose that a program is running. To continue, it needs a datum to be entered by the computer user. An example of this could be some accounting software that needs an invoice total while running. It will display a message asking the user to enter the invoice total. Let's say it takes the user five seconds to read the message, analyze it, and enter the requested number. During these five seconds, in a single-programming environment, the CPU has to wait and is not able to do anything useful. It could have executed, say, five billion instructions if it was able to switch to a ready-to-execute process and then switch back to the first process once the data is entered.

II. In another situation, suppose you need some information from the Internet and have issued a request to your browser program. Due to the tremendous amount of processing involved and the low Internet connection speed of your local network, this is taking a long time. What would you do until the information is displayed? One thing we usually do in such situations is to stare at the monitor, which is definitely not a constructive way to spend one's time.

Multiprogramming is a technique that allows more than one program to be ready for execution (process) and provides the ability to switch from one process to another, even if the former is not yet completed. Of course, sometimes in the future we will have to switch back to the first process and resume (not restart) its computation. This technique works for both **single-**

A computer with one CPU and one or more input/output processors or math coprocessors is not a *multiprocessor* computer. A *multiprocessor computer* has to have more than one general processor. In a single-processor system, the general processor is called the CPU, but in a multiprocessor system each general processor is called a *Processing Unit* (PU).

processor (like some personal computers) and **multiprocessor** (such as large main frame) computers. We know that operating systems usually creates a **process** to run a program. This process persists until either the execution of the program is normally completed or it is aborted. In rare situations where a process is withdrawn from the system before being completed or aborted does not interest us. We will, therefore, respect this meaning of the program and process from now on.

If you think clearly, you will notice that we should have used multiprocessing, instead of multiprogramming, in this chapter. This is true. Unfortunately, the term "multiprogramming" is recognized for this technique of the operating system and we will stick to it. On the other hand, **multiprocessing** is used for systems with more than one general purpose processor. Processors, in such a system, can collectively run many tasks simultaneously.

The feature of multiprogramming is mainly accomplished by the operating system. The hardware provides some specific circuitry that may be used by the operating system in the course of facilitating multiprogramming. Multiprogramming is very important as it may increase the utilization of the computer by hundreds of times, depending on the computer we are using. For a personal computer, this factor is much lower, but is still very desirable. In this era of computer usage, every general-purpose operating system must have the following three properties:

1. It must provide an environment to run processes in a multiprogramming fashion.
2. It must act as a service provider for all common services that are usually needed by computer users, such as copying files, making new folders, compressing information, sending and receiving messages from other computers in the network, etc.
3. Its user interface must be easy to use and pleasant to work with.

Older operating systems, such as DOS, that do not have all the aforementioned properties, are no longer used and are being replaced by modern operating systems.

To answer the question that was raised at the end of the previous section, i.e., how much is processor utilization increased with multi-programming, we will follow the case of $w=0.9$. When there are two processes in the system, the approximate CPU wait time is computed as;

$$w' \cong w^2 = (0.9)^2 = 0.81 .$$

For this case we would say that the degree of multiprogramming is two. The CPU busy fraction becomes 0.19. The CPU utilization is increased to 19%. The overall CPU performance is increased by

$$\frac{0.19 - 0.10}{0.10} * 100 = 90\%$$

A more accurate CPU wait fraction when there are n processes in the system could be computed from

$$w' \cong \frac{(\frac{w}{1-w})^n}{n! \sum_{i=0}^{n} [\frac{1}{i!}(\frac{w}{1-w})^i]}$$

For a reasonably large n, the approximate formula gives satisfactory results, rendering the more accurate formula to be seldom used.

The *degree of multiprogramming* is defined as the maximum possible number of simultaneous processes in the system. For a multiprogramming operating system, this value is large enough not to worry about.

When there are five processes in the system, the CPU wait fraction becomes

$$w' \cong w^5 = (0.9)^5 = 0.59 ,$$

The general approximate formula is:

$$w' \cong w^n \qquad (3.2)$$

Where n is the number of processes in the system.

In Table 3.1, when w is 0.6, w' for different values of n from two to ten are computed. It gives a feeling about how fast w' approaches zero.

Table 3.1: w' for different values of n

n	2	3	4	5	6	7	8	9	10
W'	0.36	0.216	0.13	0.077	0.047	0.028	0.0168	0.01	0.006

It is worth mentioning that, by switching from single-programming to multiprogramming, we intuitively expect a lower CPU wait factor than what is given by (3.2). Take a simple example where $w=0.5$ in single programming. We expect w' to be zero for two process cases. This is not possible because there are situations when both processes are doing I/O operations and the CPU has to wait and sit idle until at least one process completes its I/O. The CPU wait factor, from equation (3.2), will be 0.25 which is much better than 0.50. There is a 50% decrease in CPU wait factor, or a 50% increase in CPU utilization.

Multiprogramming is the central issue in the design of any modern operating system. All technical materials of the book are aimed at providing a multiprogramming environment that is efficient, smooth, and where simultaneously running processes do not interfere with each other. In this chapter, we will briefly discuss some of these subjects. There will be specific chapters for the areas not covered in this chapter.

3.3 Process State Transition Diagram

The number of **process states** in a multiprogramming environment is at least three. These states are: **ready**, **running**, and **wait/blocked**. This means that, at any given time, a process is in one of these three states. The actual number of states may vary from one operating system to another. If one knows the meaning of these three essential states, the reasons for every **state transition**, and the actual method with which a transition takes place, then the roles of new states in a given operating system is easily comprehensible. Think of a human being. He may be a child, i.e., a childhood state, a youngster, an adult, or an old person. The difference between a process and a human being is that a process may transit between the states many times, while a human being transits is only in one direction with no returns. When a process is created, its state is ready. In this state, the process is *ready* to use the processor (or one of the processors) to execute its operations. In the **running** state, the process is actually executing its instructions. This means, the processor is assigned to this process to execute its instructions. In the **wait/blocked** state, the process has either blocked for its input/output operations to be completed by an I/O processor or it is waiting for some other event to occur before which further execution of its instructions is not possible. A **transition** from one state to another state takes place when certain conditions are satisfied. For example, when the processor is free, one of the processes (if there is any) from the ready state will be picked up for execution and its state will be changed from ready to running. This is called a state transition for that process and it occurs when the processor becomes free.

Some researchers call the state transition diagram in Figure 3.2 a five-state model, while we call it a three-state model. They count the state before process birth and the termination state, too. We prefer not to count these states because they are not part of process's living period. Similarly, the state before a human's birth and the state after his death are not part of his life.

In a multiprogramming environment, there can be more than one process in the ready state. These processes are usually put in a queue, called *ready queue*.

In a system with one general-purpose processor, i.e., a system with one CPU, only one process can be in the running state. Under some circumstances, e.g., when there is no process in the system, there may not be any processes in the running state. The technique of multiprogramming is also used in systems with more than one general-purpose processor. For this kind of system, if there are *n* processors there can be, at the most, *n* processes running at one time. A process may be withdrawn from the running state and put back into the ready state for many reasons. One may be when the process has been using the processor for an extended period of time and as a result, other ready processes have been waiting an extraordinary amount of time for the chance to use the processor.

While running, a process may need a service that is given by a special-purpose processor; it may require a device that is not presently available. It may have to wait for certain circumstances to arise. In this case, it will be withdrawn from the running state and put to wait/blocked state. Figure 3.2 depicts the process state transition diagram. The link that is connecting the running to the wait/blocked state is a one-way connection. It therefore is just not possible for a process to go from a wait/blocked state to a running state. If a process' intent is to transit to a running state from a wait/blocked state then it must transit to the ready state and wait there until its turn to use the processor. There are three states in the mentioned state transition diagram hence it is called a three-state state transition diagram. Some authors include the states before birth and after death and call it a five-state state transition diagram. Figure 3.2 also represents the life cycle of each process. The life cycle consists of states ready, running, and wait/blocked states. These states may repeat many times during execution of a program before the process is completed. It could be compared to the simplified life cycle of a person consisting of eat, work, and sleep.

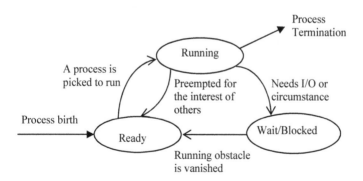

Figure 3.2: The process state transition diagram in multiprogramming

3.4 Process Switching

To facilitate multiprogramming, the processor must be able to **switch from one process to another**, while still not having completed the current process. The general name for this task is **context switching**. If the processor is supposed to switch from process *A* to process *B*, we might think of loading the **Program Counter** (PC) register with the address of the first instruction that is to be executed in process *B*. True, it would do the switching, but we would lose all temporary values of process *A* that were in the CPU registers just before the switch. Since we would not have saved process *A*'s **Location Counter** (LC), we would not be able to switch back to process *A* and continue its execution, but rather we would have to restart process *A*. It would not work well for process *B* either, if it were not the first time it was picked for execution.

Assuming we want to switch from process *A* to process *B*, the following six steps must be taken in the order provided for a systematic and correct course of action to switch from one process to another.

1. Current value of the PC register is saved and control is transferred to the operating system.
2. All temporary data, results, and control values of process *A* are saved in main memory. These values include, but are not restricted to: stack pointers, flags, **Program Status Word** (PSW), and general register contents.
3. The state of process *A* is changed from "running" to either "ready" or "wait/blocked," depending on the reason for switching.
4. All temporary data, results, and control values of process B except its LC are loaded into their proper places within the CPU. If it is the first time that process *B* is given the chance to use that CPU,

The *stack pointer* of a process is a datum that points to a location of a special memory area called stack. The stack, itself, is found in the main memory in order to store managerial information for a process. The type of information stored in the stack is *last-in-first-out*. For this type of information stack is the best data structure. It is the responsibility of the operating system to build one (or more) stacks for every process. Stack construction is performed during process creation.

The *flags* are a set of bits that explains the current status of the CPU and/or the status of previously executed instruction. Not all instructions affect flags. A flag that is set/reset by the execution of some instruction will always represent the effect of the execution of the last such instruction.

The *Program Status Word* (PSW) is a register that contains current operation mode, flags, mask bits, LC, etc. of the currently running process. In some processors, this register may not exist, if all of this information is provided by other means.

some of these places will be initialized by the ope-rating system.

5. The state of process B is changed to "running."
6. The PC register is filled with the address of process B's first instruction to be executed next.

Process switching is sometimes called *context switching* because conditions that determine the course of action may change in order for the instructions of a new process to be executed next.

3.5 The Interrupt System

In a multiprogramming environment, there are one or more general processors and many I/O processors. In addition, several processes may be active at any given time. Of course, being active does not mean that the process is currently using the CPU.

Consider a process that was performing an I/O operation and that the operation has just finished. How could the CPU know that it has finished its I/O operation, so as to schedule the remaining computational ope-rations? In other words, if you are a manager and have assigned a task to one of your employees, how would you be informed that he or she has completed the task?

There are two general approaches to find out when a task that was assigned to a peripheral processor, e.g., I/O processor, has been completed. These are **polling** and **Interrupt**. Polling means periodically checking the peripheral processor to see when the assigned task has been completed. Interrupt, on the other hand, is a mechanism where the peripheral processor sends a

A *device driver* is a program that facilitates the communications between the corresponding device and the device user. Every device type has its own driver to maximize device utilization efficiency and accuracy.

A *clock* is used to keep the time-of-day. Every personal computer has a battery-driven hardware clock. The clock keeps working even if the computer is turned off. We can adjust this clock by means of CMOS update facilities or from within the operating system. This clock is called a *hardware clock*. Some operating systems (like Linux) prefer to have a software clock, too. The *software clock* is set by the hardware clock during the system startup and reset. From then on, it is updated every time a specific interrupt is generated, so as to show the correct time. Accessing the software clock takes less processing time than accessing the hardware clock.

A *timer* is used to keep track of the elapsed time since it was last reset. An important usage of timers is to make sure one process does not use the processor for a long time. This kind of timer is called an *interval-timer*. It is set to periodically send an interrupt to the processor and to remind it that it is the time for process switching.

signal whenever it finishes the task. Many of the *device drivers* are **interrupt-driven**, but some are polled. We will provide further information on how the interrupt system works after the meaning of interrupt and the situations in which interrupts occur are clarified.

Interrupt is a signal that is sent to the CPU to capture its attention. It may be issued by different sources, for example:

- By an I/O processor that wants to inform the CPU of the completion of the assigned task
- By a user that may press special keys such as "break" at any time or move or click mouse keys
- By the real-time clock that wants to inform the CPU that it has been working on the current process for a long period of time (perhaps one thousandth of a second) and that it is time to switch to another process
- By a fault detecting hardware that is trying to informs the CPU of a malfunctioned circuit
- By a monitoring circuit within the ALU that controls the acceptability of the data size for the operation being performed and, consequently, the operation result size

Interrupt signals are of different urgency and importance. While a hardware error interrupt is highly urgent and crucial, an interrupt issued by an I/O processor to inform the CPU of a task completion, is neither urgent nor very important. It, therefore, makes sense that the CPU's reaction differ according to the type of interrupt.

Interrupts are usually categorized into a small number of classes, each of which containing interrupts sharing equal priorities and/or a similar nature.

When the processor receives an interrupt and decides to process the interrupt, it will have to switch from the current running process to a part of the operating system that is responsible for interrupt processing. This part is called the **interrupt handler**. The interrupt handler has a collection of interrupt handling routines, one per every interrupt class, or at times, one for every specific interrupt. Safe switching from the running process to the interrupt handler requires following the context switching steps. A must is to save the content of the PC register (the currently running process's LC.) This register points to the next instruction of the running process that has to be executed when the processor later switches back to it. When the process switches back, it will continue its execution by fetching and executing the instruction pointed out by the LC. Therefore, the processor cannot cease the execution of the current instruction at the exact time that an interrupt is received. First, it has to complete the current instruction. Technically speaking, the interrupt signal reaches the CPU and is stored in some flag. The flag is ignored until the execution of the current machine instruction is completed. This is disrespectable of the interrupt's priority or urgency. There are very few exceptions. One example is the *move* instruction in some computers that is supposed to move a big chunk, say 256 bytes, of data from one location of main memory to another. This instruction is a machine instruction, but it is of a multi-instructional nature as it includes many memory reads and writes. Such an instruction is professionally implemented to make it **interruptable**. In the case of *move,* for example, the source and destination addresses of the instruction are modified whenever each word of data is moved from source to destination.

The CPU always looks for interrupt signals just before fetching a new instruction to execute. If there are any interrupt signals, the CPU handles them in the order of priorities and urgencies.

What if you want to completely ignore some interrupts? Suppose you are running a program and in your program (process) there is a "divide by zero" operation. This would cause an interrupt and, as a result, the system would cancel your process. You may want to know what happens if the program ignores the "divide by zero" operation and continues execution.

Some interrupt types can be masked. Masking an interrupt type means ignoring every interrupt signal of the type. Of course, there are interrupts that cannot be masked by the programmer. For example, a programmer cannot mask the hardware error interrupts. These interrupts are called **Non-Maskable Interrupts** (NMI). However, there are many **maskable** interrupts such as "divide by zero" and overflow. A **privileged instruction** called a **disable interrupt** can disable all interrupts, but it cannot be used in the user mode of system operation. The **enable interrupt** operation reactivates the interrupt system after it has been disabled by a disable interrupt operation.

An *overflow* occurs when the result of an instruction is larger than the maximum storable value of its corresponding data type. For example, this occurs when two numbers of large integer type (64 bits) are added and the result is supposed to be stored in a 64 bit location. The result, however, is too big to be stored in that location, causing an overflow. The ALU circuitry recognizes this overflow and sends an overflow interrupt signal to the corresponding interrupt flag.

An *underflow* occurs for a negative result that is not storable in the anticipated location.

With the introduction of interrupt, Figure 1.1 has to be modified to make the computer listen to the user's new requests and facilitate context switching. At the beginning of each fetch-execute cycle it has to check for any outstanding interrupt signals. If there is one, a context switching is made from the currently running process to the interrupt handler. Another context switching may take place from the interrupt handler to the process whose execution was interrupted after the interrupt handling is completed.

3.6 Direct Memory Access

The main memory of a computer is a shared place for all processes, their data and results. In a multiprogramming environment, accessing the main memory becomes a new challenge as one or more processors and many peripheral processors are simultaneously active and trying to get into main memory to read or store information. The following two basic solutions are used for collision-free access to main memory.

1.   The **Programmed Input-Output** (PIO) method
2.   The **Direct Memory Access** (DMA) method

In the PIO method, the CPU is the owner of the main memory. Any data transfer between I/O devices and the main memory has to go through the CPU. An example is when some information is to be transferred from the keyboard to the main memory. Whenever a key is pressed, an interrupt is generated and the CPU executes the corresponding interrupt handler. The interrupt handler obtains the data (the pressed key) and transfers it to the CPU, from which point the data goes to the main memory. This mode of operation is only used for slow devices such as mouse and keyboard.

In the DMA method, information is directly transferred from the device to main memory and vice versa, without first going to the CPU. To facilitate this mode of operation, a bus ownership resolution is required. In one approach, it is assumed that the CPU is the bus owner and needy devices must steal bus cycles, one cycle at a time, from the CPU. The device that possesses the bus will use it and the main memory for one cycle to transfer only one word of data to or from main memory. This mode of operation is called **cycle stealing**. For every bus cycle, the following operations have to be performed.

- Every device that wants to use the next cycle of the bus (and main memory) has to send a request to the **bus arbiter**. Here, a bus cycle is assumed to be the same as a memory cycle, both in duration and start/end.

- The bus arbiter decides which device will use the next cycle of the bus to access main memory. The decision is based on the priorities that are assigned to the devices directly connected to the bus. Because devices are assumed to steal bus cycles from the CPU, it is assumed that the CPU has the highest priority.

> *Bus arbiter* is the collection of hardware circuitry that is responsible for choosing the device that will use the next memory cycle and, of course, the bus, to transfer one datum from the main memory to another device, or vice versa. It uses fixed, rotating, or completely random priorities for the requesting devices. In the cycle-stealing mode, the CPU is exempted from these priorities. The CPU always is given the highest priority over all other devices.

- The winning device is then informed to use the next cycle of the bus and main memory.

The operations involved in cycle stealing are all performed by hardware circuitry, once for every memory cycle. These operations do not noticeably increase the memory cycle time.

The cycle stealing mode is not appropriate for fast devices like hard disk drives, DVD drives, and high-resolution graphic cards. These devices may be given more than one cycle of main memory per one request. These periods may be as long as 32 memory cycles, or even longer, depending on the speed of the device and system restrictions. When such a period is given, bestowed the device can use the bus and main memory continuously for the whole duration. This mode of operation is called **burst mode**. A process similar to the cycle stealing mode of operation is followed to possess the bus and main memory.

A new mode of operation called **ultra DMA** has recently been invented. With this mode of operation, more than one unit of data can be transferred in each clock cycle.

3.7 Multitasking

When working with a computer, users like to have many application programs simultaneously operational. This is necessary because some application programs require long processing times before the desired results can be produced. It is true that by having more than one application program operational, the time that it takes for each process to complete its task increases compared to when the application program runs alone. However, the overall system productivity and, as a result, overall user gain will increase. These simultaneously executing programs are usually called **tasks**. Therefore, a system with the capability of **multitasking** allows users to activate more than one task, or application program, at a time. An Internet browser that searches for some information is an example of a task. A word-processing software that is activated to perform the word-processing task is another application. The computer user can switch back and forth between active task windows to see results, enter a new request or data, etc. The operating system will switch between tasks based on the tasks current states and their requirements.

Multitasking is only possible when the operating system supports multiprogramming, i.e., when **multiprogramming** is the fundamental capability of simultaneously executing pieces of software. Multitasking and multiprogramming are sometimes used interchangeably. Most modern operating systems, like **UNIX** and Windows, support multitasking.

3.8 Multithreading

Up until now, a process has been the only operating system identifiable functional and active object within the computer and is created to run a program to perform a duty. What if we need to perform two similar duties? One way to take care of this situation is to create two of the exact same process; each assigned to handle one of the two duties. Similarly, for more than two similar duties the appropriate number of identical processes has to be produced. This is a correct solution, but it spawns two major problems:

1. As the numbers of duties increase, the number of processes increases too, and very soon we will either run out of main memory or, in the case of virtual memory, we may reach an inefficient state of main memory, or, at least one with very low efficiency.

2. By increasing the number of processes, the number of objects that compete for computer resources increases, too. This could lead to an undesirable state of the system in which many processes cannot complete their duty because they do not get the chance to use the resources needed.

A better solution is suggested by **thread** methodology. Thread refers to a path through a program's instructions during its execution. We know that, the instructions of a program are not executed in the same order of their physical appearance within the process. Depending on the input and the environment data, some instructions may never be executed and some may be executed over and over again. Without the **multithreading** methodology, there is only one thread of execution per every process. At any point in time, the front of the thread shows where we are right now and what the status of the related process is, based on the current contents of registers and control signals.

Corresponding to every process is an address space. The **address space** of a process is the set of all memory locations that the process is allowed to read from and write to. This would also include the many CPU registers and flags the process uses while running. In addition, the machine language instructions of the program, data, results, and stacks, are parts of this address space. The **physical address space** of a process is the set of all main memory locations occupied by the process at any given time.

Multithreading methodology allows more than one thread of execution for every process. All threads of a single process share the same address space. They use the same global data, i.e., all data that is within the process but not defined to be thread-specific. Threads of the same process use the same files for storing and/or reading information. They also use the same resources that are assigned to their corresponding process. For example, if a tape drive is assigned to a process all its threads are able to use it.

A **multithreading operating system** is one that is capable of handling processes and threads at the same time and in which every process is allowed to generate more than one thread. In such an operating system, there must be facilities for thread creation, deletion, switching, etc. Such an operating system allows users to generate more than one request to a process at a time. For example, a browser can be made to search simultaneously for more than one topic, even though there is only one copy of the "browser program" in main memory.

The multiprogramming methodology and technique are essential in the implementation of multithreading. In this new environment, a thread becomes the smallest functional and active object to which CPU (or a PU) is assigned.

For more details about thread methodologies, benefits, and implementation techniques, please refer to Chapter 5.

3.9 Multiprocessing

A computer may have more than one processor. Every processor can independently take a process for execution. A process scheduler is usually responsible for defining what process is to be executed by which processor. The main memory, in such systems, is common to all processors and all processes (partially) reside in main memory. Every processor may have its own small cache memory for holding a copy of some parts of processes. Because the cache size is much smaller than the size of main memory, a cache can only store a limited amount of data and/or code. **Multiprocessing** and multiprogramming can simultaneously exist in one system. Compared to single-processing multiprogramming systems, in multiprocessing multiprogramming systems, there can be more than one process in the running state. In such a situation each process is using a different processor for executing its instructions. If there are, say, n processors in the system, there could be at the most n running processes at any given time.

3.10 Summary

The ultimate goal in the design and implementation of an operating system is to produce a handy software program that manages computer resources in the most efficient way so as to serve computer users correctly, reliably and fairly. It is recognized that this is not achievable in single-programming environments. Modern operating systems are built with the capabilities of multiprogramming, multitasking, and multithreading. Providing these capabilities require many hardware and software methodologies and techniques. A good understanding of process creation, life cycle, and termination, along with its state transition conditions is most essential in elucidating the needs of different mechanisms within the operating system. Some of these mechanisms, namely process switching, interrupt system and handling, and direct memory access, are briefly explained in this chapter. Multithreading, as an offspring of multiprogramming, has become an essential part of all modern operating systems.

3.11 Problems

1. If the fraction of CPU idle time, w, is 0.25, what is the fraction of CPU idle time when there are four processes in the system, using the approximate formula? What is it if we use the exact formula?

2. For $w=0.4$, compute w' for $n=2$, 3, 4, 5 using both the approximate formula and the exact formula. Compare the results.

3. In a three-state state transition diagram, if the wait/blocked state is broken into two states, i.e., wait and blocked, develop a four-state state transition diagram.

4. If an interrupt is generated while the processor is in the middle of executing (or fetching) a machine instruction, the interrupt will not be handled before the execution of the instruction is completed. Are there any exceptions to this rule for your computer processor? If the answer is yes, and the interrupt causes the processor switching, what does the system save for the location counter of the process that it has switched from?

5. For the processor of your personal computer, name all machine instructions for which when each one is being executed if an interrupt occurs the processor can switch to the interrupt handler to take care of the interrupt and then return to the instruction and complete its execution.

6. What are the differences between multiprogramming and multiprocessing techniques?

7. Design a logic-level circuitry for diagnosing overflow, underflow and dividing by zero.

8. Find out how many interrupt classes are there for the processor of your personal computer. Name these classes in order of priority.

9. Research. Find a reference that has calculated the more accurate CPU-wait-time formula for a multiprogramming environment. Make every effort to comprehend the discussion.

Recommended References

The multiprogramming and layered structure concepts of operating system are well presented by Dijkstra [Dij68a], Brinch-Hansen [Bri70] and Madnick and Donovan [Mad74].

Process states and state transitions, in general, are discussed by Stalling [Sta11]. Specific considerations of this subject for UNIX and Windows is presented by Vahali [Vah07] and Solomon and Russinovich [Sol00], respectively.

Stalling [Sta05] has treated direct memory access methodology in detail.

Thread concepts are covered by Lewis and Berg [Lew96]. Specific implementation of thread for Windows 2000 is given by Solomon and Russinovich [Sol00].

Chapter 4

Process

Inside a computer there is a little society of processes. Processes are born, live, and die. Even the operating system, itself, is a set of processes. When we turn the computer on, we actually generate the booting process. It boots the operating system process (see the side box) and the booting process fades away. Computer users, application programs, or application processes, and the operating system may create new processes or they may destroy existing ones. This society of processes needs a governing body that is the operating system. The governing body requires a complete set of information for every process in the system, in order to identify and manage processes. This set of information is collectively called **process attributes**.

There are three concepts upon which operating system kernels are organized: process, thread, and agent. Consequently, we have process-based, thread-based and agent-based operating systems. We will talk about process-based operating systems in this chapter. Thread-based operating systems are covered in Chapter 5. Agent-based operating system design is very new and its concepts, methodologies and techniques are still being developed. In a process-based operating system, when the system starts (or restarts), many operating system processes are created to serve application processes. Therefore, the operating system is composed of, not only one process, but a collection of processes.

4.1 Process Attributes

Like in human societies, upon its creation, a process has to be registered. Registration involves recording all information necessary to identify a process and to differentiate it from other processes in the system. This information, called **process identification information**, is recorded right after the process is created or born. Usually, every process is also given a unique identifier, called a *process ID*, in order to make future references to it easier and unambiguous. We can think of this ID of something similar to a person's social security number or a comparable national number. Process identification information is usually static, which means it does not change as time goes by and as the process moves from one state of life to another. Therefore, this information does not reflect the current state of the process. For that purpose, the system will record **process state information**. Process state information is dynamic and it is frequently changed, especially when the process is not idle. It includes, among others, temporary data of the process found in special and/or process-visible registers (i.e., registers which can be directly used by a running process), process status data, and pointers to different memory areas that are used to build dynamic stacks for storing peripheral information about the process. Yet this is not enough. The administrating body needs one more set of information called **process control information**. This information is mainly for management purposes. To control a process, the governing body should know the current state of the process, what resources it has, and what it needs. Although we will provide a typical **process attributes** table, in which information is categorized into three sections, namely identification, state, and control information, the goal is not to learn and/or memorize to which category each piece of information belongs. Rather, our aim is, to clarify what types of information are needed for every process and what purposes this information serves. To summarize, we have identified the following three categories of information that is recorded and kept up to date by the operating system for every process in the system:

    Process identification information

    Process state information

    Process control information

A program is a collection of instructions and data. At the same time, process is an active program. Hence, instructions, data, results, and temporary values are actual parts of a process. On the other hand, for example, the numeric identifier of a process, or process ID, is not an actual part of a process and is only attached to the process for the operating system's sake in order to uniquely identify every process. This data is called **meta-data**. It is similar to a person's social security or national number which is issued for official transaction. It is clear at least that, process meta-data has to be kept by the operating system and not by the process. Going back to the process attributes subject, we realize that some attributes are parts of the process body while others are parts of the process meta-data. The process body and its meta-data are collectively called the **process image**.

    Process attributes have to be stored and kept track of. The operating system collects all the attribute information of every process in a structure called **Process Control Block** (PCB). There is one PCB per process. Without being very specific, a PCB will generally have the elements shown in Table 4.1.

When a process starts/restarts running, i.e., its state changes to running, some PCB elements move to temporary locations of the CPU. For example, the location counter moves to the program counter register and the process' visible register contents move to corresponding CPU registers. While the process is running, changes to these contents will not be immediately transferred to its PCB, but the PCB will be updated periodically or whenever the process' state is changed from running to a new state.

The PCBs of all processes are embedded in a table called the **Process Table** (PT). In other words, there is one process table within the operating system body, with one entry for every process control block. The process table is a data structure of the operating system. It is, therefore, part of the operating system address space and not part of any process's address space. Because of its frequent usage, the process table is always kept in main memory and it is not swapped out to auxiliary memory.

A real scenario will help us understand how different fields of the PCBs are used to design and implement process management concepts. We provide an example of how linking fields of the PCB is used to create a single link list in order to make a queue of all the processes in the ready state. For this queue, there will be a variable that points to the rear of the queue and one variable that points to the front of the queue. These variables are two new operating system variables that must be taken care of. Otherwise, access to the queue becomes impossible. Of course, these variables are not stored within the process table, itself. This is to preserve the neat structural symmetry of the process table.

Table 4.1: Attribute fields generally kept for every process

Fields	Some possible usage
Process identification information	
Process ID	For unique and simple referencing by the operating system.
Parent process	For accounting purposes of CPU time, I/O time, etc.
User identifier	For process ownership resolution
Group identifier	For process sharing between members of a group

Process state information	
Process-visible registers	To keep temporary values while process is running
Location counter	Will be needed, as a continuation point, when the process restarts running
Condition code flags	To reflect the state of some previously executed instruction
Stack pointers	To point to the stack of procedure and system calls that is used to keep track of sequence of such calls
Process control information	
Status	Process status (Ready, Running, …)
Priority	The precedence of the process with respect to other processes, to be used for scheduling purposes
Process start time	For accounting and scheduling purposes
CPU time used	For response time calculation and scheduling purposes
Children's CPU time used	For accounting and scheduling purposes
Scheduling parameters	To be used for scheduling the process to use required resources and the CPU
Links	To make lists, queues, stacks etc. of processes with respect to their future needs and the order by which it will receive
Process privileges	To be able to assign specific permits to specific processes for using system resources
Memory pointers	To keep track of memory locations assigned to the process
Interprocess communication information	To keep track of pending signals, messages … from/to other processes to be taken care of, later
Devices assigned to the process	To free all the resources possessed by the process, before terminating the process
Open files	To flush all unwritten data to files and close them before process termination
Flags	For different purposes, for example the interrupt flag will inform the system of an existing pending interrupt signal that must be processed in the future

The threading of ready PCBs, i.e., rows of the process table with states being *ready*, are one-sided with two pointers *front* and *rear*, to make the addition of a new process to the end of queue possible that is when a process is born or the state of an existing process is changed to ready and, similarly removal of a process from the front of queue possible when the process is chosen to become the new running process. Figure 4.1 presents a process table composed of ten TCBs. If we represent P_i as the process whose PCB is stored in row i of the process table, then this figure shows the processes and their respective positions in the ready queue. Symbol Λ stands for the end of a link thread.

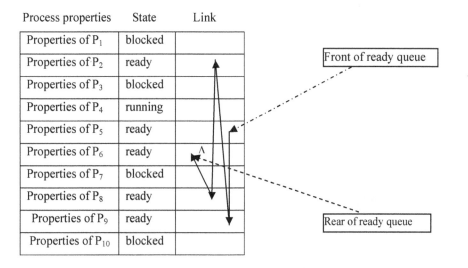

Figure 4.1: A simplified process table with links for implementing a queue

In Figure 4.1 the links connecting all processes in the ready queue are drawn. The ready queue is organized in the form of a special queue with one pointer to the front of the queue and one pointer to the rear of the queue. This kind of list is appropriate for the **First-In-First-Out** (FIFO) process scheduling method in which a newly arrived process to the ready queue will be added at the rear of the ready queue and the next process to run is removed from the front of the ready queue. A different link list may be needed for other scheduling methods. The arrows starting from the front of ready queue show the order according to which processes will be picked up to use one round of the CPU, based on the FIFO policy. The order will be P_5, P_9, P_2, P_8, and P_6. The pointer to the rear of the queue helps in adding new items to the queue without having to start from the front of the queue and finding out where the rear of the queue is.

When process P_5 is picked to use the CPU, the front of the ready queue pointer is updated to point to process P_9. Similarly, if process P_{10} becomes ready, a link will be generated to point from process P_6 to process P_{10} which will cause the null symbol at the link field of process P_6 to be removed, the pointer field of process P_{10} is set to null, and the pointer to the rear of the queue is updated to point to process P_{10}.

The link field of the process table can also be used to thread blocked processes and, depending on the reason for blocking, many queues may be set up using this link field.

When a process is terminated, its PCB is removed from the process table and the space will be used for a new process in the future.

4.2 System Calls

Great efforts are put into making a robust fault-free efficient kernel. With no doubt, it is the kernel that makes some operating systems superior over others. When the computer is up and running, many managerial processes, that are not created by any application program are alive and on duty. Some of these are created from the instructions embedded within the kernel. This is not the only role of the kernel's embedded instructions. There are codes, or instructions, that are usually asleep, or not a part of a live process which can be made active when called on by either an operating system's process or by a user process. These codes are organized in a set of routines, each capable of performing a little function. For example, a bunch of kernel instructions may be organized to close an open file, when activated.

Although files are kept on disks (floppy, hard, CD, etc.) and not in main memory, vital information such as name, size, location on disk, etc. of every open file is kept in main memory. One reason for closing a file when we are done with it is to let the operating system, or the close file routine of the kernel, vacate main memory locations occupied by the file to be used for other processes that need main memory. The "close" routine can be used by an operating system process (including a kernel process) or by an application process that feels responsible for closing its open files which are no longer needed, so as to ensure its quota for the number of open files is not violated and the file is safely closed before process termination. Therefore, we can think of the **close file** routine as a more primitive set of instructions than an operating system process or an application process. Although it is not an independent process, other processes could use it and, by doing so, becomes part of the calling process' body. Routines such as the *close file* routine are called **kernel services**. Kernel services are carefully designed, implemented, and tested to be correct and to do exactly what they are meant to do, without any detrimental side effects. To improve the efficiency of the kernel and to reduce its size, every service is made to do only one action. For example, the kernel service **open file** only does what is meant by opening a file. It is not made to do anything else like reading something from a file or writing something on it.

Some kernel routines are usable by application programs and some are not. Calling some routines directly from the user level is made possible even in a strict hierarchical operating system, in which we expect higher level codes to observe the hierarchy and access a kernel service via levels in between their own level and the kernel level. In the design of operating systems, principles like layered, structured, readable, object-oriented, etc. are respected as far as they do not decrease the system efficiency, i.e., speed, size, and minimal resource usage. Calling a kernel service from the application program's layer, while observing the layered structure, is a very inefficient method, especially when the need for doing so is highly frequent. Writing kernel services requires such a high degree of expertise that most application programmers lack the ability to write routines that are similar to kernel routines. Therefore, they have to rely on prewritten primitives within the kernel.

> *Trap* is one way of getting the operating system's attention. Interrupt is another way of invoking the operating system. A trap is issued by a running process for asking the operating system to execute a kernel service. The calling process, i.e., the process that issues a trap, provides enough information for the operating system to identify the kernel service. This information is stored in registers and/or an operand of the trap instruction. The operating system will collect the trap instruction's operand (if any) from the instruction register.

Some kernel services are made available for direct use by application processes. For kernel service, a **system call** or **supervisor call** (SVC) to a function is necessary. The function prepares the arguments and executes a **trap** instruction. A trap instruction is a software interrupt that is generated by a software application.

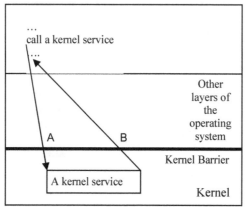

Figure 4.2: The kernel barrier is busted twice as shown at points A and B

Connecting the two different worlds of the kernel and application processes requires a regulated mechanism called a **protocol**. Figure 4.2 demonstrates the calling and hence, executing and returning of a system call from a user process. When this is done, the barrier separating the **user mode** and the **kernel mode** is busted twice: once when entering from the user mode to the kernel mode and once when returning from the kernel mode to the user mode.

Having in mind that the kernel is a highly protected environment, the following steps must be observed for every kernel-routine execution.

1. The application programmer should know what system calls are available for him and use these with correct syntax.
2. When translating the user program, the program translator (assembler, compiler, etc.) will insert extra codes to prepare the system call identification and its parameters for the kernel. This set of instructions will include the **trap** instruction. The trap instruction informs the operating system that it wants to execute a kernel primitive.
3. During the execution of a user program and when the trap instruction is executed, a **software interrupt** is generated. In response to this interrupt, an interrupt service routine is activated to change the mode of execution to the kernel mode and prepare for the system call execution.
4. The system call is executed.
5. The execution mode is changed to the user mode and a regular return to the user program is performed.

Careful examination of steps 1 to 5 will reveal that it is not the application process that goes into the kernel to execute a kernel service. Rather, after the trap instruction, the user process has no control on what and how his request is executed. It has to wait (or is perhaps blocked) until the return from the kernel is completed by the operating system. Therefore, when a user process is in control, it is always in the user mode with limited privileges corresponding to that mode.

A brief list of some common **system calls** are given in the Table 4.2. To make the list realistic, the system calls are taken from the UNIX operating system.

Table 4.2: A brief list of UNIX system calls

System Call	Description
Process Management	
pid = fork()	Create a child process similar to this process
pid = waitpid (pid, &static, options)	Wait for your child process with the numeric identity "pid" to terminate
s = execve (name, argv, envp)	Replace the process's memory image with the "name" process, i.e., run a new program in this process
exit (status)	Terminate this process and return its status value
s = kill (pid, sig)	Send a signal to the process with the "pid" identification
pause ()	Suspend the calling process until the next signal
wait (&status)	Wait for the child process to exit and get its status
alarm (sec)	Set the next SIGALRM for "sec" seconds later
Interprocess Communication	
qid = msgget(queueid, rights)	Create a message queue or get the system-wide identification of the existing queue "queueid"
msgsnd(qid, &mymsg, size, flags)	Send my message of size "size" to the queue of system-wide id "qid"
msgrcv(qid, &mymsg, size, type, flags)	Receive a message from queue "qid" into "&mymsg" buffer
semid = semget(key, nsems, rights)	Create a semaphore with key "key", if it does not already exists
semop(semid, operation)	Perform the operation "operation" to semaphore with identification "semid"
File System	
fd = create (name, mode)	Create a new file and return the handle for future access

fd = open (file, how)	Open a file with the given handle for read and/or write
s = close (fd)	Close the file with the given handle
n = read (fd, buffer, nbytes)	Read data from the file into the buffer
n = write (fp, buffer, nbytes)	Write data to the opened file from the buffer
pos = lseek (fd, offset, whence)	Move the file pointer to a new place within the file
s = stat (name, &buf)	Read and return status information of "name" file
s = mkdir (path, mode)	Create a new directory
s = rmdir (path)	Remove the given directory
s = link (name1, name2)	Make a link from "name1" directory to "name2" directory (or file)
s = unlink (name)	Remove the named directory (or file) link from this directory
s = chdir (name)	Change to the named directory
s = chmode (name, mode)	Change the file's protection mode

In this table, the return value of system calls is the integer 0, if the system call is completed successfully. Otherwise, it is the integer -1. The abbreviation *pid* is for process identification. *fd* is for file descriptor (the identifier that is used to refer to a resource). *opts* is for options, *execve* for the execution of a program with provided arguments and environment, *argv* is for the arguments vector, *envp* for array of environment pointers, and & for pointer reference.

4.3 Process States and State Transition Model

In Section 3.3, we examined the process life cycle. Three states were recognized and a state transition model, composed of these states, was developed. That model is the most essential state transition model for all modern multiprogramming operating systems. New states can be added and corresponding transitions may be developed to produce more complex models that are tailored to reflect new requirements. Before doing so, we would like to talk about rationales behind the need for dealing with process states and state transition models.

System analysis is an essential part of any software system development process. The operating system could be looked at from the process's point of view to determine what could be done for a process to run correctly, smoothly, and efficiently without doing any harm to other processes and the system. To do so, it is essential to identify the different states of a process during its life cycle and state transitions. Actually, we do not just recognize the states but rather we, as the designer of the operating system, make the decision on what states to use and what transitions to allow. This is the reason why all operating systems are not exactly the same in regards to the state transition models. Essentially, they all have the three indispensable states: ready, running, and wait/blocked.

While a process resides in a specific state, it does not require a tremendous amount of services from the operating system. However, services are considerable when transferring from one state to another. Sometimes the process dictates state transition, for example when a running process needs to read some data from a disk. Sometimes, however, it is the operating system that makes the decision to change the state of a process, e.g., when a process has been using the CPU for a long time and there are other processes waiting to use the CPU. In either case, it is the operating system that goes through all the necessary formalities.

The basic three-state state transition model is redrawn in Figure 4.3. Most contemporary operating systems utilize a state transition model with more than three states. The purpose of this chapter is to develop a more detailed model in which an operating system's responsibilities becomes more apparent. As a result, system design and implementation complexity reduces. This also improves efficiency due to shorter and more specific data structures that keep track of processes in the system. For example, UNIX uses a nine-state state transition model with the following states: **created**, **ready to run in memory**, **ready to run swapped**, **kernel running**, **user running**, **sleep swapped**, **asleep in memory**, **preempted**, and **zombie**.

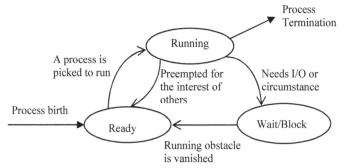

Figure 4.3: The three-state process state transition diagram

In UNIX process states, it is clear that the running state of the three-state model is broken into kernel running and user running. Similarly, the wait/blocked state is divided into sleep swapped and asleep in memory. Furthermore, zombie is similar to the terminate state and reflects the case in which the process is no longer active and will not become active in the future, either. In this state, a trace of the process is left for possible usage by its parent process. We can assume that the state of the process in the process table is changed to zombie, or a dead process. However, its PCB is not cleared and may be used by its parent process and/or the operating system. Table 4.3 presents a rough description of the UNIX states and their corresponding mother states in the three-state model.

Table 4.3: UNIX process states and their relations to the three essential states

State name	Mother state in the 3-state model	Meaning
Created	---	Process is created, but with the fulfillment of some other requirements will become ready
Ready to run – in memory	Ready	Process is ready to run, it is up to the dispatcher when to make it run
Ready to run – swapped	Ready	Process is ready to run, but is currently swapped out of the memory and if it is swapped in, its state will become Ready to run – in memory. It is then up to the dispatcher to decide when to choose it for running
Preempted	Ready	Process was in kernel running state before the system decided to switch to another process
Asleep – in memory	Blocked	Process is waiting for an I/O to be completed, for a device to be granted, and/or an event to occur
Sleep – swapped	Blocked	Process is waiting for an I/O to be completed, for a device to be granted, and/or an event to occur at the same time it is swapped out of memory and it has to be swapped in, first
User running	Running	The process is running.
Kernel running	Running	The process is executing a kernel service routine, i.e., some kernel instructions are being executed in behalf of the process
Zombie	-----	The execution of the process is completed but its PCB and process table entry is not removed, yet

To exercise a practical design problem, let's suppose we would like to break the running state of the three-state model into two states, namely kernel-running and user-running. In other words, a process in the kernel mode having extended privileges would be distinguished from a process in the user mode which has restricted privileges. From Chapter Three, we learned that it is not possible to directly change the mode of a process from user to kernel, thus allowing the process to execute kernel procedures. This mode change is accomplished indirectly by the operating system as a response to a **system call** requested by either the running process, a clock interrupt, or an I/O interrupt. Even then, the process is not within the kernel to do whatever it desires to do. Rather, some part of kernel is executed on behalf of the process. In the kernel running state, things may happen that cannot take place in the user running state. Also, the process will need different services from the operating system than if it were in the user running state. For example, the process may be in the kernel running state as a result of an interrupt and then another interrupt may come about. This situation cannot arise in the user running state.

Let's examine transitions that cause the entering and leaving of the running state of a three-state transition model. We will see the equivalent transitions for when the running state is broken into two states (kernel running and user running) and when the terminate state is replaced by zombie.

1. *Ready* to *running* in the three-state model becomes *ready* to *kernel running*, because initial preparations take place within the kernel.

2. *Running* to *ready* in the three-state model becomes *kernel running* to *ready*, as this happens in response to a clock interrupt which is processed within the kernel.

3. *Running* to *terminate* in the three-state model changes to *kernel running* to *zombie*, because final

> *Context switching* is the set of actions taken to safely switch from the running process (thread or agent) to a ready to run process. This action enables the system to run the latter process from the exact point where its execution was discontinued, if it is not the first time it uses the CPU. Moreover, the execution of the former process will be resumed when later in the future when the scheduler picks this process to swich to.

process termination operations are performed by the kernel. The system call used for this purpose is either *exit* or *abort*. Zombie state in the UNIX operating system represents the process execution termination. Zombie is a state in which a process has died but is still not buried. Such a process will be buried when some information, e.g., its total execution time, is collected. Therefore, the equivalent transition in UNIX will be *kernel running* to *zombie*. The transition from kernel running to zombie takes less processing time (for the time being) than running to traditional terminate state.

4. While in the kernel running state, a high priority interrupt can occur. To process the interrupt a reentry to kernel running will be performed, hence *kernel running* to *kernel running* transition takes place.

5. When a process is in the kernel running state in order to handle an interrupt and then another high priority interrupt occurs, a reentry to the kernel running state takes place. This was explained in Item 4. After handling the latter interrupt, the point of return is where the processing of the former interrupt was left off, i.e., the kernel running state. Hence, once again, there is the *kernel running* to *kernel running* transition.

6. The *running* to *wait/blocked* in the three-state model becomes *kernel running* to *wait/blocked*. This is because the final stages of making a process wait for an interrupt are performed in the kernel.

7. To complete the diagram, whenever a process is in *user running* state and needs kernel service, the process state is changed to *kernel running*. The process then returns to the user running state when kernel service is completed.

The resulting state transition diagram is presented in Figure 4.4. We are now very close to a real UNIX state transition model. We need to clarify three more concepts before we can actually arrive at the complete model. These concepts are: **process creation**, **process swapping**, and **process preemption**.

We will talk about process creation later in this chapter, but a brief discussion here will explain why the **created** state in UNIX is different from the "ready to run" state. In response to certain actions, a process is created. These actions, in modern operating systems, are: system power on or system reset, a process create system call like *fork()*, or a user launch of a program by a command or activation of an icon. In the UNIX operating system, the kernel performs the following actions during process creation:

Allocating a row in the process table for the process being created
assigning a unique identification number for the process being created
Allocating space for the process image
Initializing the process control block of the process being created
Returning the numerical identification of the created process to the creating process and a zero value to the created process.

The status of a newly created process will be "created." It is neither "ready to run – swapped nor "ready to run – in memory". This is not because the process cannot belong to one of the two ready states. Rather, it is because UNIX operating system designers wanted to have a "created" state giving them the opportunity of generating processes without yet scheduling them to run in the future.

Primitive UNIX-like state transition Model

Corresponding states in the three-state model

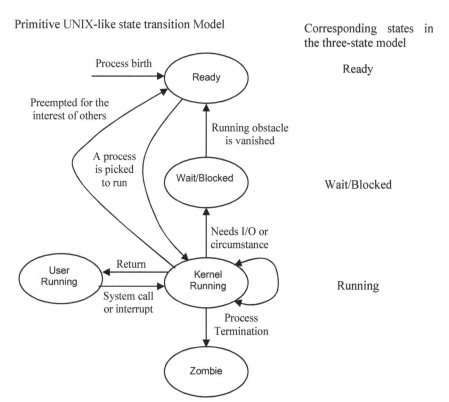

Figure 4.4: A hypothetical state transition model with five states

Swapping out a process is the action of removing a process that has not yet been terminated from main memory and transferring it to secondary memory. *Swapping in* a process is the reverse action, bringing the process that has been swapped out of the memory back again into main memory. **Process swapping** (in and out) originates from a specific **virtual memory** methodology that was chosen for the UNIX operating system. The discussion of main memory management, especially when virtual memory is used, is a vital part of any operating system text book. It is considered in the forthcoming chapters.

Without delving into the memory management issue, the easiest way to understand the need for process swapping is to investigate when swapping is performed in the UNIX operating system. When enough free space is not available in main memory and further execution of a running process depends on the assignment of more free space, two phases of memory freeing are performed one after the other. First, parts of main memory that are occupied by existing processes and satisfy certain conditions are evacuated. The evacuation process is done according to an algorithm called the **page removal algorithm**. Second, if not enough memory is freed, then some processes are chosen and rolled out of memory. UNIX calls such a process a "swapped out" process. A *swapped out* process will be swapped in, in the future, to let it complete its task. Actually, the UNIX operating system always likes to have certain amount of free memory to prevent frequent process swapping. Therefore, once memory freeing starts, it continues until a specific amount of memory is freed. The amount of freed memory is often much more than what was immediately needed.

Let's distinguish between two types of processes. One, which is ready to immediately run and has not used the CPU since it was created or transferred from a wait/blocked state to the ready state. The other, which was running and could have continued running, but, for some reason, the CPU was forcefully seized from it. The state of the former type processes is called the "ready to run – in memory" and the state of the latter type processes is called "preempted." We can identify many reasons for differentiating between these two states. For example, in an *interactive* environment we wish to answer any short query as soon as it arrives, without waiting for its *turn* to come. Once a request is generate it is not clear whether the request is short or long. Therefore, right after a request is generated (if possible) a process is created to take care of the request. The state of this process is set to ready to run - in memory. CPU scheduler immediately schedules this process to run for a predefined fixed time slice. If the process is completed in one time slice the corresponding request is considered a short one. Otherwise, it is considered a long request and the CPU is taken away from the process and its state is changed to "preempted". Processes in the preempted state receive their turn to use the CPU according to a different scheduling strategy. In another episode, a process that is forcefully evacuated from the running state and put into preempted state has a higher desire to use the CPU. Hence, we may prefer running such a process when CPU utilization is low. Therefore, adding a new state called *preempted* opens up a new horizon for implementing better scheduling strategies that increase the performance of the system.

Now, let's turn to possible transitions in the nine-state UNIX model, the states being *created, ready to run-swapped, ready to run-in main memory, preempted, sleep-swapped, asleep – in main memory, kernel running, user running,* and *zombie.*

A process is born in the created state when a means of running a program is needed. If enough initial main memory is assigned to a created process it will transfer from the *created* to the *ready to run in memory* state. Otherwise, the process will transfer to the *ready to run swapped* state.

A *ready to run in memory* process may be swapped out of memory due to a memory shortage and when indicated by the memory management algorithm. Such a process is *ready to run swapped*. This process will be swapped in when the scheduling algorithm decides to do so. Then, the process' state will again become *ready to run in memory*.

It is from *ready to run in memory* that a process can move to the running state. The initial activities of preparation are performed by kernel routines. Therefore, a process will transition to the *kernel running* state first and, from there, to the *user running* state.

A *user running* process will move to the *kernel running* state to perform any protected mode operations like system calls or interrupt handling.

Under certain conditions, some scheduling policies such as *round robin* may attempt to force a process out of the *user running* state. In this case, the process will go through the *kernel running* state to the *preempted* state. A Preempted process is a kind of ready to run in memory process. It is neither newly created ready to run process nor a process that has needed an I/O operation or has had to wait for some conditions before continuing its execution in a previous round of CPU usage. Such a process is, roughly speaking, called a **CPU-bound** process. The distinction between CPU-bound and **I/O-bound** processes will help to better schedule processes with the aim of achieving a more balanced system, or, a system in which all devices are kept busy working most of the time. A *preempted* process will be given CPU time to continue its execution in the future and its state will become *user running*.

> A *CPU-bound* process needs processing time much more than input/output time. This characteristic identifies the process whose performance is limited by CPU usage.
>
> An *I/O-bound* process, on the other hand, uses much more I/O devices as oppose to the CPU.

A *user running* process may need to read some data from input devices, may output results to disks or other output devices, or wait for some event to occur, for example receiving a message from some other process before continuing its execution. In such a case, the process has to be evacuated from the user running state and transferred to *asleep in memory* via *the kernel running* state.

An *asleep in memory* process may be swapped out of memory due to memory shortage. It then becomes *sleep swapped*. When the wait/blocked reason is gone the *asleep in memory* and *sleep swapped* processes will be transferred to *ready to run in memory* and *ready to run swapped*, respectively.

When an interrupt occurs for a process, interrupt handling is performed when the process' state is changed to *kernel running*. A new unmasked interrupt with higher priority than the one being processed forces a reentry into the *kernel running* state. After this new interrupt is handled, the process will return to the *kernel running* state again to complete the handling of the first interrupt. In another situation, a process may call a kernel service, thus going to the kernel running state. If, during the execution of the kernel service, another kernel service is called by the current running kernel service the process will reenter into the kernel running state.

Note that, for the purpose of state model development, it is assumed that it is not possible that two state changing events to occur simultaneously. For example, a transition from the *sleep swapped* state to the *ready to run in memory* state cannot happen, because it requires two events to occur at the same time: the termination of the sleeping condition and the termination of the main memory restriction for this process.

Along with these transitions, the UNIX state transition is shown in Figure 4.5.

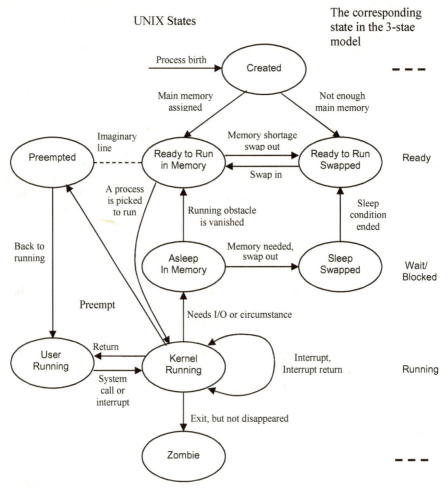

Figure 4.5: The UNIX state transition diagram

An attractive feature of Figure 4.5 is that the states are divided into five rows. For these, the equivalent state from the essential three-state state transition model is given, opposite the corresponding row.

4.4 Process Creation and Termination

The topic of process creation and termination is best dealt with by discussing the answers to the following questions clearly, precisely, and on an individual basis. We will follow this guideline and will present the necessary information in the order in which the questions are raised.

1. Why are processes created?
2. When is a process created?
3. What is done to create a process?
4. What are the tools for creating a process?
5. What are common in parent and child processes?
6. What are different between parent and child processes?
7. How is a process terminated?

4.4.1 Why are Processes Created?

Processes are the means of running programs to perform tasks. All required processes are not created when the computer is started (restarted). As computer users decide to run new programs, the system has to provide the proper environments to do so, i.e., create processes. For example, if we plan to run an Internet explorer program, the system must create a process to run this program. The program has been (previously) compiled and linked and is, so called, executable. Besides the code and data that have been embedded into the program, many other requirements must be fulfilled to do the job. Some of these facilities are embedded into the process that runs the program (see Table 4.1). Processes use hardware devices such as the CPU and main memory to execute instructions. They also rely on operating system facilities. In fact process is an active entity that performs actions. In doing so, it uses CPU, main memory, cache etc. It may be compared to a human who is active and say writes an article using paper and pencil.

4.4.2 When is a Process Created?

Generally, processes are created due to these three circumstances:

1. Computer start or restart
2. Explicit request by a computer user to start a new process by double clicking on or opening an executable program file, issuing a command to run a program, etc.

3. In response to a request from a running process to create a child process
The first two types of process creation are often in response to an offline action and seldom occur when the computer is automatically restarted. The third process creation type is an online action and occurs when a running process submits a request to the operating system to create a new process by calling a supervisor service. This new process will presumably carry out some duty for the process that requested its creation. The new process is called a child process of the creator process. The creator process is called the parent process.

4.4.3 What is done to Create a Process?

There is a list of actions necessary to create a process. The following presents these actions in the order in which they are usually carried out, although this order is not fixed and slight variations are possible. The first action is to make sure we have not already reached the limit for the number of existing processes. Although advances in computer hardware and operating systems have enabled us to set this limit, which is called the **degree of multiprogramming**, to a very high number, we still must check to make sure it is observed. This limit is directly related to the maximum size of the process table. The next action is to generate a process ID for future references that uniquely identifies the process that is being created. This and the following step, the allocation of a process control block, may be combined because the generation of the process ID may somehow be related to where about the PCB is in relation to the process table. These list of actions are summarized as:

1. Ensure the degree of multiprogramming, that is maximum possible number of processes, has not been exceeded
2. Generate a unique process ID to be used for addressing the process in the future and insert it into the process table
3. Allocate space for the process control block and the process context, i.e., places to store CPU register contents, and to initialize proper fields; then make the connection between the corresponding row of the process table and this PCB
4. Allocate space for other preliminary structures such as stacks and stack pointers and initialize the related fields
5. Put the process in one of the queues, usually ready queue, corresponding to process states, in order for the operating system to be able to track the process

4.4.4 What are the Tools for Creating a Process?

Creating a process is one of the responsibilities of the operating system kernel. A system call, or kernel service, is usually provided so that it can be used by programmers and/or within the operating system to create a new process. The name and arguments of this system call varies from one operating system to another. For the UNIX operating system, the *fork()* system call creates new processes. The syntax for the *fork* system call is:

retval = fork();

When the *fork()* system call is called a child process is created for the calling process. The process within which the *fork()* system call is called is actually the parent process of the process being created. The child process is a copy of the parent process, except for some attributes that are discussed later. The returned value *retval* is the integer zero for the child process and it is the child's process ID for the parent process in order that the parent knows the child's process ID. The parent and child processes will continue to execute the same code after the *fork()* instruction. However, it is possible to check the *retval* value and let the parent and child processes follow different paths of instructions. It is safe to assume that an exact copy of the parent process's data and code (program instructions), is made for the child process. However, for the UNIX operating system this is not quite true.

In UNIX, a program and its data are broken into pages of equal size, for example 2 Kilo Bytes (KB). A child

> Capital letters K, M, G, T, P, E, Z, and Y are used for kilo, mega, giga, tera, peta, exa, zetta, and yotta that correspond to 1000, 1000^2, 1000^3, 1000^4, 1000^5, 1000^6, 1000^7, 1000^8, respectively. However, in computer, they are used for 1024, 1024^2, 1024^3, 1024^4, 1024^5, 1024^6, 1024^7, and 1024^8, respectively, which we will use, too. In another convention, other abbreviations, namely K_i, M_i, G_i, T_i, P_i, E_i, Z_i, and Y_i, are used, and new names, namely kibi, mebi, gibi, tebi, pebi, exbi, zebi, and yobi, are generated for 1024, 1024^2, 1024^3, 1024^4, 1024^5, 1024^6, 1024^7, and 1024^8, respectively. In this convention, letter *i* stands for the word *binary*.

process shares the same page set of the parent process until a change in a page is going to be made by either the parent or the child. Right before the change is made, a copy of the corresponding page is made for the child process. From then on, each of the child and parent processes uses its own page. This technique is called **copy on write**. With this technique, main memory is better utilized as the parent and child processes are logically (but not physically) memory-independent. Be careful not to mix this technique with the thread methodology that will be discussed in the next chapter. For all practical purposes you may assume that parent and child processes each have its own separate and independent data, result, and code memory. Copy on write is just for increasing memory efficiency.

In the following, by using the *fork()* system call, a child process is created. The parent process will then execute procedure "proc1" and wait for the child process to terminate. The child process will execute "proc2" and will exit with the status "status".

```
void main(void)
{
    int  pid;
    int  retval;
    int  status;      // Pointer to the value returned by the child process
    pid = fork();     // It is assume that, there is no obstacle in creating
                      // the child process
    if (pid != 0)     // This is the parent process
        {
            proc1;  // Parent process will continue running procedure proc1
            wait (&status);  // Wait until the child process is terminated
        }
    else
        {
            proc2;  // Child process will continue running procedure proc2
            status = ...; // Provide a valid value for the returned status
                          // to the parent process
            exit (status);
        }
}
```

The program just presented is a very simple one but it shows how a process and its child can cooperate by each performing part of a job.

4.4.5 What are Common in Parent and Child Processes?

The most important piece of information that is the same (but not common) for parent and child processes is the source code of the program that is executed by both processes. It should be mentioned that when a child process is created, a (logical) copy of this information is made for the child process during its creation. From then on, each one will use its own piece of code. It is possible that the codes may differ as a result of replacing existing instructions with new ones. This is because the stored program concept allows a process to change its own code. It is also possible for parent and child processes to follow different paths of execution and they may execute different procedures and even different programs. The procedures are parts of the common code, but the programs are not. Data and results that exist right before the creation of a child process will be common for both parent and child processes. Once again, from this point on, each of the processes may input its own data and/or may produce its own results that do not exist in the other process or are different from the other process's data and results. Code, data, and results are collectively called **process image.**

For the UNIX operating system, a parent's permissions and rights are passed on to its children. Right after the point of child process' creation the working directory, root directory, and open files of both parent and child processes are the same.

4.4.6 What are Different between Parent and Child Processes?

While the parent's CPU usage is surely greater than zero when a child process is created, the child's CPU usage is set to zero.

A parent process can wait for a child process to complete its task using **wait()** or **waitpid()** system calls, but a child process cannot wait for its parent to complete its task. This means that a parent process is able to create a child process to do a certain task and to report the status of its completion to the parent. However, this is not possible the other way around.

The child process does not inherit any locks and alarms that may have been set by the parent. It will not have any pending signals right after being created. Therefore, the child is not notified when an alarm, set by the parent, expires.

A child process can be made to run another program by using one of *execve*, *execv*, *execle*, and *execl* system calls. If a child process starts to execute a new program, it will have a new image and will no longer remember its previous image. In this case, when the new program is completed, the child process completes and exits. It will not return to the previous process image.

4.4.7 How is a Process Terminated?

When the execution of a process is completed, it is logically terminated. For the physical termination of a process, all memory occupied as process images and stacks are first freed. Then, the process control block is freed and the process is removed from the process table. The physical termination of a process is started after its parent process becomes informed of the logical termination of its child. The parent process might have been waiting for its child to terminate by calling *wait()* or *waitpid()* system calls. Logical termination of a process takes less processing time than its physical termination. For logical termination it suffices to change the terminating process's state to *terminated* and to actually add this process to the set of terminated processes. Physical termination of a process, on the other hand, involves physical removal of the process and the corresponding controlling information from main memory, registers, etc.

4.5 Process-Based Operating Systems

In a layered operating system like UNIX, Windows, Linux, etc., higher layers of the operating system are organized as independent modules, each capable of performing a major managerial function. The kernel may be a huge "monolithic" process or it could be a collection of modules each capable of performing one managerial function. Besides, it consists of a set of primitives used by many kernel modules, higher layer modules, and perhaps user processes. Monolithic structuring of the kernel is a thing of the past and it is no longer an acceptable method of kernel design. Therefore, for modern operating systems, active modules can be processes, threads, or **agents**. A process-based operating system is an operating system in which the kernel is composed of a set of independent processes and a collection of primitives. Each process in such a system is given a unique responsibility. This concept does not mean that in such a system we cannot create threads. Rather, it clarifies the way we look at the operating system in terms of design and implementation purposes. Although UNIX is a process-based operating system it provides a collection of application accessible procedures for creating user-level threads. This kind of threads is explained in the next chapter.

In a process-based operating system, the centre of attention is the process. We shall later provide managerial rules and regulations for processes, the synchronization method of processes, the scheduling of processes, and so on.

4.6 Summary

Processes are one of the central issues of every operating system. Processes are created, managed, and destroyed by the operating system. They are created as an environment for running user programs. The process state transition diagram is one way to model processes and to study the requirements within every state and during transitions from one state to another. The request to create a process could come from a user, an application process, or the operating system itself. On the other hand, the same requesters could order the destruction of a process or it could be terminated automatically when its duty is finished or when a fatal fault has occurred. A process that requests the creation of another process becomes the parent process and the created process is called the child process. A child process goes its own way right after it is created. It is the parent process that may wait until after the execution of its child process to collect, for example, accounting information for an accounting system. As UNIX is a process-based operating system, this chapter was able to use actual examples from this operating system.

4.7 Problems

1. What are the purposes of system calls?

2. Explain the reasons for the two transitions from the kernel to itself, in the UNIX state transition diagram.

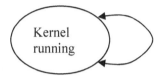

3. Write a program that creates two child processes. Each created (child) process has to execute a separate executable program.

4. Using system-calls such as *create*, *open*, and *read*, develop a program to make a copy of an existing file.

5. In order to find out whether system calls consume more CPU time than regular procedures, develop a program that calls a kernel service one thousand times and a procedure the same number of times. Calculate the CPU time spent in each case. Compare the results and present an argument that supports the results. You should pick a system call that has approximately the same number of instructions as the procedure.

6. Develop a C (C++ or C#) program which when starts running inputs the value of the variable x and then creates a child process. The father process then doubles the value of x and sends it to the output device. On the other hand, the child process triples the value of x and sends it to the output device. Explain the output of the program.

7. Find out whether Linux is a process-based operating system or a thread-based one.

8. Find out how we can create a child process to run a different program (not a different procedure).

9. Name one more operating system which is process-based.

Recommended References

Horning and Randal [Hor76] have treated the concept of process independent of any operating system. For the general treatment of processes within UNIX refer to Vahalia [Vah07]. McKusick et al have presented a specific treatment of processes for Berkeley 4.4BSD UNIX [Mck96]. [Bac86] is a good reference for the treatment of AT&T UNIX. Linux process management is discussed by Beck et al [Bec02] and O'gorman [Ogo01]. For sample implementations of the concepts of this chapter see reference [Crow96].

Chapter 5

Thread

A system, that is composed of processes structured in a parent-child hierarchy and a governing body named the operating system, works very well running our programs. However, what are the problems with this type of system that inspired operating system scientists introduce a new species of living objects called **threads**?

Consider a situation in which a process is needed by many users. It might be a file server that is in constant demand by many processes to *create*, *open*, *read*, *write*, *see* and/or *change attributes*, *copy*, *delete* files etc. What do we do when we have only processes and no threads? For every request to the file server, a child process of a file server process is created and the responsibility of handling the corresponding request is passed on to it. As stated in the previous chapter, to create a child process a copy of the parent's memory image must be made for the child. Even if only parts of a parent's image, for every child process, are retained, main memory will soon be in high demand, thus decreasing its efficiency. Another very important issue is resource allocation. Computer resources are limited. A majority of the time, in multiprogramming environment resources are highly sought after. In a multiprogramming single-processor system, there is only one CPU, which many processes would like to snatch in order to conduct their duties. A personal computer might have one hard disk, even though many processes are in constant need to read or write on files. Even with more than one hard disk, the situation may become challenging. A similar

> A *file server* is a software program that provides file services to users, usually within a network of computers. A file server is a kind of multi-user software that takes requests from many processes, does the requested file service, returns the results, or stores the information provided by the users, on files.

scenario may arise for other resources and even for software resources like compilers.

Creating many processes and letting them compete for limited resources causes the system to spend much time mediating and resolving conflicts. It also increases the chance of **deadlocks**, a situation where two or more processes are each waiting for a resource that another holds and the waiting creates a loop. The thread concept and technology was introduced to solve these dilemmas. It also has other benefits.

By using threads, we can make many parts of a program execute concurrently. This concurrency is more effective when the system is of multiprocessor/multi-programming nature. In the case of multi-programming systems with one processor, as described in Chapter Three, the overall system utilization also increases. When a system is better utilized in running a process, the process will be completed in a shorter period. For instance, for a word-processing software, one thread could be assigned for information input and display function, one thread for spell checking, one for periodical transfer of the information to its permanent place on a disk, and yet another for pagination purposes. All these threads can run concurrently or in a multiprogramming fashion. A similar situation can be arranged using only processes. However, by using threads, resources such as open files and main memory information, are shared. One more benefit of threads is that, in sharing many resources of a process, thread creation and destruction takes less system time which in turn improves the overall system efficiency. A process' threads are regularly set up to cooperate and make the job faster and more appealing to the user, whenever the computer user is present during a job execution. With this in mind, processes usually work in a competitive, not cooperative manner. They try to grab more resources and CPU time to get their own job finished sooner.

> *Deadlock* refers to a situation in which two or more processes are each waiting for a resource that is currently in the possession of another process. A closed loop is formed by the waiting. Forcefully taking these resources from the processes is not permitted. In such a situation, an intervention by the operating system is inevitable, although this intervention may kill some processes out of interest for the others. Although deadlock is a rare event, it could be very harmful. Hence, its prevention is very desirable.

5.1 Thread Types

The implementation of threads is not without difficulties. Any change to a shared, or global variable, or the status of a resource, by one thread affects all **sibling** threads, i.e., threads that share the same executable code. For example, a thread may free up a tape drive which some other thread will need in the future.

It is possible that there will be timing conflicts in using common resources like data buffers. These are new challenges in the development of thread-based operating systems.

Threads are sometimes called **Lightweight Processes** (LWP), because thread creation and termination by the operating system is less time consuming than process creation and termination. The name LWP does not mean threads are smaller than processes. We will stick with the preferred and more commonly used term "thread" in our discussion.

There are three different views on thread implementation. Threads could be implemented at the user level. A **user-level thread** is known only to the user or actually the process that has created it. A process has to handle all aspects of managing the threads it created. These tasks include but are not restricted to: CPU assignment, device assignment, state transition, etc. To be clearer, the operating system will not know that a process has created any threads and hence cannot help managing them. What the operating system does, in respect to user-level threads, is to provide a set of basic routines for creation, manipulation, and destruction of threads. These can be used by the user whenever needed, without any managerial responsibility as the part of the operating system.

The **kernel-level thread**, on the other hand, is a thread that is created by the operating system in response to a request from a user. The operating system knows this thread, has given it a unique identification number, and it takes complete responsibility for managing it (compare to process management). This kind of thread is the most common one and will be the center attention of this chapter.

The third type of thread implementation is **hybrid implementation** that is the implementation of a combination of user-level and kernel-level threads. The managerial responsibility of this kind of thread is performed partially by the user who has created the thread and partially by the operating system.

User-level threads have many advantages and few disadvantages. We are not planning to discuss the pro and con details of user-level threads. Rather, we would like to ignore user-level and hybrid thread implementations and concentrate on kernel-level thread implementation. We think this is where the operating system plays a significant role, which is worth considering in an operating system context. Of course, by discussing kernel-level implementation of threads a great deal of hybrid thread implementation is covered. With this in mind, the forthcoming discussion covers kernel-level methodologies and design ideas.

The discussion of threads is most natural within the context of a **thread-based** operating system. In the previous chapter, we presented the process concept and many of the actual situations discussed were taken from the UNIX operating system, an agreed upon process-based operating system (with thread supporting capabilities.) In this chapter, we will present actual examples from the contemporary Windows operating system which is the closest to a completely thread-based operating system among commonly used operating systems.

In a thread-based operating system, a process is no longer the active species of the environment. Rather, the responsibility of running programs is transferred to threads. A process plays the role of a house in which threads live. As there are no empty houses, as soon as a process is created a thread is also created from the process. Therefore, there is at least one thread for every process but there might be more than one thread living in a house, i.e., a process. A hierarchy of parent-child processes is perfectly acceptable in thread-based operating systems. To make the case simple and practical, we assume that all threads of a process are **siblings**. There is no hierarchy among themselves even though a parent-child relation may exist among some of them in regards to thread generation. This is a safe assumption since there is usually no major difference between the thread that is generated by a process (the primary thread) and threads that are generated by other threads, as long as they are within one process.

A **multithreading operating system** is the one that is capable of handling many processes and threads at the same time. Every process is allowed to generate more than one thread. In such an operating system, there exist facilities for thread creation, deletion, switching, etc. Such an operating system allows users to generate more than one request to one process at the same time. For example, a browser can be made to search simultaneously for more than one topic, even though there is only one copy of the "browser program" in main memory.

> In a *thread-based operating system*, a process cannot execute a program. To execute a program, the system must create a thread. For example, when a computer user double clicks on an executable program, a process is created. Immediately after the creation of this process, its first thread is created, too. This first thread is usually called the primary thread.

Multiprogramming methodology and technique are essential in the implementation of multithreading. In the new environment, a thread becomes the unit to which the CPU (or a PU) is assigned.

Now that the fundamentals have been covered, we can continue with other aspects.

5.2 Common Settings for Sibling Threads

The process that has generated sibling threads provides the common ground on which these threads perform their tasks. Figure 5.1 shows the model of a process and its threads. The process provides the address space and all shared items, like global variables, open files, and other resources. Every thread has its own private items such as stacks, stack pointers, register contents, condition codes, priority,

CPU time usage, scheduling parameters, and various flags. The most important piece of information, the program counter, shows the location in the shared code where this thread is running or will run. All threads of one process can access the process's common address space without any restrictions or protection. A thread's private items are not part of the common settings.

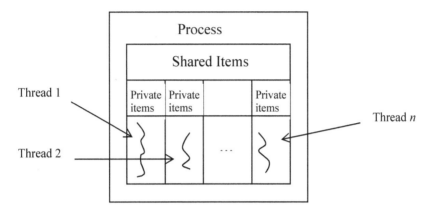

Figure 5.1: The model of a multithread process

For all sibling threads, the corresponding process provides "sibling thread's common settings." The settings are not the same as a process attributes. Rather, they are the process's code, data, open files, file attributes, and resources such as tapes, CDs, etc. Other process attributes may not be usable by its threads and therefore do not belong to sibling threads common setting. One example is accounting information. A thread need not know the collective execution time of all sibling threads. This may very well be the process' private piece of information. Table 5.1 summarizes sibling threads common setting.

Table 5.1: Sibling threads common setting.

Subject	Description
Address space	Code, (parts of) data, and (parts of) results
Open files	Open files, file attributes, and means of referencing files
Resources	Tapes, CDs, and many other hardware or software resources that are assigned to the process

5.3 Thread Attributes

Similar to processes, threads have their own attributes. These attributes serve three purposes: identification, status clarification, and thread controlling. Typical information would be: register contents, stacks, stack pointers, condition codes, priority, CPU time usage, scheduling parameters, various flags, and the location counter. The specific operating system's designer may add new items or even remove some depending on how the thread concept is to be implemented in the operating system. Table 5.2 shows some of the fields used in Windows operating system for **thread attributes**.

Table 5.2: Windows thread attributes.

Fields	Some possible usage
Thread identification information	
Thread ID	For unique and simple referencing by the operating system
Thread state information	
Thread-visible registers	To keep temporary values while thread is running
Location counter	Will be needed, as a continuation point, when the thread restarts running
Condition code flags	To reflect the state of some previously executed instruction
Stack pointers	To point to the stack of procedure and system calls that is used to keep track of sequence of such calls
Thread control information	
Base priority	The lowest precedence of the thread's dynamic priority with respect to other threads to be used for scheduling purposes
Dynamic priority	The current precedence of the thread's priority with respect to other threads to be used for scheduling purposes.
Thread processor affinity	The set of processors that the thread is allowed to be scheduled to use, for execution of its instructions
Thread execution time	Total execution time used, so far, for the thread, for accounting and scheduling purposes

Suspension count	Total number of times the threads execution has been suspended and not yet resumed
Impersonation token	A temporary authority token, to perform an action on behalf of another process
Alert status	An indicator of whether the thread has executed an asynchronous procedure call and it is in a position to be interrupted when the results are ready
Termination port	A channel to send a message to when the thread is terminated
Thread exit status	How the thread was terminated. Thread's completion condition, to be reported to its creator

The corresponding process attributes of Windows are shown in Table 5.3. It is worth mentioning that this section is not the proper place to show process attributes. However, this is done to clarify that process attributes complement thread attributes in order to make control and management of threads possible.

Table 5.3: Windows process attributes.

Fields	Some possible usage
Process identification information	
Process ID	For unique and simple referencing by the operating system
Process control information	
Security descriptor	User who created the process, users who can use it, and users who are forbidden to use it. For security and protection purposes
Base priority	The baseline priority for execution of threads of the process. Priorities of threads are dynamic but a baseline is respected
Default processor affinity	The set of processors that the thread of this process is allowed to be scheduled to use, for executing their instructions
Quota limit	Maximum number of resources, size of memory and secondary memory, CPU time, etc. the process or its

	threads are allowed to use, collectively, to make sure it does not use more than its credit.
Execution time	Total execution time of all its threads, for accounting and scheduling purposes
I/O counters	The number and types of I/O operations performed by process's threads
VM operation counters	The number and types of virtual memory operations performed by process's threads
Exception/debugging port	The port to which a message is sent per every exceptions caused by the process's threads
Exit status	Shows how the process is terminated

5.4 Thread States and the State Transition Model

A thread can have states similar to process states. In addition, there is no need to remove a state or add a new one. *Ready, running*, and *wait/blocked* states or simple variations of these are just as fundamental to any *active program* as they are for threads. State transition diagrams provide the basis for analyzing an operating system's requirements for handing threads. The procedure for developing a thread state transition diagram will not be discussed here since it is very similar to the procedure for developing a process state transition diagram which was discussed in the previous chapter. Instead, we simply present the **thread state transition diagram** of a contemporary operating system, such as Windows. A brief description of states and the interpretation of state transitions are provided. In Windows, a thread could be in one of the states listed in Table 5.4.

Table 5.4: Windows thread states

State	Description
Ready	The thread is ready to be picked up for execution.
Standby	Ready and chosen to run on a particular processor, next.
Running	Using a processor and executing program instructions
Waiting	The thread is waiting for an event to occur
Transition	Ready to run but needs some resources other than processor
Terminated	Thread's execution is finished, but it is not yet completely removed, from the system

The state transition model of thread is depicted in Figure 5.2.

When a thread is first created, it is in the *ready* state. The scheduler can pick a ready thread to be executed next in one of the processors. The state of this thread becomes *standby*. From the standby state, the thread's state changes to *running* when the corresponding processor picks the thread for execution. When the thread uses its current share of processor time, it is *preempted*, i.e., the processor is taken away from the thread.

A *running* thread may need to input data, output results, or wait for some event to occur, such as receiving a message from some other thread before further continuing its execution. It such a case, the thread has to wait and its state is changed to *waiting*. From this state, it can move to the *ready* state when the reasons for waiting no longer exist and required resources are assigned. The thread will move to the *transition* state if the reasons for waiting no longer exist, but all the required resources are not assigned. From the *transition* state, a thread moves to the *ready* state when its required resources are reassigned.

Finally, a thread *terminates* upon completing its execution.

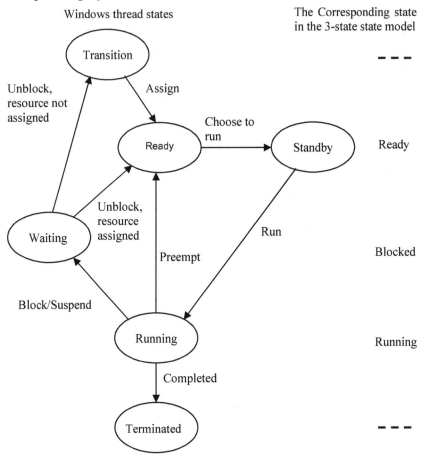

Figure 5.2: Windows thread state transition model

5.5 Thread Creation and Termination

The philosophy behind thread creation and termination in a thread-based operating system is similar to process creation and termination in a process-based operating system. We will discuss this by providing the answers to the following questions:

1. Why create threads?
2. When is a thread created?
3. How is a thread created?
4. What are the tools for creating a thread?
5. How is a thread terminated?
6. What is done after thread termination?

5.5.1 Why Create Threads?

In a thread-based environment, threads are the only means of running programs. Without threads user tasks will not be accomplished.

In a process-based environment where multithreading is possible, threads are created instead of child processes for resource sharing and address space sharing among sibling threads. This technique increases the availability of main memory and resources for other processes and threads. As a positive side effect, the chance of deadlock is decreased because there are fewer processes to compete for resources. Compare this to a similar system in which child processes are created instead of threads. It should be noted that threads do not compete for many types of resources. However, their parent processes do.

5.5.2 When is a Thread Created?

When a process is created, its first thread, sometimes called the **primary thread,** is created by the operating system. Refer to the previous chapter for a discussion on when a process is created. There are other circumstances in which threads are created. Regardless of the reason, a process or a thread may make an explicit call to a **system service** that is designed to create threads. Therefore, the following two circumstances cause thread creation:

1. Whenever a process is created, its first thread, sometimes called the primary thread, is created
2. Whenever a running process (in process-based operating systems), or a running thread, explicitly requests the execution of a service call that creates a thread.

5.5.3 How is a Thread Created?

Kernel-level threads, which are the focus of this chapter, are managed by the operating system. As in process registration, any thread that is created must be registered with the operating system for future references. Recall that a **process table** was used to hold the **process control block** information of all processes in the system. The identification, state, and control information of a thread are kept within a structure (or an object) called the **Thread Control Block** (TCB). There is one TCB for every thread in the system. There is one entry for every thread in a structure called the **Thread Table** (TT). The thread table, like the process table, is kept in main memory and is not swapped out to **secondary memory**, in order to facilitate fast future references. Although the exact steps taken for thread creating depend on the specific operating system, the following are the general steps taken for this.

1. Make sure the total number of threads created so far has not reached the limit
2. Allocate a unique thread identification
3. Allocate space for the thread control block and thread context, i.e., places to store the CPU register contents, and initialize appropriate fields
4. Allocate space for other required structures such as stacks and stack pointers and initialize proper fields
5. Put the thread in one of the queues corresponding to the thread states.

We will still have the **process table** and **process control blocks** in both thread-based operating systems and process-based operating systems with thread creating facilities.

5.5.4 What are the Tools for Creating a Thread?

It is customary to provide a system call for creating a thread. A **system call**, or a **system service** as some operating system specialists call it, is a routine of the operating system kernel that is made available for use within the kernel itself, by the upper layers of the operating system, and application programmers. To generate a new thread, a system call is activated with proper arguments. The calling method is usually the same whether called by a programmer or some part of the operating system.

We have decided to provide a balanced quantity of materials of Windows, UNIX, and Linux operating system in this book. In accordance with this commitment, specific examples of this chapter are based on Windows operating system. The actual system call for creating a thread in Windows is not known. Windows designers have not revealed system calls so that they are able to change them at any time, without affecting user programs. The Win32-API (Application Programmer Interface), sometimes called the 32-bit API, is an environment for Windows application programs and contains hundreds of procedures. As a Windows programmer, you will somehow tell the system that you are using this environment. Within this environment, there is a procedure called **CreateThread** for creating a new thread. Whether or not this is actually a **system call**, reveals the different ways a thread creation routine is called either by a programmer or by the operating system. If this is a system call, then the inner layers of the operating system will also call **CreateThread** to create a thread. However, if this is not a system call then it is a procedure, within which one or more system calls will be called to create a new thread.

CreateThread has few arguments. Properties like who can access the thread, the size of the thread's stack, the program that the newly created thread will run, etc., are passed on to the **CreateThread** procedure so that a thread with specific properties is created. The calling statement looks like this:

HandleVar = CreateThread ("list of arguments separated by comma");

When a thread is created the system will return a pointer to the caller. In Windows this pointer is called the **thread handle**. The handle is the means of accessing the created thread. For example, if we want to destroy the thread later, we can identify that particular thread by its handle. In our example, *HandleVar* is chosen as the variable that will accept the created thread's handle. Of course, **CreateThread** is the name of the Win32-API procedure that creates a thread. All arguments needed for the thread's properties have to be listed inside a pair of parenthesis and separated by comma. The **CreateThread** procedure can be called from anywhere within a user's program. Whether or not a procedure with the same name is called from within the Win32-API to create our thread, or many little system calls are called in a specific order to collectively create the thread, is not clear.

The following is the implementation of a particular and simplified patient monitoring system using three threads. In this system, a ward nurse is supposed to check her patients every 15 minutes and regularly evaluate their vital signs. She is also responsible for administering patient drugs based on their doctor's recommendations. Two threads are designed for these purposes. First, a thread which beeps, displays a message, sleeps for 15 minutes, and repeats this sequence. Second, a thread which beeps, displays a message which is different from the message displayed by the fist thread, asks the operator to input the time span to sleep before displaying the next message, sleeps for the given period, and repeats this sequence. Both threads are created and started by a main program.

```
#include <windows.h>
#include <stdio.h>
void  RegAttendance (void)   // Regular attendance
{
    while (1)
    {
        Beep (500, 10);  // Make a beep sound
        printf (" It is the time for the regular patient attendance \n ");
        Sleep (15*60*1000);  // Sleep for 15 minutes
    }
}
void  ScheAttendance (void)     // Scheduled attendance
{
    int TimeSpan;
    while (1)
    {
```

```
    Beep (500, 10);  // Make a beep sound
    printf (" Enter the time span before next scheduled attendance\n ");
    scanf ("%d", &TimeSpan);
    Sleep (TimeSpan*60*1000);  // Sleep for "TimeSpan" minutes
  }
}
int  main(void)
{
  HANDLE thread1, thread2;
  thread1=CreateThread(0,0,(LPTHREAD_START_ROUTINE)
        RegAttendance,NULL,0,0);
  thread2=CreateThread(0,0,(LPTHREAD_START_ROUTINE)
        ScheAttendance,NULL,0,0);
  Sleep(INFINITE);
  return 0;
}
```

Program 5.1: Thread-based simplified patient monitoring system

Program 5.1 is an application program but similar schemes can be used to create threads within the operating system. In Windows every process starts with one thread called the **primary thread,** which can create other threads using *CreateThread*. As seen in Program 5.1, *thread1* is directed to execute the "RegAttendance" routine. *Thread2*, on the other hand, will run the "ScheAttendance" routine. Recall that a primary thread is also created to run the main program which will create the two other threads and will assign their responsibilities.

A thread can be created directly in the main body of the main program or it can be created in the body of a routine that is going to be executed by another thread. We can talk about a parent-child hierarchical structure for threads that are directly or indirectly created within the large body of a process. Often, threads of one process are considered to be on the same level, or siblings, irregardless of where and when they were created.

5.5.5 How is a Thread Terminated?

All threads that are created within the large body of a process are terminated when the process is terminated. A thread can terminate itself by explicitly calling proper system calls or Win32-API routines such as *ExitThread*. The third method for terminating a thread is by calling Win32-API routines such as *TerminateThread* form another thread in the same process, or another process if this process has the permission to do so, and has the handle to access the thread.

Handle is a pointer that indirectly points to an object, i.e., the pointer points to a pointer which, in turn, points to the object. The benefit of using handles in our program is that, if the address (or location) of the object is changed by the operating system, we can still use the handle to access the object. This is possible by the operating system updating the contents of the pointer that the handle points to.

5.5.6 What is done After Thread Termination?

After thread termination, some handles used by the thread are freed and others are freed when the thread's corresponding process is terminated. The thread's TCB is freed and its corresponding entry in the thread table is removed. If a thread is the last thread of a process to terminate, the process terminates, too. Specific steps for process termination depend on the operating system used.

5.6 Thread-Based Operating Systems

All contemporary operating systems support thread methodology and technique. However, it is the designer of the operating system that decides on a process-based or thread-based system. In a thread-based operating system, the thread is the only active object and the process is just the container of threads. Procedures, routines, primitives, etc. are all passive collections of instructions that are only useful when they become parts of a thread and are executed with the thread execution.

In a thread-based operating system, there is at least one thread for every process, which is called the primary thread. This thread is created as soon as its mother process is created. For an operating system to be classified as thread-based, this methodology must be well adhered to within the kernel. Therefore, a thread-based operating system is an operating system in which kernel activities are performed by a set of threads. Each thread belongs to a process with a given responsibility. A kernel may still have many primitives with very low level responsibilities. Every primitive can become a part of many threads. By doing so, code reusability is achieved and kernel size is reduced. Contemporary Windows are the most widely-used near thread-based operating systems.

5.7 Summary

Threads, in a thread-based operating system, are active objects that follow program instructions in order to perform tasks (or subtasks). Thread methodology boosts operating system efficiency through better utilization of main memory and reduction of competing objects for resources. At the same time, thread methodology increases collaboration between related program objects. The threads of a process are not as independent as processes. Threads can share many items such as address space, resources, global variables, etc., while still possessing their own location counter, status, stack, and stack pointer, etc.

Threading technique has its own difficulties, too. One thread may try to free a resource although its sibling threads have yet not finished with the resource. A thread may try to close a file that is needed by others. Another difficulty is having a thread change a global variable while its sibling threads are unaware of. In any case, we are sure the specialists will overcome these drawbacks.

5.8 Problems

1. Define the exact thread-creation steps taken by Contemporary Windows.

2. The UNIX operating system uses the copy-on-write technique in order for the parent and child processes to share memory until the point where one of them tries to modify a page frame of the shared memory. Just before the modification takes place, the system makes a copy of the frame and allocates it to the child process. State the similarities and the differences of this technique as compared to thread methodology.

3. In a thread-based operating system, if the primary thread of a process terminates, is it possible for threads of this primary thread to continue running?

4. In a thread-based operating system, for each one of the following attributes state whether it is a process attribute, a thread attribute, or both.

     I.   Location counter
     II. Condition code flags
     III. Dynamic processor affinity
     IV. Execution time
     V.   ID
     VI. Default processor affinity
     VII. Quota limit
     VIII. Visible registers
     IX. Exit status
     X.   Assigned resources

5. Give two reasons for using thread concept when we can use process and child process concepts.

6. Highlight the differences between the thread concept in Windows and the thread concept in Unix.

7. Name one more operating system which is thread-based.

Recommended References

For a conceptual treatment of thread methodology, read the text by Lewis and Berg [Lew96]. See [Pha96] by Pham, [Sol98] by Solomon, and [Sol00] by Solomon and Russinovich for threads in Windows. Mauro and McDougall have described developments in threading in Solaris 2 kernel [Mau01].

Chapter 6

Scheduling

From a purely conceptual viewpoint, a job is a request for a computation. However, from the scheduling point of view, a job is a computation that has to be scheduled for execution. This computation is organized as a sequence of instructions, collectively called a program. A program could be stored on removable media, such as floppy diskettes, compact disks, flash disks, etc., that may or may not be conncted. A program may be stored as well on media such as hard disks or a disk pack that is currently connected to the computer. In any case, a program is not an active object. When a program is activated, it becomes a process. A process is therefore, a live creature that is made to follow the instructions of a program in order to perform a task. In doing so, a process will use many computer resources such as the CPU, main memory, secondary memories, etc. In a thread-based system, the thread is the living object and the process becomes the environment within which threads live, similar to a house in which one or more people live in. In such an environment a process is composed of the program, resources, open files, etc., that are used by its threads. This much we already learned from previous chapters.

In job scheduling, the next job is selected from amongst a set of available jobs to become a process. This involves determining the order in which jobs become processes. Process scheduling is the policy of selecting the next process to run from amongst ready processes. The order in which processes will run is thus determined. In thread scheduling, the next thread to run is selected from amongst ready threads. Consequently, the order in which threads will run is determined. Job scheduling, process scheduling, and thread scheduling are conceptually and technically different, but sometimes the term *job scheduling* refers to all these concepts. We will make proper distinctions as necessary.

There are many criteria that a job scheduler may be based upon. We will first introduce these criteria, later talk about specific scheduling strategies and then discuss their properties.

6.1 Scheduling Criteria

Scheduling criteria are properties of entities, like jobs, processes, and threads, which can influence the order in which these entities are selected to use computer resources especially the CPU. These criteria and a short description of each one are discussed below.

6.1.1 Request Time

Request time is the exact time a demand to do a task is received. The task may be to compile a source program. A process (or thread) has to be formed to do the compilation. In this case, the compiler does the compiling process. A request may be to find out whether a certain book is available at a library. A request may require long or short execution time. Sometimes the actual time a request needs is not important but its relative arrival time, in respect to other requests' arrival time, is an important scheduling criteria. It is usually the case that the earlier the request time, the sooner the job must be done.

6.1.2 Processing Time

The processing time needed by a job is the time taken for its corresponding process to be executed to completion. Often, a job with a shorter processing time is executed sooner than a job with a longer processing time. A similar situation is frequently observed in every day life when one waits in a queue for service. For example, in a supermarket checkout queue, a shopper with one or two items may be given permission to checkout first.

6.1.3 Priority

It is possible to assign priorities to jobs. With a priority-based scheduler, a job with higher priority has the opportunity to be scheduled before a job with a lower priority. Sometimes, priorities are assigned to users. In such a case, a request by a person with higher priority has preference to be executed sooner than that of a person with lower priority. **Static priority** is when priority does not change with time and is fixed under all circumstances. Priorities that are assigned to users are usually of this type. Based on **dynamic priority**, the priority of a process may vary with time and changes in circumstances. Consider the case where the priority of a task increases as its waiting time to service increases. Sometimes, priorities describe the degree of urgency to do a task. For example, on the Internet, the priority of a message determines how soon the message is to be delivered. Voice messages for a videoconference over the Internet are delivered sooner than ordinary search result messages. In this case the deadline id the sum of request time and deadline parameter.

6.1.4 Deadline

The deadline of a job is the time by which job execution must be completed. A deadline is often expressed by either one of the two values: (1) the exact time the execution completion of a job is requested and (2) the maximum time limit in which the execution of the job must be completed after it is requested. The latter is called the job's **deadline parameter.**

6.1.5 Wait Time

The wait time of a request is the time that has elapsed since the request was submitted. Wait time is a dynamic value and increases as the time goes by. A closely related factor to wait time is the **response time**. This is the length of time from the instant a request is submitted until the first reaction of the system to the request. Usually, the reaction must be visible by the requester.

A *scheduling policy* describes the guideline for selecting the next process (job or thread) from among all processes that need a computer resource like the CPU.

A *scheduling algorithm* is a finite set of clearly stated unambiguous stepwise operations that when applied to a finite set of processes that are waiting to use a computer resource like the CPU, either one or more of these processes are selected or a time table for the resource usage is produced. Similarly, there exists program, thread, and I/O scheduling algorithms.

A *scheduling mechanism* determines how to do every step of the scheduling algorithm in order to reflect the actions needed. For example, the exact steps to be taken to modify a process-queue and process state are defined by a scheduling mechanism.

6.1.6 Preemptability

When a process is picked up for execution, it may not be allowed to switch to another process before the execution of the former process is completely finished or the process is self blocked. The inability to switch to another process may depend on the nature of the process, in which case the process is called non-preemptable. Inability may also depend on the type of adapted scheduling policy. On the other hand, if the operating system is allowed to switch from a running process to another ready-to-run process before completion then the running process is preemptable.

6.2 Scheduling Objectives

A scheduler assigns specific times for processes to use computer resources in order to perform their tasks and subtasks. Usually, there is an enormous number of ways to schedule a set of processes to use a set of resources, especially since every process needs many resources at different times for varying time spans. Not all these options are of the same importance and lead to an equal amount of system efficiency and utilization. Different scheduling policies are designed to match different environments. A scheduling strategy is usually designed to attain a defined objective, although multi-objective strategies are also possible. Common scheduling objectives are listed and briefly defined below.

6.2.1 Throughput

The number of requests that a system can complete in one unit of time is called the system's **throughput**. We may want to set up our scheduling policy so that the total number of completed requests over a period of time is as high as possible. At first, it may seem that such a policy is beneficial to all users and that everyone get his/her work done sooner, but this is not so. Such a system will favor shorter requests over longer ones and longer requests will not be executed unless there are no shorter requests. This seems to be unfair. Tasks with reasonable input/output handling are naturally long and will be postponed when tasks with less input/output handling are present. This can reduce overall system utilization because I/O devices will be left idle most of the time and only some hardware modules, such as the CPU and main memory, will have high utilizations. Therefore, overall system utilization may be low when there is an emphasis on high throughput.

6.2.2 Deadline

In some computing environments every request has a deadline, before which time the request must be completed. Missing a deadline may in fact cause a catastrophe. In these environments, the main scheduling objective is to devise a time table or policy for the execution of requests in such a way that all deadlines are met. Examples of such environments exist in aerospace, nuclear power-plant, avionics, the automotive industry, multimedia etc. These are called **real-time** environments. A major difference between commercial and real-time systems is that a real-time system must not only be correct but it must also be timely and predictable. Real-time systems can be classified into hard real-time systems and soft real-time systems.

In a **hard real-time** system, there is an absolute requirement to executing all requests before their deadlines. However, in a **soft real-time** system, the occasional missing of a deadline will not cause a total system loss or catastrophe. Even so, in a soft real-time system, the main objective is to meet all deadlines.

6.2.3 Turnaround Time

Excellent **Quality of Service** (QoS) is answering every request within a reasonably short time. **Turnaround time** of a request is the time span starting from when a request is submitted to the system and ending whenever the requesting execution is completed. The turnaround time of all requests is usually not the same and may vary from one request to the next. It is not possible to judge on the quality of a scheduling policy based on the turnaround time of one or a few requests. A better measure would be the **average turnaround time** of requests. This may be used to estimate the expected time length in which a request is completed after being submitted to the system.

If a request requires 5 seconds to be executed, is picked for execution right after its submission, and is executed without any interruption, its turnaround time will be 5 seconds. Similarly, if a request requires one second of execution time, is picked up for execution right after its submission, and is executed without any interruption, its turnaround time will be one second. Although our response to both requests is exactly the same, i.e., every request is picked for execution right after submission, the net result turnaround time is different. Therefore, one way to achieve a better measure is to normalize the turnaround time of all requests. A **normalized turnaround time** is obtained by dividing the turnaround time of every request by its execution time. This normalized turnaround time is called a **weighted turnaround time**. We now can recognize an **average weighted turnaround time** as a positive objective in the design of a scheduling policy. However, this objective has its own disadvantages. For example, a newly arrived request is preferred over a request that has been waiting its turn for execution. This is because such a decision leads to a better average weighted turnaround time. Shorter requests are also favored over longer ones submitted at the same time.

6.2.4 Response Time

Response time is a very similar factor to turnaround time. The **response time** of a request is the time span from when the request is submitted to the system until the first (user visible) reply to the request submitter is generated. When this reply is received by the submitter, he will know the request is accepted by the system and the system has started its execution.

6.2.5 Priority

Priority is one of the scheduling criteria that are described in the previous section. Respecting priorities may be the sole scheduling objective. Priorities may be given to either: user groups, users, jobs, processes, or threads. When priorities are assigned to one of these entities, lower level entities will usually inherit the same priority. For example, if priorities are assigned to users, then the jobs, processes, and threads of a user will usually carry the priority of the user. Sometimes priorities of lower level entities are not exactly the same as the priority that is assigned to their parent or ancestor entities. Rather, it may be computed by a complex algorithm. When priorities are dynamic, there may be a base priority that is inherited, but the actual priority may change as time progresses and circumstances change. On the other hand, if the priority is static, the priority that is assigned to a process (or thread) stays the same for the lifetime of the process.

6.2.6 Processor Utilization

The most advanced technology and expensive materials are used to make processors. Consequently, the processor is the most valuable module of every computer. A scheduler can be designed to make computer processor's utilization as high as possible. Such a scheduler will have to favor **CPU-bound** processes over **I/O-bound** ones. A quantitative measure of utilization is the **Utilization factor**. If the processor is always busy by doing our requests for the period of interest, the utilization factor for that period is one. In other words, it is fully utilized. However, if the length of the period is r and the processor is busy doing our requests for a total length of e in that period, then processor utilization is e/r for the period.

6.2.7 System Balance

A good mix of processes can utilize most devices simultaneously, namely devices such as the processor, main memory, I/O processors, disk drives, printers, etc. A scheduler with the objective of balancing the utilization of system modules will have to distinguish I/O-bound from CPU-bound processes and schedule them so that valuable devices are kept busy most of the time.

6.2.8 Fairness

It is difficult to design a set of scheduling rules so that system resources are fairly distributed among all users. Actually, the concept of fair may mean different things in different environments. A user may write a program so that it creates many processes (including child processes) and threads. These processes will all independently compete with other processes (and amongst themselves) to grab system resources. Threads will also compete with other threads to obtain CPU time. Therefore, an application with many processes and threads benefit from the ability to use more resources and CPU time than an application with one or very few processes and threads.

One way to approach fairness is to use a method called **fair share scheduling**. With this kind of scheduler, each user is assigned a share of the system, especially a share of the processor or processors. This share is expressed in the form of a fraction of resource utilization. However, it may not be easy to ensure that every user will receive its exact share of resources.

6.3 Scheduling levels

The level of scheduling depends on the type of entities to be scheduled. The system has to have a policy for accepting new requests from the outside world. All the requests that are accepted by the system need computer resources, especially CPU time, in order to be answered. All requesters like to receive their answers in the shortest possible time. Actually, there is a silent competition going on among processes that are generated to fulfill their corresponding requests. The scheduler also has the responsibility of preparing the order in which processes use the processor or processors. All scheduling decisions are made having the global scheduling objective in mind. Three levels of scheduling are described next.

6.3.1 High-Level Scheduling

The decision to choose one or more jobs (requests) from amongst all available jobs and to transform them into processes is called **high-level scheduling**. This level of scheduling, also called **long-term scheduling** prepares subjects to be further scheduled for execution in the future. One important factor, that directly affects the decision to choose or not to choose new jobs, is the degree of multiprogramming. This is the maximum number of processes (or threads in a thread-based operating system) that can exist at the same time in the computer. For contemporary operating systems, this number is so high that all requests are usually accepted by the system as soon as they are received. As a result, high-level scheduling is losing its importance compared to other levels of scheduling. However, we always have to make sure this limit is observed, because some hardware registers and operating system structures may have been designed with this limitation in mind.

Some scheduling objectives may entail not accepting new jobs for execution even though the system is not yet saturated with respect to its degree of multiprogramming. For example, where the objective is user priority, a job from a low priority user may not be accepted if there exist processes from a high priority user in the system.

Many events may prompt new scheduling decisions. Such events include the arrival of a new request from one of the users, the completion of a request, and the state in which a fraction of processor idle time is more than a certain predefined value. In an interactive environment, every new request is admitted as soon as its corresponding process is received and it is given one slice of CPU time at the earliest possible time. The admission of the request is a long-term scheduling decision while permission to let a process use the processor is a low-level scheduling decision.

6.3.2 Medium-level scheduling

For some operating systems, such as Linux and UNIX, when there is an extreme shortage of main memory, one or more processes may be removed from the main memory and put into secondary memory. The operating system will bring back the process into main memory when the circumstances are resolved and other factors, like the degree of multiprogramming, allows us to do so. When the process is brought back to main memory and is scheduled for execution, it will continue from where it left off. The act of temporarily removing a process from main memory is called process swapping (or swapping out). Many processes may be swapped out of main memory at one time in order to increase the amount of free main memory to a certain level. The decision of choosing which process or processes to swap out of main memory is a **medium-level scheduling** decision.

6.3.3. Low-level scheduling

Actual processor assignment to processes is determined by low-level schedulers. Non-ready processes are not considered for scheduling at this level rather, only ready processes are scheduled to use the processor. The scheduling objective is the most influencing factor in the deployment of a specific scheduling policy. Without having this in mind, it is not productive to discuss choosing a scheduling policy. However, there are some guidelines that are usually considered, disrespectful of what the specific scheduling algorithm is.

In an interactive environment, most queries are usually very short and it is the nature of such an environment to execute a short query soon after it is received. Otherwise, the system cannot be classified as an interactive system. To accomplish this goal a CPU **time-quantum**, i.e., a very short period of the CPU time, is assigned for the execution of every newly received query. This is accomplished in the shortest possible time after the query is received. Recall that we may not know whether the query is short or long when it is generated.

It is not customary to assign a long continuous time span to one process when many other processes are awaiting execution. Assigning long continuous time spans to some processes may have negative effect on criteria such as average response time, average turnaround time, deadline meeting (if applicable), average wait time, etc.

6.3.4 Input/output scheduling

Input/output scheduling, or I/O scheduling for short, encompasses the methodologies and techniques for the correct and efficient arrangement of input-output operations. It covers a wide range of I/O devices such as the display, hard disk, flash disk, optical disk, scanner, printer, floppy disk, mouse, light pen, keyboard, etc. The scheduling of information transfer within the **Local Area Network** (LAN), **Wide Area Network** (WAN), the **Internet,** etc. is also included in I/O scheduling. However, one general policy and one scheduling algorithm does not work (well) for all devices and communication medias.

Three techniques, namely **programmed I/O, interrupt-driven I/O**, and **Direct Memory Access** (DMA), are available for the actual implementation of an I/O operation after it is scheduled.

With **Programmed I/O**, the process that has issued an I/O

> A *local area network* is composed of a collection of computers located in close vicinity of each other and which are connected together using twisted pairs, fiber optic cables, or even wireless devices. There are many connecting topologies like the bus, ring, tree, etc. Communication speed ranges from one megabit per second to multiple megabits per second for LAN. Every computer is a standalone independent system with its own operating system, system software, and application programs. The overall system facilitates information and resource sharing, electronic mail, and multi-user application development.
>
> A *wide area network* connects many computers that may be geographically very far away from each other. The communication media includes among other devices, communication processors, routers, bridges, telephone lines, mobile devices, satellites, modems, communication protocols, and routing algorithms to facilitate message passing and information exchange. WAN provides similar capabilities to LAN but in an area as wide as the whole world.

operation waits until the operation is completed. While waiting for I/O completion, CPU time that is assigned to this process is actually wasted. This type of waiting is called busy-waiting.

Interrupt driven I/O is the second implementation technique of I/O operations. The process which has issued an I/O operation may continue its execution, but when the I/O operation is completed, the process is interrupted. After the I/O operation is issued, the decision of either waiting or proceeding depends on whether the operations following depend on this I/O operation or not.

If the process decides to wait, it will go to sleep and will be waken up after the interrupt is received. The advantage of going to sleep is that, while sleeping no CPU time is assigned to the process.

Direct memory access refers to a method of directly transferring blocks of data between main memory and the I/O device. With this method, a (hardware) module, called the DMA unit, takes care of transferring the data, independent of both the CPU and the process that has requested the I/O operation. When the I/O operation is completed, an interrupt is issued to the corresponding process. The process could meanwhile go to sleep. The word "direct" in the term *direct memory access* means that the data will not go through the processor during the transfer, as opposed to the other two methods in which data goes through the processor.

I/O devices are classified into three categories. The first category consists of all **dedicated devices**. A dedicated device is a device that is assigned to only one process at a time in a non-preemptable fashion. In other words, when a device of this category is assigned to a process it will not be taken away from the process until the process no longer needs it, upon which time the device is released. The second category is for **shared devices**. A shared device is a device which many processes concurrently use it in a time-sharing fashion. This occurs within a reasonably long period of time when more than one process uses the device. The device can be temporarily taken away from one process and assigned to another even though the former process has not yet finished with it. The third kind of I/O devices is the **virtual device**. This is assigned to a process in place of another device. The assigned device is a virtual device of the original. The two devices do not necessarily have similar characteristics. For example, a process is to originally transfer its output to a printer. However, a file is assigned to the process instead. The file is then the virtual printer in this context.

We will not be able to present all scheduling methodologies and techniques for all kinds of devices, due to the vast amount of information that has to be covered and the fact that this book is not intended to be the text for an advanced course for computer science graduate students. Disk I/O scheduler will be covered in a later sections.

6.4 Scheduling Algorithms: Single-Processor Systems

In this section, our focus is on medium-level or medium-term scheduling algorithms, i.e., the policy for ordering the processes or threads to use the central processing unit. Processes are generated from programs and threads are generated from processes. A high level scheduler decides which programs to pick to transform them into processes, before being scheduled by a medium or low level scheduler. Scheduling criteria and objectives are discussed in previous sections and in this section we will present actual scheduling algorithms. Real-life practical examples in this chapter will be taken from the **Linux operating system**. It is not quite possible to present actual scheduling algorithms without any notion of states and the state transition diagram of the underlying operating system. Figure 6.1 presents the state transition diagram for Linux. Again, we have followed our guidelines of illustrating the diagram in a level-based fashion so that, for every level, the corresponding state in the fundamental three-state diagram is evident.

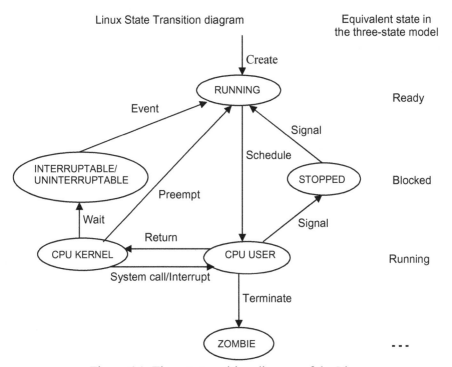

Figure 6.1: The sate transition diagram of the Linux

The task control block of a Linux task contains the fields that are shown in Table 6.1.

Table 6.1: Linux process attributes.

Fields	Some possible usage
Process identification information	
pid	A unique ID which is hashed into process table which in turn points to process structure (i.e., PCB)
uid	The ID of the user who created this process
gid	The ID of the group which the process' owner belongs to
Process state information	
state	Current state of the process which is one of the states shown in Linux state transition diagram
tss	The save area structure which is used to save all volatile information of the process (LC, flags, user visible registers…) when the process (temporarily) stops running
exit_code	The exit (or termination) code of the process; which is used by its parent
exit_signal	The exit signal, if the process was terminated by a signal
Process control information	
policy	The policy is one of the SCHED_FIFO, SCHED_RR, and SCHED_OTHER scheduling policies
priority	The static priority of the process that is assigned when the process is created
start_time	Time when the process is started
times	Times spent in user mode and kernel mode
counter	Number of remaining scheduling clock ticks in this epoch
*next_task	Pointer to the next task in the task structure linked list
*prev_task	Pointer to the previous task in the task structure linked list
*next_run	Pointer to the next task in the running (i.e., ready in three-state methodology) queue
*prev_run	Pointer to the previous task in the running (i.e., ready) queue
*p_opptr	Pointer to process which created this process
*p_cptr	Pointer to the last created child process, for this process
*wait_chldexit	Pointer to a wait queue structure, for a process that is waiting for its child to terminate

*pidhash_next	Pointer to the next item in the process table which is a hash list
*files	Pointer to the structure of open file list of this process
*mm	Pointer to the structure of the complete memory management pyramid of this process
*sig	Pointer to the structure of signal actions (i.e., signal handlers) of this process
signal	Set of pending signals
blocked	Set of masked signals

We could go about defining every term that is used in Table 6.1. Although this is very informative and useful, it is not a part of our goal. Rather, we intend to design a text-book that is short and at the same time discusses all the necessary concepts for a first course on operating system methodologies and design.

6.4.1 First-Come-First-Served

The most natural scheduling algorithm is **First-Come-First-Served** (FCFS). Banks, airport check-ins, post offices, and barber shops are common places that serve people according to the FCFS policy, whenever there is more than one person that requires service at one time. Based on the FCFS strategy, when a person's turn comes up, he must be completely served before starting to serve the next person in line. Thus, this policy is inherently non-preemptive. We are so accustomed to this policy that we believe it is the fairest. Any disregard of this is considered cheating. With this policy, anyone waiting in a FCFS line is pleased if the service is fast enough. However, people become concerned when one person takes up more time from the server. After this person, the service to those in the queue will be delayed by the amount of service time used by the person. This is the major weakness of the FCFS algorithm.

A process has to be in the ready queue in order to be scheduled to use the CPU. Otherwise, the process is either using the CPU, or it is not in the position to immediately use the CPU, even if the CPU has been assigned to it. It is worth mentioning that the ready queue may be divided into a few sub-queues each having a different scheduling priority. For example, in UNIX the ready queue is broken into three sub-queues: preempted, ready to run - in memory, and ready to run - swapped.

Suppose that people who need service arrive on a regular basis. Either one of the following two circumstances can arise:
1. The server, e.g., a CPU that gives processing services, is not capable of serving people as fast as they arrive. In this case the request queue will become increasingly longer, with no limits, this is an indication that a more powerful server is required

2. The server can serve people faster than their arrival rate. In this case, a queue will not be formed if the server starts working no later than the first person's request arrival time, which is usually the case.

Therefore, for regular arrival, either there is no need for a queue or the system is not well-designed and a more powerful processor should replace the existing one. The irregular arrival of requests is the main reason for exploiting queues. It is usually the case that the arrival of service requests is not regular. During breakfast, lunch, and dinner hours, more people go to restaurants than any other hour. Bank customers arrive in higher numbers from 10:00am to 12:00pm compared to other working hours. Similarly, computer users do not necessarily log on nor submit their requests on a regular basis. Therefore, a queue should be set up to hold requests when they arrive at a faster rate. To save memory space, a FCFS queue could be organized using a single-linked list. In such a list, each link points from each node to the node corresponding to the previous request. In addition, one pointer points to the front of the queue and another pointer points to the rear of the queue.

The advantage of the FCFS policy is its nature of serving users according to the turn of their request. From an implementation viewpoint, it is very simple to implement a queue in which every newcomer is appended to the end of the queue and the next user to be served is removed from the front of the queue. This kind of structure is a linked list in which one pointer points to the rear of the queue. The disadvantage of this structure is that, in order to remove an item, the whole list has to be traversed to find the item at the front of the queue. A better dynamic structure is a doubly linked list with two pointers, one pointing to the rear of the list and one pointing to the front of the list. When an item is removed from the front of the list the backward chain will help to update the front pointer to point to the new item in front.

The disadvantage of the FCFS policy is when the task at the front of the queue requires a long execution time. Then, all other requests' turnaround times will be increased by this process' execution time. As a simple example, consider two requests with execution times of 20 seconds and 1 second. If the request with a 20 seconds execution time is received just before the request with a one second execution time and these requests are scheduled according to the FCFS policy, then the turnaround time for these requests would be 20 and 21 seconds, respectively. The average turn around time would be $(20+21)/2 = 20.5$ seconds. If, on the other hand, the order of execution time is changed so that the request with a one second execution time is served before the request with a 20 seconds execution time, then their turnaround time would be 1 and 21 seconds, respectively. In this case, the average turnaround time is $(1+21)/2 = 11$ seconds. A lower average turnaround time means users are expected to wait a shorter time in order to obtain the required service from the system.

FCFS policy is one of the three policies that are used in the **Linux** operating system. Linux calls it **SCHED_FIFO**. It may also be preempted by a higher priority process of the type SCHED_FIFO or SCHED_RR. When the process returns from either the STOPPED or INTERRUPTABLE/ UNINTER-RUPTABLE state, it has to compete with other processes in order to use the CPU again. The SCHED_FIFO policy is reserved for **real-time processes** which are supposed to be the most urgent processes. Since there are three scheduling policies in Linux, the priority of tasks is designed so that the priority of a non-real-time process never becomes greater than the priority of a real-time process.

6.4.2 Shortest Job Next

The **Shortest Job Next** (SJN), or **Shortest Process Next** (SPN), policy is best applicable when there is prior knowledge about the execution time of the processes that are waiting to use the processor. SJN, or Shortest Job First (SJF), is a non-preemptive algorithm like the FCFS algorithm, in that when a request is picked for execution by a processor, it will not be put aside in favor of another request. We can think of a preemptive version of the SPN if that policy allows a newly arrived process with a shorter execution time into the ready queue to preempt the running process with a longer execution time. However, this leads to infinite switching between two or more processes with equal remaining execution time, hence it is not practical.

To implement the SPN policy we can make use of a double linked list with two pointers that point to the two ends of the request list; one pointer is called the *front* and the other the *rear*, similar to the FCFS algorithm request list. The only difference is that the SPN list is in order of the required execution time of the requests, so that the request with the lowest execution time is always in front of the list and the request with the highest execution time is at the rear of the list. Keeping the list in proper order requires extra overhead from the system. Whenever a request arrives at the ready queue, the list has to be scanned, starting from the rear and going towards the front (or vice versa) in order to find the proper place to insert the new request. For a long list, this search may take a reasonably long time.

The advantage of the SPN policy is the fact that it leads to the shortest possible average turnaround time. Therefore, the SPN policy is an optimal non-preemptive scheduling policy with respect to the average turnaround time. Another of its advantage is the throughput boost up. By serving the shortest requests first, the chance of delaying the execution of long requests and even not executing them at all increases. This results in execution of a higher number of requests in one unit of time. There are three disadvantages for the SPN algorithm. First, we need to know upfront the required execution time of the requests. The second disadvantage is the extra time taken for the request queue to maintain its order based on execution time of requests. Third, in constantly favoring short requests over longer ones, a long request can be pushed back to **starvation** by continuously arriving shorter requests. Starvation is the condition in which a process indefinitely waits for one or more resources without ever getting it.

6.4.3 Shortest Remaining Time Next

In a multiprogramming environment where preemption is allowed and a process may repeatedly enter and leave the ready queue, the **Shortest Remaining Time Next** (SRTN) policy can be used to schedule the processes in the ready queue. This is done by selecting first the process with the shortest time needed for completion. A newly arrived process to the ready queue may preempt a process which is currently being executed because its remaining execution time is lower than the one running.

An accurate implementation of the SRTN requires that, whenever a new request arrives, the remaining execution time of the running process be updated to reflect its current value. A decision is then made to continue the former process or to start (or restart) the new process for running.

The advantages of the SRTN policy are very similar to the advantages of the SPN policy, namely a short average turnaround time and a high throughput. The disadvantages are also similar to the SPN algorithm. To be explicit, there is (1) the prior need for the execution time of the requests, (2) the extra time it takes for the request queue to maintain its order based on the requests' remaining execution times, (3) the priority of short requests over longer ones which constantly push back a request with long execution time, towards starvation when there are continuously arriving shorter requests, and (4) the overhead involved in keeping the remaining execution time of the running process (or running processes for multiprocessor systems) constantly updated and in switching two processes whenever the remaining execution time of a newly arrived process is less than the remaining execution time of the running process.

6.4.4 Highest Response Ratio Next

A major disadvantage of both SPN and SRTN is their disregards for requests with longer execution times. **Highest Response Ratio Next** (HRRN) policy tries to remove this disadvantage. With this policy, the waiting time of a request directly affects its response ratio based on which requests are scheduled. The **Response Ratio** (RR) of a process is defined as:

$$RR = \frac{w + e}{e}$$

Where *w* is the length of the time in which process has been so far waiting, and *e* is the expected execution time of the process. The *RR* of a process which has just been requested is always one. However, just after that, when two processes are created simultaneously and have not yet received any execution time; the one with a lower execution time will have a higher response time. The wait time of a process increases as time passes. Therefore, even a process with an expected long execution time will reach a point when it gets its turn for processor usage. As a matter of fact, the response ratio of a previously created process is always greater than the response ratio of a just-created process, disrespectful of their respective execution times.

The response ratio is a dynamic value. Both the passing of time and the CPU usage by a process influence its response time. Thus, RR must periodically be updated.

Whenever the processor is ready to pick a new process from the ready queue, in order to start or resume its execution, one process with the highest response ratio is selected. This means the HRRN policy can be used in a multiprogramming environment with preemptable and/or non-preemptable processes. It does not matter whether it is scheduling processes or threads, the HRRN policy works for both.

For the implementation of the HRRN policy, we must pay attention that although the RR of a non-running process may become greater than the RR of the running process the running process is not preempted. But if a running process is blocked the next process to use the CPU is the one with highest, or one of the highest, RR.

The advantages of using the HRRN algorithm are: short average turnaround time and high throughput. Its disadvantages are similar to the SRTN algorithm, requiring overhead for updating the *RR* similar to updating the remaining execution time.

6.4.5 Fair-Share Scheduling

From the two previous chapters, we know that a user can write an application program so that when it runs, many child processes are generated. All processes that are generated for an application can compete with processes of other users (and among themselves) to receive more CPU time. As a result, an application with many processes can usually consume more CPU time than an application with less processes. The same thing is true for threads that are created for one application in a thread-based operating system. In a multi-user environment, professional computer users can use this opportunity to increase their share of CPU time and by doing so decrease the chance of nonprofessional users to get hold of the CPU. **Fair Share Scheduling** (FSS) is based on defining a fraction of CPU time to be used by every user, or a group of users, and on trying to respect this fraction. If the fraction is assigned to groups of users, a similar situation can arise in which some user within the group may be able to generate more processes and consume more CPU time than others. This in turn could be resolved in a similar manner.

6.4.6 Round Robin

Perhaps one of the most widely used scheduling policies is **Round Robin** (RR). A time quantum (or time slice) is defined and a real-time clock (i.e., interval timer) is set to send an interrupt whenever the time quantum has passed, since the timer is set or reset. This interrupt is used for process switching. In order to repeat this cycle, the interval timer is reset again right after the interrupt is generated. Whenever the processor is ready to pick a new process for execution, it picks the process from the front of the ready queue. This can run for maximum of one time quantum and the real-time clock will send an interrupt as soon as the time quantum has passed. In response to this interrupt, the operating system stops the execution of this process and inserts it at the end of the ready queue. The scheduler then picks another process from the front of the ready queue. While a process is running it may want to do an I/O operation, may need a device which is not available, may like to wait for a message from another process, or may like to wait for an event to occur. The operating system will evacuate such a process from the CPU even if its time quantum has not completed and a new process will be picked up for immediate execution. To start a new time quantum for this process, the **interval timer** will be reset right before the new process is picked up.

The length of a time quantum is not dynamically changed but there are ways to compensate for the unused portion of a time quantum given to a process. One way is to insert the process somewhere within the ready queue (not at the rear of the queue), when the process becomes ready to use the CPU time again.

Practical schedulers of contemporary operating systems are often a combined version of a few of the policies that are discussed in this section. It is possible to combine priority and round robin. We may define more than one ready queue, one for every priority level. Then, round robin is only applied to the highest non-empty priority level queue.

In an interactive environment, users like to receive prompt response to short requests. One way to respect this need is to assign a time quantum to any request as soon as it arrives and after the current quantum has finished. Since there may be more than one such request at one time, we can plan a specific queue for every process' first time quantum.

The last point about the RR scheduling strategy is the choice of time quantum length. An extremely long time quantum will practically degenerate the RR algorithm to the FCFS algorithm. A very short one, on the other hand, will reduce system efficiency. Efficiency could become very low depending on the length of the time quantum. In practice, the faster the processor, the shorter the time quantum is chosen. A good choice for time quantum should be long enough to complete an average-length interactive transaction, in one CPU time quantum.

The implementation of the RR policy is reasonably simple. A singly linked list with two pointers to its rear and front, similar to the FCFS algorithm, can be used to implement the ready queue. If we plan to sometimes insert a request somewhere other that the end of list, a doubly linked list should be utilized instead of a singly linked one. The real-time clock, or as it is some times called interval timer, and its interrupt handler are also needed. The timer is either implemented by hardware or by software. If it is implemented by software, it is basically a down counter that down counts hardware timer ticks. If it is set (reset) to say n, every time a hardware-timer tick is generated the counter is decremented. When the counter becomes zero, a round robin interrupt is generated and the counter is reset to n again. If it is implemented by hardware, the ticks are generated by an oscillator and are sent to a register with down-counting capability. Whenever the content of this register becomes zero, an interval-timer interrupt is generated. The register is reloaded whenever it becomes zero or as the system decides.

It seems that the RR scheduler has many positive properties: a quick response to interactive requests, longer waiting times for processes that require longer CPU times, the possibility of defining many priority levels, etc. The task switching overhead is its main disadvantage.

The round robin scheduler is another one of the three scheduling policies that is adapted by the Linux operating system. It is called **SCHED_RR** and is used for real-time processes. The priority of a SCHED_RR process is static, or fixed, and does not change during the lifetime of the process. The priority of a SCHED_RR is assigned when the process is created. A round robin process, i.e., a process that is to be scheduled based on the SCHED_RR, is considered preemptable. This means that its execution can be stopped at any time and be withdrawn from the CPU in favor of a higher priority process. Actually, a running SCHED_RR process will run until one of the following events occurs:

(1) Further execution of the process depends on some data or resource which is not yet available, or if the process has to synchronize itself with another process. In this case the reason for the discontinuation of the execution is internal. This process will be moved out of the ready-to-run queue.

(2) A higher priority process, a process which has to be executed before this process, has just arrived to the ready-to-run queue. This lower priority process will be evacuated from the processor and will be moved to ready-to-run queue.

(3) It has used up its current time quantum. Similar to Events (2), the process will be evacuated from the processor and moved to the ready-to-run queue.

The SCHED_FIFO is different from SCHED_RR in that only Event (1) and (2) are applicable to SCHED_FIFO.

6.4.7 Priority scheduling

The only criteria for scheduling processes may be priority. At any scheduling point the highest priority process amongst all priority-based processes is picked for execution. A preemptive scheduling policy evacuates a running process from the processor as soon as a higher priority process arrives at the ready-to-run queue. Priorities can be either static (fixed), or dynamic (variable.) In the **dynamic priority** case, the priority of processes is periodically recalculated and updated.

The third scheduling policy of Linux is the priority scheduling policy called **SCHED_OTHER**. It is designed for non-real-time processes. Every process is given a static priority when created and will gain/lose scheduling credit as time goes by, depending on whether it is waiting for execution or is being executed. The overall scheduling goodness of a process, at any given time, is the sum of its static priority and its **gained credit**. We can say that SCHED_OTHER is a **credit-based scheduling** policy. The credit of a process could go as low as zero, in which case it will not be eligible to use the processor until the system decides to give new credit to it.

Process scheduling in Linux as a whole, as a case-study, is discussed next, along with the discussion of the concept of scheduling goodness.

6.4.8 Process Scheduling in Linux

There are three scheduling policies in Linux, or we can say there are three types of processes as discussed earlier in this chapter, SCHED_FIFO, SCHED_RR, and SCHED_OTHER. The type of a process, or its scheduling policy, is stored in the *policy* field of process attributes. Every process, no matter what type, receives a fixed priority which is an integer in the range of, say, 1 to 99. The static (fixed) priority of a process is stored in the *priority* field of process attributes. This fixed priority is not the only factor upon which the overall scheduler picks a process to execute next. The overall measure is called **scheduling goodness**. A higher goodness value means that the corresponding process deserves to be executed earlier than a process with a lower goodness. It does not necessarily mean that the process with a higher goodness value will be completed before a process with a lower goodness value. The goodness value is static for both SCHED_FIFO and SCHED_RR processes. It is dynamic for SCHED_OTHER processes. To guarantee that the scheduling goodness (or goodness, for short) of a process of either of the types SCHED_FIFO or SCHED_RR is always higher than the goodness value of SCHED_OTHER processes, the goodness values of the formers are defined as its priority plus a large constant number, say, 1,000. For a SCHED_FIFO or SCHED_RR process,

$$goodness = priority + 1000.$$

For a SCHED_OTHER process, we have to introduce a new parameter before calculating its goodness. In Linux, time is divided into frames called **epoch**. At the start of every epoch, the scheduler calculates every SCHED_OTHER process' CPU share of this epoch, by an integer number of scheduling-clock ticks. For a process in the ready queue (or running queue in Linux), this value, which is called the "credit" of the process, is equal to the static priority of the process. The credit of a process is stored in the *counter* field of process' attributes. The epoch length is considered to be a fixed value when processes share is being calculated. However, for many reasons, in practice it may end earlier or later than what is calculated at the start of a new epoch. For example, a process may not be able to use all its credit in this epoch because it needs some data to be read from a disk. As a result, the process is evacuated from the ready-to-run queue. This will cause the epoch to become shorter. In another case, a process may arrive at the ready-to-run state coming form the STOPPED or INTERUPTABLE/UNINTERRUPTABLE states. It deserves to get its processor share in this epoch, if it has some credit left from its previous epoch. This will enlarge the current epoch. For every scheduling-clock tick, the credit counter of the process that is using the CPU is reduced by one, i.e., the process loses one credit. A process with its counter equal to zero can no longer use the processor in this epoch. Therefore, it is preempted and the next process in the queue is picked for execution.

An epoch ends when the counter (credit) of all processes in the ready-to-run state, i.e., RUNNING state in Linux terms, becomes zero. At this point, another epoch starts and the scheduler will allocate new credits to processes. Once again, the credit of a process in the ready-to-run state is set to its static priority.

The credit of a process in the wait queue, i.e., with a STOPPED or INTERRUPTABLE/UNINTERRUPTABLE state, will usually increase with respect to its current credit, every time credit recalculation is performed, i.e., once at the beginning of each epoch. Its new credit is computed as:

$$credit = priority + \frac{credit}{2}$$

Note that every time the credit of a waiting process is calculated one half of its previous credits are forgotten. For example, if the current credit of a waiting process is 12 and its priority is 8, successive recalculation of its credits at the beginning of four consecutive epochs will produce 14, 15, 15, and 15, respectively.

To summarize, the goodness of ready-to-run real-time processes, i.e., SCHED_FIFO and SCHED_RR, are always well above other ready-to-run processes. These processes will be executed before any SCHED_OTHER process. The Linux scheduler is priority-based and higher goodness SCHED_FIFO ready-to-run processes will be executed before any lower goodness SCHED_FIFO processes. Similarly, a higher goodness SCHED_RR ready-to-run process will be executed before a lower goodness SCHED_RR process. Equal goodness SCHED_RR processes are executed in a round-robin fashion with each process receiving one time quantum every time its turn comes up. It is obvious that a higher goodness SCHED_FIFO ready-to-run process will be executed before a lower goodness SCHED_RR process and vice versa. Recall that, for SCHED_FIFO and SCHED_RR processes, the difference between goodness and priority is the constant number, 1,000. Therefore, in the absence of SCHED_OTHER, for these sets of processes, the word "goodness" can safely be replaced by "fixed priority." For example, when we say a higher goodness real-time process can preempt a lower goodness CPU-using process, we mean a higher priority real-time process can preempt a lower priority CPU-using process. We must make sure that in comparing real-time with non-real-time processes, their goodness is compared.

The system is implemented such that SCHED_OTHER processes are scheduled when there is neither any SCHED_FIFO nor any SCHED_RR processes. A SCHED_OTHER process can use all its credit in every epoch, when its turn comes. In every epoch, all ready-to-run SCHED_OTHER processes are scheduled to use the CPU, disrespectful of their priority or goodness. The priority of such a process affects the number of scheduling clock ticks of CPU time that it can use in this epoch. The goodness of processes affects the order in which processes will be served during the epoch. Recall that a SCHED_FIFO process is nonpreemtable which means when it is picked up for execution it will continue running until completion unless it voluntarily goes to either STOPPED to wait for an event to occur, or goes to the INTERRUPTABLE/UNINTERRUPTABLE state to wait for an I/O operation to complete.

6.5 Analysis of Scheduling Algorithms[1]

The objective of analyzing a scheduling algorithm is to evaluate its performance. One way to evaluate the performance of a scheduling algorithm is to **model** the system with respect to the objective. This model hides unnecessary features of the system that are not related to the modeling objective and provides a simplified structure of the whole system. Queuing models are often used for this purpose. The heart of this kind of model is composed of one or more queues. However, for our discussion, we will concentrate on simpler models with one queue. Arrival patterns to the queue, departure patterns from the queue, service rates, and request rates are vital information to the analysis of the system.

Arrival and service patterns are often assumed to obey **Poisson distribution**. The reason is that assumptions leading to Poisson distribution are reasonable assumptions which are applicable to most computing systems under investigation. These assumptions are:

(1)   Arrival of new requests is independent of the history of the system and the current status of the queue

(2)   We can always define a time interval dt so small that the probability of more than one arrival within any period $(t, t+dt)$ is negligible. The probability of one arrival in such an interval is equal to λdt. Here, λ is a constant which is called **arrival rate**

With these assumptions, it is possible to show that **inter-arrival time** distribution satisfies Poisson distribution.

Suppose that t represents the inter-arrival time random variable and $P_0(t)$ represents the probability that there is no arrival within the interval $(0, t)$,

$$P_0(t) = Pr\ [\ N(0, t\ ) = 0].\quad (6.1)$$

In (6.1), $N(0, t)$ is the number of arrivals in the interval $(0, t)$. Therefore, $[N(0, t)=0]$ is the probability of number of arrivals in the interval $(0,t)$ being equal to zero. Using this notation for the interval $(0, t+dt)$, we will get:

$P_0(t+dt) = Pr\ [\ N(0, t+dt\ ) = 0]$

$= Pr\ [\ N(0,t) = 0\ AND\ N(t, t+dt) = 0].$

According to Assumption (1), the probability of arrivals in two non-overlapping intervals is independent, and hence:

$Pr\ [\ N(0,t) = 0\ AND\ N(t, t+dt) = 0]$

$= Pr\ [\ N(0,t)=0]\ Pr\ [\ N(t, t+dt) = 0]$

---

[1] One reason for presenting this section is to show there are precise analytical computations in designing any efficient and reliable operating system and just talking is not enough. The reader may skip this section altogether. The following sections are not directly related to this section.

$$= P_0(t) \ (1 - \lambda dt).$$

Therefore:

$$P_0(t+dt) = P_0(t) \ (1 - \lambda \ dt) \qquad (6.2)$$

Or

$$\frac{P_0(t+dt) - P_0(t)}{dt} = -\lambda P_0(t) \qquad (6.3)$$

The left side of equation (6.3) is the definition of the derivative when dt approaches zero, thus:

$$\frac{p_0'(t)}{P_0(t)} = -\lambda$$

Or, from differential equations

$$\ell n \, P_0(t) = -\lambda t + c \qquad (6.4)$$

But $P_0(0) = 1$ because it represents the probability of having no arrivals at the exact time of zero. By replacing t by zero in (6.4), we will get:

$$\ell n \, P_0(0) = -\lambda \times 0 + c$$

Which leads to $c = 0$ and (6.4) will become:

$$\ell n \, P_0(t) = -\lambda t$$

Or

$$P_0(t) = e^{-\lambda t}.$$

The distribution function of the random variable t is defined as:

$$F(t) = Pr \ (T \leq t)$$

$$= 1 - Pr \ (T > t)$$

However, $Pr(T > t)$ is the probability of interarrival time being greater than t which is equal to $P_0 \ (t)$, that is, the probability of no arrival within the interval $(0, t)$. Hence,

$$F(t) = 1 - P_0(t) = 1 - e^{-\lambda t} \qquad (6.5)$$

The **probability density function** (*pdf*) of the above distribution is:

$$f(t) = F'(t) = \lambda e^{-\lambda t} \qquad t > 0, \ \lambda > 0 \qquad (6.6)$$

The expected value of the random variable t is:

$$E(t) = \int_0^\infty t \, f(t) dt = \frac{1}{\lambda} \qquad (6.7)$$

The net result is that the *pdf* of inter-arrival time is exponential and we expect to receive a new arrival every $\frac{1}{\lambda}$ time.

A very similar discussion to inter-arrival time can be presented for inter-service time. If we do so, the probability distribution (pdf) for the inter-service time will be computed as:

$$f(t) = \mu \, e^{-\mu t} \qquad t > 0, \quad \mu > 0 \qquad (6.8)$$

The expected value of the random variable *t*, in this case, will be:

$$E(t) = \int_0^\infty t \, f(t) dt = \frac{1}{\mu} \qquad (6.9)$$

Equation (6.9) means, we expect the system to complete one request every $\frac{1}{\mu}$ time.

To get a feeling of how an actual case is analyzed a system of *n* users and one processor can be investigated and the **average response time** of the system calculated. The average response time is an important measure of a scheduler's performance.

6.5.1 Average Response Time

A model of *n* computer users that continuously request services and one processor that serves users by executing their requests is depicted in Figure 6.2.

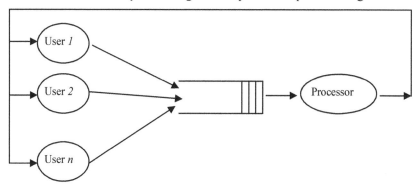

Figure 6.2: The multiprogramming model of *n* users and one processor

We have assumed that when a user starts to analyze the situation and generate a request it will generate it after a time *t*, which is a Poisson random variable with the expected value of $\dfrac{1}{\lambda}$. After the request is submitted, it will take the system, on the average, a period of length R to send a reply to the user.

The processor picks the requests from the queue in a FCFS fashion and the execution time of every request is a Poisson random variable with the expected value $\dfrac{1}{\mu}$.

The overall time of generating, waiting for the response, and analyzing the response is:

$$\frac{1}{\lambda} + R$$

The number of completed requests in one time unit for every terminal is:

$$\frac{1}{\dfrac{1}{\lambda} + R}$$

Let's assume that the probability of the queue being empty is P_0. The processor will be busy whenever there is at least one request in the queue (including the one that is being executed). The probability of the queue being not empty is $1-P_0$. Since the processor's service rate is μ, the systems service rate is $\mu(1 - P_0)$. The system is a closed one which means a new user request cannot be generated until his previous request is completed and the response is received by the user. Therefore, in the steady state, the number of requests generated per unit of time by n terminals (n users) is equal to the number of requests completed per unit of time.

$$\mu(1 - P_0) = \frac{n}{\dfrac{1}{\lambda} + R} \qquad (6.10)$$

From (6.10), R is computed as:

$$R = \frac{n}{\mu(1 - P_0)} - \frac{1}{\lambda} \qquad (6.11)$$

For example, for n=5, since μ=10, p₀=0.2, and request rate λ=4, response time is equal to R=0.374.

This section is presented with the goal of showing how sophisticated the performance analysis of a scheduling algorithm can be. The analysis that was shown here is for a very simple system that has only one queue. Real multi-users, multiprogramming, multiprocessor systems, with multiple I/O processors could have many queues and various interconnections of these queues. Analyzing such a model for the purpose of calculating system parameters can become a very complex job. Such an analysis is more appropriate for an advanced book on operating systems, not this one.

6.5.2 Numeric Computation of Turnaround Time

In this section, we focus on the computation of turnaround time as the only performance measure of scheduling algorithms. The goal is to compute the average turnaround time of a set of requests, or processes as they are informally called in this context. The example which is considered throughout this section is a set of three processes. For each process two attributes, arrival time and CPU burst (or CPU time needed), are given. The set of processes with their attributes is presented in Table 6.2.

Table 6.2: Three processes and their attributes

Process	Arrival time	CPU burst
P_1	10	4
P_2	11	3
p_3	12	2

If FIFO scheduling algorithm is applied to this set of processes in a non-preemptable single-programming fashion, then the final results concerning turnaround time computations are shown in Table 6.3. In this case, the **Average Turnaround Time** (ATT) is approximately 5.66.

Table 6.3: Single-programming and FIFO scheduling

Process	Arrival time	CPU burst	Completion time	Turnaround time
P_1	10	4	14	4
P_2	11	3	17	6
P_3	12	2	19	7

Average turnaround time = 17/3 = 5.66

Table 6.4 represents similar results when **Shortest Process Next** (SPN) scheduling is applied to the same set of processes. In this case, after process P_1 is completed process P_3 is picked up. This is because, at that time, even though both processes P_2 and P_3 are ready, process P_3 has a shorter execution time than process P_2. When a scheduling decision has to be made, the SPN scheduling strategy makes the decision based on available information. Therefore, it was not possible to wait for the arrival of process P_3 (we actually did not know such a process will arrive) when process P_1 was picked up to be executed at time 10.

Table 6.4: Single-programming and SPN scheduling

Process	Arrival time	CPU burst	Completion time	Turnaround time
P_1	10	4	14	4
P_2	11	3	19	8
P_3	12	2	16	4

Average turnaround time = 16/3 = 5.33

According to the regular round robin scheduling strategy, the CPU is repeatedly given to every qualified process for a very short time quantum in a circular fashion. The time quantum is so short (less than one millisecond) that for a reasonable time interval we can safely assume that each qualified process gets t/n of CPU time, where t is the length of the interval and n is the number of qualified processes. Figure 6.3 shows how the CPU would be shared by processes within each recognizable time interval.

In Figure 6.3, the numbers on each horizontal line represent the actual CPU time which is consumed by the corresponding process in the matching time interval. For the computation of these numbers, the overhead time, due to process switching, is ignored. Processes P_1, P_2, and P_3 are completed at 19.0, 19.0, and 18.0, respectively. The average turnaround time will thus become (9.0 + 8.0 + 6.0)/3 = 7.66.

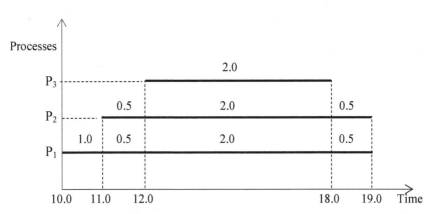

Figure 6.3: Round robin scheduling of three processes

It is not clear which one of the three scheduling strategies, FCFS, SPN, and round robin, always leads to a better average turnaround time. It depends on the combinations of the processes, arrival times, and CPU bursts.

The advantage of multiprogramming is its generally better performance when processes not only need CPU time but also have to do some I/O operations. This case is discussed as follows.

The computation for processes which require both I/O time and CPU time is somewhat complicated. It involves considering every process's CPU wait fraction, w. For example, if the execution time of a process is five seconds, of which 40% is I/O time, then its CPU burst would be $(1 - w) \cdot 5 = 3$ seconds and its I/O time would be $w \cdot 5 = 2$ seconds, where w is 0.4 here.

If the average CPU wait fraction is *represented* by w, when there are n qualified processes running in multiprogramming fashion, the CPU wait fraction is approximately w^n. For $w=0.4$ Figure 6.4 presents the Gantt chart of the CPU usage by processes in Table 6.2. To obtain this figure, the **simulation** clock is set to the time when the first event occurs. In this case, the first event is the arrival of process P_1 which is at time 10.0. We then repeatedly perform the following until there is either no process in the system or we decide to terminate the simulation process. The exact time the next event will occur is found. Events of interest are either completion of an existing process or arrival of a new process. Initial start of the system which happened once is also an event. The system is analyzed from the time the simulation clock was last updated (or set), i.e., the time of previous event up to the time of the new event. Especially, the CPU usage of every process is computed and the remaining CPU burst of processes is updated. The simulation clock is modified to show the exact time of the new event. See Figure 6.4.

For example, suppose we have processed the event of time 11.00, the next event will be the arrival of process three at time 12.00. Between time 11.00 and 12.00 there are two active processes p_1 and p_2. The CPU wait fraction for this period is $w'=w^2=(0.4)^2=0.16$. Therefore, the CPU busy fraction is $1-w' =0.84$. Within this interval the useful CPU time is $(12.00-11.00)*(1- w')=0.94$, i.e., 0.42, half of which will be given to each of processes p_1 and p_2. At time 12.00 we have three processes p_1, p_2, and p_3 with remaining execution times 2.98, 2.54, and 2, respectively. We are now done taking care of the event which occurred at time 12.00.

From Figure 6.4, the completion time of processes P_1, P_2, and P_3, are 20.46, 19.79, and 18.41, respectively. Average turnaround time, in this case, is equal to 8.55.

In this example, we cannot compare the multiprogramming results with those of the single-programming which was discussed earlier because here we have included an extra time for the I/O processing for each process. In the cases of single-programming, no I/O operation for any of the processes was assumed. However, recalculation of average turnaround time for FCFS and SPN schedulers, considering the new situation, is possible. The reader can take it as an exercise and perform the calculations.

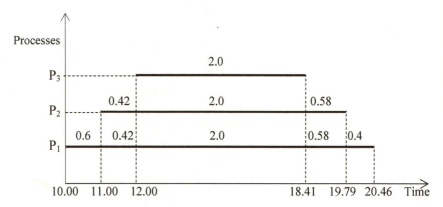

Figure 6.4: Gantt chart of CPU usage by processes

6.6 Multiprocessor Scheduling

The environment under investigation of this section is a multiprocessor, multiprogramming one that covers a wide range of systems. Some specific characteristics of the environment, that influence the type of scheduling strategies to be adapted, are first identified in the following subsections.

6.6.1 Processor Types

Two general categories of multiprocessor systems are identifiable. Category one covers multiprocessor systems that are built using only one type of processor with the same instruction set that the every one can execute the operating system code. These processors should have exactly the same architecture, the same resources like cache memory, the same speed etc. A computing system that belongs to this category is called the **Symmetric Multi-Processor** (SMP) system. An SMP system is also called a **homogeneous system**. On the structure side, all the processors are in the same level, each processor can run the operating system and there is no master-slave kind of relation between processors. In contrast, an **asymmetric multiprocessor** is composed of more that one processor in which processors are not necessary the same or not all processors can perform the same kind of tasks. This type of system is also called a **heterogeneous system**. Scheduling processes in an SMP system is quite less complicated than in nonsymmetrical multiprocessor systems.

6.6.2 Processor Affinity

Another concept that has to be discussed regarding multiprocessor systems is **processor affinity**. A process may be attracted to use a specific processor to run its program. Such a process is said to have affinity toward that particular processor. A **hard affinity** will force the scheduler to only schedule the process on that processor. A **soft affinity**, on the other hand, does not forbid the scheduler from letting another processor run the process. However, when there is an option available, the process will be scheduled on the processor with affinity. When processor affinity is defined for processes, the threads of a process inherit the affinity of their creating process. No affinity gives the scheduler the freedom to assign any processor to run any process or thread. It is worth mentioning that the processor affinity concept is applicable regardless of the type of multiprocessor computers, that is, SMP or Asymetric Multiprocessor (ASMP).

The soft affinity of a thread (or process) to a specific processor will increase the chance of assigning the same processor to the preemtable thread over and over again. As a result, if the processor has its own cache, the cache reloading overhead is decreases. The benefit increases if the thread is CPU-bound and, as a result, is frequently scheduled to run. Another benefit of processor affinity is when there are at least two threads which we do not want to run simultaneously. In this case, the hard affinity of both threads is defined to a unique processor. Since there is at the most one thread running on one processor at one time, the nonparallel execution of threads is guaranteed. Sometimes we like to leave a certain amount of processing power for an application. We can put aside as many processors as we like for this application and define the processor affinity of other processes to the remaining processors. Such a situation is more likely to be\applicable when the system load is light. The disadvantage of hard affinity is the possibility of increased thread response time, creating a negative effect on the overall system balance.

6.6.2 Synchronization Frequency

When a program is being run on more that one processor, we may have to define rendezvous points where all or some parallel sections of the program meet, before advancing forward. Three levels of synchronization are defined based on how often parallel segments are synchronized. These levels are expressed in terms of parallelism grain size.

(1) **Independent parallelism**: Here, processes are completely independent and they do not communicate with one another during the execution. It is not important whether they belong to one application or more or even one user or more, as long as there is no communication between them. These processes do not need to synchronize during execution.

(2) **Coarse-grain parallelism**: For this type of application, processes are suppose to synchronize every once in a while. The exact synchronization period is not fixed but it is approximately every 1,000 or more machine instructions. The usual synchronization tools, such as semaphores and messages, are applicable for these processes.

(3) **Fine-grain parallelism**: Fine-grain parallelism occurs in applications where frequent synchronization is required. Every few high-level instructions all or some parallel executing sections have to reach a common point to be synchronized and from there a new parallel step may start. A common tool for implementing fine-grain parallel applications is the thread tool. The programmer has to take care to define parallel steps and synchronization points. For every set of instructions that can run in parallel, a thread is defined. Once again, the exact synchronization step size is not fixed and it could vary from one program to another. It is safe to assume that parallel sections are less than 1,000 machine instructions each. If parallel sections are composed of very few machine instructions, say 10, then the overall efficiency of the system will be very low. Consequently, we do not gain a lower overall turnaround time compared to the non-parallel version of the program.

6.6.3 Static Assignment versus Dynamic Assignment

A processor may be assigned to a process for the whole duration of its execution. If the processor assignment model is to assign a fixed processor to every process and the process is only allowed to run on the specified processor, then the model is called a **static assignment**. On the other hand, if the scheduler is not required to always assign the same processor to a process whenever it is ready to use that processor, then the scheduler is following a **dynamic assignment**.

The two concepts of static processor assignment and hard processor affinity should not to be considered the same. Although they may look similar, there are conceptual differences between them. The former is fixed while the latter is dynamic. In hard processor affinity, it is possible to change the affinity of a process (or thread) during its life time. In addition, a process's hard affinity may define a set of processors. The scheduler is allowed to choose any one of these processors, whenever the process is to be scheduled to run. Processor assignment helps in better analyzing the behavior of a scheduling strategy and even in checking the safety of a real-time system. The hard affinity concept looks for benefits like decreased cache reload, parallel execution of threads, etc.

6.7 Scheduling Algorithms for Multi-Processors

The scheduling objectives of multiprocessor systems are similar to the ones in single-processor systems. For a list of objectives refer to Section 6.2. As following, some scheduling policies applicable to multiprocessor systems are presented. For those that were defined earlier in the single-programming environment, only a brief discussion is given and the focus is on the ways these policies are adapted to multiprocessor systems.

6.7.1 First-Come-First-Served

All processes are put in a single queue and when a processor is ready to pick a process for execution, it picks the process that has arrived earlier than all ready-to-run processes. This scheduling policy is non-preemptive. When the execution of a process is started it will continue until either the process is terminated or it is blocked due to waiting for some resource or an event to take place. In other words, the processor is taken away from the process when the cause of execution discontinuation is internal to the process. With **First Come First Served** (FCFS), when a processor becomes idle, a process with the earliest arrival time is chosen to run on this processor.

6.7.2 Shortest Job Next

Based on **Shortest Job Next** (SJN), or **Shortest Process Next** (SPN), policy, the process that requires the least amount of time to completion will always be picked for execution. This policy is also considered non-preemptive, i.e., the running of a process will not be halted in favor of a just arrived process with a shorter execution time requirement than this process. When a processor becomes idle, a process with the shortest execution time is chosen to run on this processor. The preemptive version of this policy is called shortest remaining time next, and is described next.

6.7.3 Shortest Remaining Time Next

Shortest Remaining Time Next (SRTN) policy works like its counterpart for single-processor systems. However, any process can be assigned to any processor, if it confers with processor affinity restriction. The shortest remaining time next policy is preemptive. If the newly arrived process to the ready-to-run queue has a shorter remaining time to completion than the remaining time of one of the running processes, the execution of the running process with the highest remaining time is stopped and its corresponding processor is assigned to the newly arrived process, if processor affinity restrictions allow. Therefore, for each new arrival we should compute the remaining execution time of all those running processes that may have to be preempted. This overhead imposed is a disadvantage of SRTN scheduling policy.

6.7.4 Fair-Share Scheduling

The behavior of a **Fair-Share Scheduling** (FSS) policy for multiprocessor systems is similar to that of the single-processor environment. However, processors altogether are the resources that have to be shared fairly amongst all users.

6.7.5 Round Robin

The **Round Robin** (RR) policy for multiprocessor systems is the natural extension of the same policy for single-processor systems. A time quantum is assigned to every qualified ready-to-run process. The assignment is repeated in a circular fashion. The scheduler could observe other restrictions such as processor affinity.

6.7.6. Gang Scheduling

Parallel execution of a process, which is composed of many parallel threads, is best achieved when all parallel threads are simultaneously scheduled to run on different processors. Such scheduling has many benefits as opposed to scheduling these threads in a multiprogramming fashion on one processor.

(1) The time span from process start to process termination is shorter, so time sensitive applications will run safer.

(2) The overall processing overhead is less because there will be fewer context switching. In a multiprogramming environment, when two threads are going to synchronize, one thread has to run to the point of synchronization and then it must be preempted. The execution of the other thread must be restarted to run to the point of synchronization. This requires frequent thread switching, if there are many synchronization points.

(3) Since resources are assigned to processes and resources that are assigned to one process are shared among all threads of the process, these resources will be utilized for a shorter duration of time and will be used in a more efficient manner.

Simultaneous scheduling of threads of one process on different processors is called **gang scheduling**. It is also called **co-scheduling** by some authors.

Analytical performance evaluation of scheduling algorithms in a multiprocessor environment is more complex than in a single-processor environment. Thus, the system under investigation is usually simulated and performance factors are measured. It is also possible to run an actual multiprocessor system and to monitor its behavior for the purpose of performance evaluation.

6.7.7 SMP Process Scheduling in Linux

Linux could be used in a **Symmetric Multi-Processor** (SMP) system. In such an environment, when a process becomes ready-to-run, the scheduler will first check to see whether or not the processor that was used to run the process the last time is available. If so, this processor will be allocated to the process. If it is the first time that the process becomes ready-to-run, or if processor last used is not available, but there is at least one other available processor, the scheduler will allocate one processor to the process.

When no processors are available and a process with higher priority than some CPU-using processes becomes ready-to-run, if the processor that was last used by this process is running a lower priority preemptable process, then the processor will be seized and assigned to this process. Otherwise, if all lower priority CPU-using processes are non-preemptable, such as SCHED_FIFO, then this process has to wait until a new scheduling situation arises. Otherwise, if there are lower priority processes running on processors (other than the processor that was last used by this process), the scheduler will check to see whether it is worth preempting a process or not. One parameter to be considered is the **hardware cache rewrite time**, that is, the time that it takes to entirely overwrite the hardware cache. If this is high, compared to the average time quantum length of this processor, preemption will not take place. In other words, it is better to bind this process to the processor last used, for the time being. Assigning a process to run on its last used processor has the benefit of using previously cached information which has not been swapped out.

6.8 Scheduling Real-Time Processes

In real-time systems every request has a deadline before or at which time the request must be completely executed. A real-time system must not only be correct but it also must be timely and predictable. Some systems are so sensitive about missing deadlines that such an event may cause a catastrophe. This type of system is called a **hard real-time system**. On the other hand, some systems may afford some missed deadlines, which may lead to some computational inaccuracy, but no crash or other kind of catastrophe is expected. This kind of system is called a **soft real-time system**.

Tasks can be periodic, a-periodic, or sporadic. A periodic task continuously generates requests at fixed intervals called request interval. Different tasks need not have the same request interval. The nature of a-periodic task's requests is their irregular occurrence. However, the minimum time between two successive requests is known. A sporadic task occasionally generates requests. The most common type of real-time systems, especially industrial ones, is real-time systems with periodic tasks. We will focus on these systems for the rest of this section.

In static priority assignment, priorities are assigned to tasks in advance, before any execution begins. The scheduler will always respect these priorities. Therefore, static priority assignment is a design-time action. Dynamic priority assignment is, on the other hand, a continuous and online activity with the scheduler making scheduling decisions as the system is running.

A preemptive scheduler can suspend the execution of the currently running request in favor of a higher priority request. However, a non-preemptive scheduler must execute the current request to completion before dispatching another request to be executed. With preemption, there is extra overhead but the chance of request overrun, i.e., a request not being executed in time, is lower if the system load factor stays the same.

Due to a wide range of systems, in the following we assume that tasks are independent and all start simultaneously. Request intervals and execution times for requests from each task are fixed. Without loss of generality, we assume, for a set of n periodic tasks that request intervals satisfy $r_1 \leq r_2 \leq ... \leq r_n$.

6.8.1 Rate-Monotonic Policy

With the **Rate-Monotonic scheduling** (RM) algorithm, priorities are statically assigned to periodic tasks. A task with higher request rate, i.e., a shorter request interval, is assigned a higher priority than a task with a lower request rate. This is a static priority scheduler, in that, priorities are assigned to tasks and are fixed. The priority of any request that is generated by a task is the priority of the task. The RM scheduling algorithm has been applied to different real time environments including control environments, fault-tolerant environments, network environments (message scheduling) etc. It has been proved that the least upper bound to processor load factor (i.e., processor utilization), for the system to be safe, is:

$$U_{lub} = n \left(2^{1/n} - 1 \right).$$

Processor load factor is defined as the sum of load factors of all tasks in the system,

$$U = \sum_{i=1}^{n} e_i / r_i \, ,$$

where r_i, $i=1,2,...,n$, is the request interval of task τ_i and e_i, $i=1,2,...,n$, is the execution time of each request created by task τ_i.

In certain situations, unnecessary preemption could have a negative effect. Consider a situation where a lower priority request is running while a higher priority request arrives. With the RM algorithm, the lower priority request is immediately preempted, no matter what the situation is. If the lower priority request has an earlier deadline than the higher priority request, it is better not to preempt the running request coming from the lower priority task. With this modification, the new policy is called **Preemption-Intelligent Rate-Monotonic** (IRM).

The IRM algorithm has the property of implementation simplicity, similar to the RM algorithm, and improvement in performance compared to the RM algorithm. It has been proved that a system of having two periodic tasks with the IRM scheduling policy is safe if $U \leq 1$. This leads to a 17% increase in the utilization factor of the processor, compared to similar situations under the RM.

It has also been proved that any system that is safe under the RM algorithm is also safe with the IRM algorithm. However, there are many systems that are safe under the IRM policy yet unsafe with the RM policy.

Figure 6.5 shows the difference in the number of request overruns for IRM and RM per 1,000,000 requests that are generated from tasks with randomly chosen properties and $U=1$.

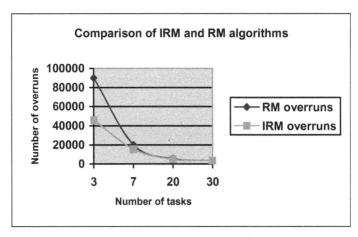

Figure 6.5: Comparison of the number of request overruns in RM and IRM

6.8.2 Earliest Deadline First Policy

Time critical tasks are very much sensitive to deadlines. A missed deadline may cause the whole real-time system to collapse. It is clear that every scheduling policy has to pay attention to requests deadlines. Compared to other scheduling policies, the **Earliest Deadline First** (EDF) pays the most attention to the exact instant when the time limit for the complete execution of a request expires. In that respect, EDF is a dynamic priority scheduler, as oppose to RM, which is a static priority scheduler. Under the EDF, there are four circumstances in which scheduling decisions have to be made. These circumstances are listed below and the actions taken by EDF are explained.

(1) If the system has just started, the EDF algorithm picks the request with the closest deadline for execution.

(2) When the execution of a request is completed, a request with the closest deadline among all pending ready requests is picked up for execution.

(3) If the processor is idle and more than one request arrives simultaneously, the EDF algorithm chooses the request with the closest deadline.

(4) Since the scheduler is preemptive, if the processor is busy running a process that is taking care of a request and a new request with a closer deadline than this request arrives, the running request is preempted and the newly arrived request is picked up.

The oldest results on the analysis of the EDF policy were produced by C. L. Liu and J. W. Layland. They proved that the EDF, or, as they called it, **Relative Urgency** (RU), is an optimal scheduling policy for single-processor systems. In other words, if a real-time system runs safely, with no request missing under any scheduling algorithm, then it will run safely under the EDF algorithm, too. In their proof the system overhead was considered to be nil. Another result reached by the same people is that any single-processor system composed of n real-time periodic tasks, with which the processor load factor is at most one, will run safely when requests are scheduled by the EDF algorithm.

The major disadvantage of the EDF algorithm is the overhead that is imposed on the system by scheduling actions.

6.8.3 Least Laxity First Policy

The **Least Laxity First** (LLF) policy makes its scheduling decisions based on the maximum time span that a request can tolerate before being picked up for execution.

The **laxity** of a request at any given moment is the time span that it can tolerate before which time it has to be picked up for execution; otherwise its deadline will definitely be missed. As a request is being executed, its laxity, or **slack**, does not change. However, the laxity of a request decreases as the request waits (either in the ready-to-run queue or elsewhere). Its chance of being overrun increases. When the laxity of a request becomes zero, it can no longer tolerate waiting.

The laxity of a request is a dynamic value that changes as the circumstances change. Four values affect its computation: (1) the absolute time of the moment when we want to compute the laxity of the request, T, (2) the absolute time of the deadline of this request, D, (3) the execution time of this request, E, and (4) the execution time that has been spent on this request since it was generated, C. The following is the simple formula for computing the laxity of a request with the aforementioned values.

$$L = D - T - (E-C)$$

Similar to the EDF algorithm, the LLF is an optimal scheduling policy. Also, a single-processor system that serves a set of periodic tasks with a load factor less than or equal to one with the LLF scheduler, is overrun-free, if the overhead is considered to be nil. The LLF belongs to the class of dynamic priority and preemptive algorithms. It has an advantageous property that it can detect request overrun before an actual overrun. Although this property is not beneficial for hard real-time systems because we should have proved the system is safe at the design time, it could be of good value for soft real-time systems. If the system detects a request will overrun, it will not start (or restart) the execution of the request. This will save the system some execution time which can be spent on other pending requests. Thus, the number of future overruns is reduced. The major disadvantage of the LLF is its excess overhead to keep the laxity of all requests updated. Recall that as a request is waiting its laxity constantly changes. Since it is not possible to constantly update the laxity of a request, the system has to periodically (very short periods) change the laxity of the non-running processes and check to see whether or not there is a request with shorter laxity than that of the running process. The fact that it is not possible to continuously change the laxity of all non-running processes overcomes the attractive theoretical property of LLF being optimal. Recall that, if two processes with the least laxity have equal laxities (at some point in time), the processor has to continuously switch between these two processes, under the LLF. However, there is a simple solution for defining a practical but approximate LLF algorithm. When a request is going to be picked up for execution, scheduler can find out whether or not the laxity of any other request is going to become zero during the execution of this task. If so, a timer is set to interrupt the execution of this task at the exact time that the laxity of such requests becomes zero. Whenever a request is to be chosen for execution, the scheduler chooses one of them with the lowest laxity. A running process is preempted by any process whose laxity has become zero. Similarly, the laxity of a newly arrived process may become zero during execution of currently running process. Therefore, the approximate LLF scheduler must consider this request, too.

6.9 Disk I/O Scheduling

Scheduling policies are also used to assign resources other than processors. For example, to write outputs on a printer, care must be taken in order not to interleave results of processes that are running simultaneously on different processors, or even processes that run in multiprogramming manner and use a common printer to output their results. Secondary storages, such as hard disks and disk packs, are I/O devices to which many simultaneous outputs are sent or from which many simultaneous readouts are demanded. It is not always wise to read or write data in the same order that is requested. There are better policies, in many circumstances.

Unfortunately, without illustrating and explaining the hardware and software structures of a secondary storage media, it is not possible to talk about I/O scheduling policies. In this section, we will first give a description of the structure of a one-plate hard disk and then present some I/O scheduling policies and corresponding algorithms.

> *Secondary storage* is a mass nonvolatile storage that is used to keep information for a long time. Primary storage (i.e., main memory) is a volatile storage that is not supposed to keep its information if the computer is shut down. All our programs and data have to be stored in secondary storage which is a permanent device. Floppy Disk (FD), Hard Disk (HD), Compact Disc (CD), Digital Video Disc (DVD), and Flash Disk (FD) are all different types of secondary storage. To run, a program must first be (partially) transferred to main memory from secondary memory.

A simple hard disk is a flat round plate with two surfaces. On every surface there is a set of concentric (imaginary or real) circles on which information is stored. Every circle is called a **track**. The capacity of all tracks of a disk is the same (of course, the storing density is different). A track is divided into an integer number of sectors. The capacity of all sectors of a disk is the same. A **sector** is the basic read/write unit. Its size is a power of 2 bytes, for example 512 bytes. To read or write information on a disk it has to be mounted on a disk drive (a hardware device) and be revolving at a constant speed, say 8,000 revolutions per minute. If there are not enough read/write heads (one per track), then the head(s) have to move from track to track to be able to read/write information on different tracks. Figure 6.6 shows a model of a one-plate one-surface disk with one moving head.

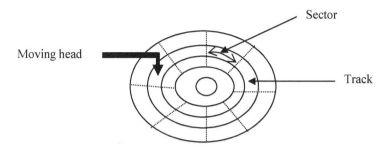

Figure 6.6: A model of a disk surface

The logical read and write unit for secondary storage is a block. Block size is an integer multiple of sector size, which, we assume it is, at the most, equal to the size of one track for the purpose of our discussion in this chapter. We will also assume that no block of data will cross a track boundary, i.e., every block of data is enclosed within only one track. The following parameters affect the reading or writing of a block of data:

(1) **Seek time:** This is the time length that it takes for the read/write head to move from its current position to the destination track from/to which data has to be transferred. This time span depends on the number of tracks to be passed over when going from the current position of the head to the destination track. With a disk of 200 tracks per surface, the longest seek time is when the head has to move from track zero to track 199 or vice versa. The seek time is composed of three parts: the initial start-up time, the traversal time from current track to the destination track, and the settling time on the destination track. The movement of the disk arm is not uniform and has to accelerate at the beginning and slow down near the end.

(2) **Rotational delay:** Rotational delay is the amount of time that it takes for the beginning of data to reach the read/write head, after the head has settled on the desired track. With a disk that rotates 8,000 **rounds per minutes** (rpm), one complete rotation takes 7.5 ms. The upper bound for rotation delay is 7.5 ms, in this case. The average rotational delay is usually considered to be half the time that one complete disk rotation takes, 3.75 ms in this case. Recall that the system will not start processing requests before the disk rotation achieves its desired constant speed, 8000 rpm in our example. Therefore, for the rotational delay, there will not be any other timing considered, except for the exact time that it takes the head to go from its current position to the beginning of the data block. Note that the worst scenario is when the head has just passed the beginning of the data block and the best is when the head is

positioned at the beginning of the data block, right after seek has been performed.

(3) **Transfer time:** The time that it takes to transfer (i.e., read or write) one block of data depends on the rotation speed, track capacity, and block size. This is equal to:

$$Block\ transfer\ time = \frac{Block\ size}{Track\ capacity} \times Rotation\ time$$

Rotational delay and transfer time is similar for all disk I/O schedulers. Thus, to evaluate their performances, we will concentrate on seek time only. To do so, in the rest of this section we will examine the efficiency of an I/O scheduler based on **total seek length**, i.e., the total number of track borders crossed for writing (or reading) one block per every track of a **track trace**

A *track trace* is a list of a secondary storage tracks corresponding to a block trace that is created by running processes, collectively, to be read or written.

A track trace is dynamically changing as new device I/O requests are generated or requests are served.

or track list. It is important to note that the track list is not produced by one process. Rather, all read/write requests (from all processes), for a specific secondary storage, are put in one queue to be processed in an order that is defined by the corresponding I/O scheduler.

6.9.1 First-In-Fist-Out

As the name suggests, tracks are accessed in the same order as their arrival. Suppose a track list (or track trace), just as it is received by the device driver of a 200-track disk, is: 34, 57, 28, 65, 190, 120, 163, 163, 180, and 46. To process this list and find out what the total number of track borders crossed is, we must know upon what track the head of the disk surface has been settled, right before starting to process this list. Let's suppose it was on track 50. From track 50 to track 34 the seek length is |50-34|=16; from track 34 to track 57 it is |34-57|=23, etc. The **First-In-First-Out** (FIFO) algorithm is the most natural algorithm to serve requests. It is simple and efficient to implement, too. The disadvantage is that, in some cases, the head may have to do long zigzag moves thus increasing the total seek length. Table 6.5 shows the order of visiting tracks of the given track trace and the total seek length.

Table 6.5: FIFO for the 34, 57, 28, 65, 190, 120, 163, 163, 180, 46 track trace

From	50	34	57	28	65	190	120	163	163	180	
To	34	57	28	65	190	120	163	163	180	46	
Seek length	16	23	29	37	125	70	43	0	17	134	Total = 494

If it takes t nanoseconds to go from one track to the next, the total seek time for the above track string is:

$$TotalSeekTime = 494*t$$

If we have the actual rotation delay and transfer time we could compute the total time for reading all blocks of the track string. Suppose that rotation delay is 3.75 milliseconds and one block's transfer time is 0.11 milliseconds then total read time for the string is:

$$TotalReadTime = 494*t + 10*3750000 + 10*110000 \ Nanoseconds$$

The shortest **seek length** (that is, the number of track boarders crossed for two consecutively served requests) for FIFO is zero. This is true for a request that is just behind the last served request in the FIFO queue of requests and it is for the same track as the last request. The longest seek length is $n-1$ where n is the number of tracks on the disk surface. This occurs when, for example, a request for track 0 has just been served and the next request to be served is for track $n-1$. A good property of FIFO is that there is no risk of starvation. Anther property of FIFO is that a new request may not be served before existing ones.

6.9.2 Last-In-Fist-Out

Based on the **Last-In-First-Out** (LIFO) policy, the last I/O request is always picked to be served first. LIFO performs well when a process requires fast access to consecutive blocks that are stored on consecutive tracks while there are some unprocessed requests from other processes. Table 6.6 is based on the assumption that the given track trace is ready at the time of scheduling and no new request is received until the processing ends. This is an unrealistic assumption since arrival of new requests and serving the existing requests are two concurrent activities not alternating ones.

Table 6.6: LIFO for the 34, 57, 28, 65, 190, 120, 163, 163, 180, 46 track trace

From	50	46	180	163	163	120	190	65	28	57	
To	46	180	163	163	120	190	65	28	57	34	
Seek length	4	134	17	0	43	70	125	37	29	23	Total = 482

The shortest seek length for LIFO is zero and occurs for a request that has just arrived for the same track as the just completed request. The longest seek length is $n-1$. This happens when, for example, a request for track 0 has just been served and the next request to be served is for track $n-1$. LIFO may cause starvation for some requests. A request that already exists may never get the chance to be executed because new requests keep coming and making the read/write head continuously busy. With LIFO, arrival of new requests causes the serving of previous ones to delay.

6.9.3 Shortest Service Time First

This policy chooses the request for track that is closest to the current location of read/write head. It is a greedy approach in selecting the best next move. Greedy algorithms are usually simple to implement and often pretend optimal, depending on the nature of the problem that they are used for. However, for the disk I/O scheduling, **Shortest Service Time First** (SSTF) does not lead to an overall optimal policy. SSTF tends to work around the current location of the read/write head and forgets about long waiting requests that are for far away tracks. Before discussing its best and worst seek length, refer to its behavior on the track list in Table 6.7.

Table 6.7: SSTF for the 34, 57, 28, 65, 190, 120, 163, 163, 180, 46 track trace

From	50	46	57	65	34	28	120	163	163	180	
To	46	57	65	34	28	120	163	163	180	190	
Seek length	4	11	8	31	6	92	43	0	17	10	Total = 222

The shortest seek length for the SSTF is zero and applies to a request that is for the same track as the last served request. The longest seek length is $n-1$. This occurs when, for example, a request for track 0 has just been served and all remaining requests are for track $n-1$. SSTF may cause starvation for some requests. A request that is far away from the current track of the read/write head may never get the chance to be executed because new requests, closer to the current track of the read/write head, keep appearing, thus making the read/write head continuously busy. With SSTF, arrival of new requests may cause the serving of previous ones to delay.

6.9.4 Scan

With the **Scan policy**, the read/write head of the disk surface moves in its current direction up (or down) and serves all awaiting service requests on the way, until (and including) the last servable request (in that direction). It then changes direction and moves back down (or up) while serving all servable requests on the way, up to (and including) the last such request. The Scan repeats this cycle as there are any requests to be served. Then, the head rests on the last track that was accessed, awaiting further requests. This is the improved version of the Scan algorithm which is called **Look** by some authors. In the earlier version of Scan the head had to move to the last track in each direction. The behavior of the Scan algorithm is very much similar to how elevators operate and, hence, is also called the **Elevator policy**. An ordinary elevator moves in its current direction, loading and unloading passengers on requested floors (tracks), until there is no servable request in this direction. Then, it changes direction and goes on to do the same again.

For the Scan algorithm, if a request is for the track which the head has just been passed and the track position is close to the returning point of the read/write head the track will be served very soon while a previously generated request may be served much later. This could be a major disadvantage of the Scan algorithm, in that the Scan algorithm favors requests that are close to the returning point of the read/write head. Also, a newly received request which is for the currently served track will be served immediately. Although this is a drawback of the Scan algorithm, a similar situation occurs with some other algorithms, too. Table 6.8 illustrates the Scan algorithm. It is assumed that the head starts from track 50 and its current direction is towards higher track numbers.

Table 6.8: Scan for the 34, 57, 28, 65, 190, 120, 163, 163, 180, 46 track trace

From	50	57	65	120	163	163	180	190	46	34	
To	57	65	120	163	163	180	190	46	34	28	
Seek length	7	8	55	43	0	17	10	144	12	6	Total = 302

The shortest seek length for the Scan is zero and occurs when a request is for the same track as the last served request. The longest seek length is $n-1$ and it happens when, for example, a request for track 0 has just been served and all remaining requests are for track $n-1$, where n is the number of tracks on the disk surface. With Scan, arrival of new requests may cause the serving of previous ones to delay. Starvation may occur for a hypothetical situation that requests for a specific track keeps coming. This is similar to a situation that an elevator is stuck in one of the floors. This is unrealistic and there are ways to overcome the situation. Therefore, Scan is considered starvation-free.

6.9.5 Circular-Scan

The **Circular-Scan** (CS), or C-Scan, algorithm acts very much similar to the Scan algorithm but with one difference. Although the read/write head moves in both directions, it only serves requests in one direction. The serving direction is either towards higher track numbers or towards lower track numbers. Here, we will assume it is towards higher track numbers. When scanning is in the direction of higher track numbers, it executes all possible requests on the way, up until the last servable request. It will then go straight back to the track with the lowest number amongst available requests. The algorithm repeats the same process in order to serve existing and/or coming requests. Since the lowest-numbered request is logically considered to be after the highest-number served track, we can think of this method as a circular method and, hence, Circular-Scan. The benefit that we get from C-Scan compared with Scan is that C-Scan does not favor requests around the returning point of the read/write head. The behavior of this algorithm on our standard track trace is demonstrated in Table 6.9. Again, we have started from track 50 and moving up.

Table 6.9: C-Scan for 34, 57, 28, 65, 190, 120, 163, 163, 180, 46 track trace

From	50	57	65	120	163	163	180	190	28	34	
To	57	65	120	163	163	180	190	28	34	46	
Seek length	7	8	55	43	0	17	10	162	6	12	Total = 320

The shortest seek length for C-Scan is zero and it occurs when the request is for the same track as the last served request. The longest seek length is $n-1$ where n is the number of tracks on the disk surface. This happens, for example, when a request for track 0 has just been served and the next servable request is for the highest possible track number, or $n-1$. With C-scan, arrival of new requests may cause the serving of previous ones to delay. As for starvation, the discussion is similar to the one for the Scan algorithm. That is, C-Scan is starvation free.

6.10 Summary

It is not always the case that every service request arrives after the previous service request has been completely served. Service requests may pile up, in which case we would like to serve requests in such an order so as to increase some metrics. This process is called scheduling. Scheduling methodologies and algorithms for single-processor systems, multiprocessor systems, and disk (or disc) I/O scheduling were studied in this chapter. Performance comparison of different algorithms for similar environments was carried out. The Linux operating system was selected to present real-world schedulers.

6.11 Problems

1. The following table gives the arrival times needed and CPU times of five processes. If the process scheduler is round robin, compute the average turnaround time of the processes.

Process	1	2	3	4	5
Arrival time	0	0	2	3	3
CPU time	8	10	6	9	12

2. Given a set of jobs that have to run in a non-preemptive single-programming fashion, which one of the two job schedulers, FCFS and SJF, always gives a better (or at least as good as the other) average turnaround time? Can you prove that this policy is optimal? Hint: look at the greedy method in the design and analysis of algorithms.

3. With respect to average turnaround time, if processes do not have any I/O needs, it is not clear whether single-programming or multiprogramming performs better.

    a. Provide an example that shows single-programming performs better.

    b. Now, provide another example that shows multi-programming performs better.

4. To implement the round-robin scheduling policy for a multiprogramming environment, an interval timer keeps track of how much time is left of the current time quantum.

    a. Can you sketch the design of such a timer?

    b. If the currently running process needs to do I/O before its time quantum is used up, how would the timer be set to start a new quantum for the next process to run?

5. Suppose that the interval timer that is used for the round-robin scheduler internally uses an oscillator with a frequency rate of one Giga Hertz. If the timer has to generate an interrupt signal every one millisecond and we use a down counter that receives the decrement signals from the oscillator and

generates an interrupt as soon as it becomes zero, what is the content of this counter at the beginning of every new quantum?

6. Three processes are running concurrently. For $w = 0.6$ (in other words, the CPU wait ratio of each one of these processes when running alone is 0.6), the following Gantt chart shows the execution start and termination of each process.

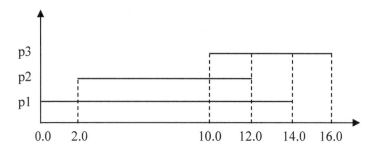

a. Compute the CPU usage of every process.

b. Compute the average turnaround time of these processes.

Hint: Use the approximate value of w for multiprogramming.

7. The Gantt chart of the execution start and termination of two processes in a multiprogramming environment is shown below. If we know that the CPU time used by these processes is 4.8 seconds and 3.2 seconds, respectively, what is w, or the CPU wait ratio of each one of these processes if running alone? Hint: Use the approximate value of w for multiprogramming.

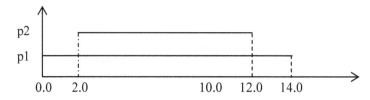

8. Is the Linux scheduling policy adequate for hard real-time systems? Explain.

9. Consider a system that runs two periodic tasks with request intervals of 8.0 and 10.0 and execution times of 2.0 and 6.01, respectively, under the rate-monotonic algorithm. Show that this is not safe and that a request overrun occurs if the two tasks start simultaneously.

10. Consider a system that runs two periodic tasks with request intervals of 8.0 and 10.0 and execution times of 2.0 and 7.5, respectively, under the

preemption-intelligent rate-monotonic algorithm. Show that this system is safe (you can assume that the two tasks start simultaneously).

11. The I/O scheduler of a one-surface-one-head disk schedules requests according to Circular-Scan algorithm. On what track must the head be if the total seek length (expressed in number of tracks) for serving the following track trace is 87.

38   12   84   48   36   95

12. The I/O scheduler is Shortest Seek Time First (SSTF). If going from one track to its adjacent track takes two microseconds, what is the least total seeks time to access all tracks of the following track-trace?

231 256 245 133 283

13. The I/O scheduling policy of an operating system is *circular scan*. For our purpose, the read-write head is on track 100. The following track-trace has to be finally processed by the scheduler. However, the whole track trace is not available before the system starts. During each disk read/write, three new requests will arrive until all requests are arrived. However, the first request will arrive alone and it will dictate the head's moving direction. What is the total seek time expressed in number of tracks?

180 190 24 199 186 142 56 84 178 146 64 82 57

14. Find out the exact differences between SCHED_FOFO and SCHED_RR.

15. Explain the exact circumstances in which the length of an epoch increases or decreases.

Recommended References

For scheduling algorithms which are used in the Linux operating system, see [Boy01] by Boyet and Cesati and O'Gorman [Ogo01]. Similarly, for Solaris and Windows 2000 scheduling algorithms, see [Mau01] by Mauro and McDougall and [Sol00] by Solomon and Russinovich. For the details of Linux kernel implementation, see [Bar00] by M. Bar. The operating system principles book by Per Brinch Hansen [Han73] is a good text for theoretical aspects of scheduling. For real-time scheduling, see [Liu73, Nag01, Nag02, Nag03].

Chapter 7

Memory Management

Main memory is a precious computer resource and perhaps the second most valuable resource, after the CPU. As opposed to the CPU, which only one process (or thread) owns it at any given time, numerous processes and/or threads may coexist in main memory at any point of time. While many main memory manufacturers compete to produce larger sized, lower priced, higher speed, and lower energy consuming main memories, it has not been possible to provide enough main memory to fulfill the requirement of handling all ready and running processes at all times. Recall that with the advancement of technology, computer users expectations have been raised, too. They anticipate running more concurrent tasks with larger sizes and more resource demanding.

Memory management policies and techniques have tremendously changed throughout the years. They have gone from single contiguous memory management technique to multilevel page table page-based memory management with virtual memory and caching capabilities. The following table lists major memory management techniques, roughly in order by the invention and usage era in operating systems. For every technique, its important properties, benefits, and restrictions (when applicable) are listed. It is quite obvious that some readers may not be familiar with certain concepts used in this table, which will be explained later in the chapter. The table acts as a reference and you may want to refer back to it when the concepts are explained. We will not give a detailed discussion of all techniques mentioned in Table 7.1, because some are no longer usable and studying some of these old techniques does not contribute to a better understanding of contemporary techniques. The only benefit might be to become familiar with the evolutionary steps of memory management methodologies and implementation. For these methodologies, a short paragraph describing the intuition is provided but to fulfill your curiosity for detailed methodologies and techniques, older operating system textbooks could be studied. The possibility of these memory management policies being used in the present embedded computers or any other special purpose computer is not ruled out.

Table 7.1: Memory management policies

Memory Management Policy	Properties, benefits, and restrictions
Single contiguous partition MM	Single-programming, easy to implement, high memory waste, low overall system utilization (especially low CPU utilization), program size limited to the size of the partition
Static partition MM	Multiprogramming, better system utilization, memory waste, program size limited to the size of the largest partition
Dynamic partition MM	Multiprogramming, better memory utilization, memory fragmentation, program size limited to the size of main memory
Multiple partition MM	Multiprogramming, multiple memory partitions for program modules, memory fragmentation, program size limited to the size of main memory
Segmentation MM	Multiprogramming, multiple memory segments for every process, memory fragmentation, overhead for address translation, program size limited to the size of main memory
Relocatable partition MM	Multiprogramming, good memory utilization, no external memory fragmentation, extra overhead for relocation, program size limited to the size of main memory
Page (non-virtual memory) MM	Multiprogramming, good memory utilization, no external memory fragmentation, overhead for address translation, program size limited to the size of main memory
Page-based virtual memory MM	Multiprogramming, very good memory utilization, little extra overhead for address translation, virtually no limit on program size, space requirement for page tables
Multilevel page table page-based virtual memory MM	Multiprogramming, very good memory utilization, little extra overhead for address translation, virtually no limit on program size, virtual memory for page tables, space requirement for page tables

* MM stands for memory management

7.1 Older Memory Management Policies

A brief introduction to some of the older memory management techniques is presented in the following.

7.1.1 Single Contiguous Memory management

The simplest memory management policy is **single contiguous** partition. The main memory of the computer is divided into two parts. One part is reserved for the operating system and the other for a program (that is, a process). The latter is called **user memory**. The user memory can hold only one program at a time and this program is kept in the memory until it is terminated. This policy is only useful for a single-programming environment, something that is completely obsolete even in personal computers. A personal computer user expects to run multiple tasks simultaneously these days. It could be useful for some special purpose computer that is used in special environments. The single contiguous policy has benefits from its simplicity of implementation, but it has major drawbacks that are mainly because of the single-programming restriction of this memory management model. Processor utilization is very low, especially when processes are I/O-bound. Similarly, memory utilization is low because a small size process occupies only a small part of the user's main memory while the rest goes unused. A program larger than the user's main memory will not be able to run on this computer. Recall that this model does not support virtual memory. When an I/O operation is performed by an I/O processor, the central processor is idle. The utilization of other devices are also low since with one process only one device (including the CPU) is active at one time and other devices all remain idle. If there are many programs to run, the average turnaround time and the wait time until completion, is very high.

7.1.2 Static Partition Memory Management

Static partition memory management goes one step forward in better utilizing the overall system. It is a fact that memory management policy particularly very much affects system utilization. In this policy, the user's main memory is statically partitioned into fixed numbers of partitions, each being a potential for keeping a process. The first step in the realization of the **multiprogramming** scheme is to be able to have more than one (active) process in main memory. This creates a foundation to switch the processor to another process when the current process needs to do an I/O operation. The number of partitions depends on many factors, for example: CPU speed, total size of the main memory, the average size of programs, the number and type of I/O processors. Partition sizes are fixed and cannot be changed while the system is executing programs, although an offline modification is possible. The partition sizes are usually not all the same in order to be able to allocate smaller partitions to shorter programs and to have larger partitions for larger programs. The number of partitions determines the **degree of multiprogramming**.

The static partition policy is also beneficial from the simplicity of implementation. It makes multiprogramming possible and hence increases overall system utilization. Average turnaround time is improved compared to that of the single contiguous memory management policy. On the other hand, there may be a program which could have been executed if the main memory had not been partitioned. It could not run now as the size of a runable program is limited to the size of the largest partitions. There is also some memory waste when a process that is allocated to a partition does not completely fill the partition. If the average program (i.e., process) size is s and there are currently n processes in the system, memory waste is:

$$MemoryWaste = m - ns,$$

where m is the size of main memory. Memory waste fraction is thus:

$$MemoryWasteFraction = (m-ns)/m.$$

7.1.3 Dynamic Partition Memory Management

The next memory management model is the **dynamic partition** memory management model. This model is similar to the static partition memory model with the exception that partition sizes are not fixed. When the computer is turned on, the whole user memory area forms one free (available) partition. If the first program becomes available for processing and its size is less than the size of the free partition, the free partition splits into two partitions. One partition is allocated to the program and the other becomes the new free partition. If the size of the program is exactly equal to the size of free partition, the whole partition is allocated to the program. Similarly, for newly arriving programs, other partitions will be allocated. It is worth mentioning that the size of main memory and allocated and free partitions are each an integer multiple of **allocation unit**. The size of a program is also rounded up to the nearest integer multiple of the allocation unit. The allocation unit is a non-negative power of two kilobytes, i.e., 2^iKB, i=0,1,2,... For the time being, let's assume the allocation unit is one kilobyte. With this restriction if a program is 1025 bytes it will be given two kilobytes of main memory. When a program is completed, its memory area is seized and becomes available to be assigned to another program. In order to prevent free partitions from becoming smaller and smaller, when an allocated partition becomes free, it will be combined with its neighboring free partitions (if any) to form a larger free partition. Since processes do not usually finish in the same order as their arrival, free and allocated partitions could interleave. In pure dynamic partition memory management, we are not allowed to move all allocated partitions to either the top or the bottom of user memory area in order to combine all free partitions into one large partition. Therefore, there are cases that we would like to load a program into main memory and its required size is less than or equal to the size of all free partitions together. However, since none of these partitions is big enough to accept the program and we are not able to combine a few of them to make enough room for the program, this program will not be accepted for execution for the time being. We then say that memory is fragmented. Memory fragmentation is a weakness of dynamic partition memory management. This type of fragmentation is called **External Fragmentation**.

> *External fragmentation* occurs when all free memory spaces combined are large enough to load a program into, but these spaces do not form a contiguous partition. Partition and segment-based memory management policies fragment main memory. In the absence of complementary compression mechanisms, external fragmentation exists.

If the degree of multiprogramming is *n* there could be, at the most, *n* allocated partitions and, at the most, *n* free partitions, if considering an allocated partition in one extreme end of main memory for the operating system itself. If the average size of a free partition is *F* kilo bytes the total external fragmentation would be $m*F$ kilo bytes, when *m* is the number of free partitions. To compute average external fragmentation, we must take into consideration that the number of free partitions is usually lower than the number of allocated partitions. This is because two adjacent free partitions merge together and become one partition while two adjacent allocated partitions hold two different programs and cannot merge into one partition. It is even possible to have three or even more adjacent allocated partitions.

On the average, the number of free partitions is considered to be one half of the number of allocated partitions. This is called **the 50% rule**. With this rule, on the average, one-third of main memory is fragmented and is wasted. The one-third rule is applicable if we assume the average program size (allocated partition) and free partition size are equal. If, for example, we take

C = (average free partition size)/(average program size),

and assume that the condition of external fragmentation holds then average external fragmentation will be:

$$ExternalFragmentation = \frac{1}{2} * k * C * r \,,$$

where k is the number of processes in a situation when no other process is acceptable by the system and *r* is the average process size.

The fraction of memory that is wasted by external fragmentation

is:
$$\frac{\frac{1}{2}kCr}{\frac{1}{2}kCr+kr}=\frac{C}{C+2}$$

The memory allocation unit is neither a byte nor a word. It is an integer multiple of one kilo byte. Let's assume it is one kilo byte. Therefore, if a program requires 1,025 bytes the system will give it two kilo bytes. The 1,023 extra bytes that are given to the program are wasted. This kind of memory waste is called **internal fragmentation**. For the allocation unit of 1K bytes, maximum internal fragmentation and minimum internal fragmentation per process is 1,023 and zero bytes, respectively. On the average, the internal fragmentation for every process is one half the size of the allocation unit. This is because internal fragmentation sould be either 0, 1, 2, …, or 1023 bytes. On the average it would be

$$\frac{1023*1024}{2*1024}\cong\frac{1024}{2}=\frac{1}{2}K$$

There may be more than one partition to accept a program for which a free partition is wanted. In such a case, a partition selecting (or placement) algorithm is needed. There is one more important topic to talk about before discussing algorithms for selecting a proper partition to house a program.

In order to run a program all modules have to be compiled and linked together to produce an **executable module**. For linking purpose, the loading address of all modules must be known. However, at this time we do not know in what area of the main memory the module will be loaded, with dynamic partition memory management. The solution was invented by International Business Machines (IBM). To explain the solution in the easiest form, compiled modules are linked as if the executable module will be loaded starting from address zero of the main memory. If it is actually loaded say in address d, the displacement or otherwise called **base address**, which is d, is kept in mind to be stored in the PCB of the process which is generated from this program. To run the program the displacement is moved to a special register called **base register**, the content of which will be added to every relocatable address that is generated by the program during running.

First-Fit

The **first-fit** algorithm assigns the first qualified partition to the program. A qualified partition is a free partition that is at least as large as the size of the program. The search starts with the first free partition and goes towards the last free partition. If, for example, the free partitions are kept in a linked list, the list has to be scanned from the front of the list towards its rear. When the partition is selected, its upper (lower) part is assigned to the program and the remaining lower (upper) part (if any) will become a new free partition. The order in which free partitions are in the linked list may not be the same as their order of appearance in main memory.

Next-Fit

The **next-fit** algorithm is very much similar to the first-fit algorithm except that, every time we want to look for a qualified partition, the search starts from where it left off the previous time. The performance of the next-fit algorithm is better than the first-fit algorithm, because it usually requires less time to find a qualified partition.

Best-Fit

The **best-fit** algorithm picks a qualified partition amongst all qualified partitions whose size is closest to the size of the program. If free partitions are ordered from the smallest size to the largest size, when scanning from the beginning to the end, the first qualified partition will be the best-fit partition.

Worst-Fit

The **worst-fit** algorithm works opposite of the best-fit algorithm. It selects the largest qualified partition and splits it into two partitions (if it is longer than the program size). One is for the program and the other is a new free partition. Here, the goal is to allow the leftover partition to be large enough to accept other programs.

Buddy System

One more partition allocation policy is the **buddy system**. The size of a buddy is $2^i{}_*K$ and it must be a contiguous partition. A partition size of $2^i{}_*K$ could split into two partitions of the size $2^{i-1}{}_*K$ which are called buddies, hence, the buddy system policy. A buddy therefore cannot start from any arbitrary address. All free and allocated partitions are of the size $2^i{}_*K$, with i being a positive integer in the buddy system. If the smallest buddy is considered to be 32K, for example, for a main memory of the size of 512M, the bubby types are 32K, 64K ... 256M, and 512M. A program the size of 70K, for example, will be given a partition the size of 128K. When this program arrives, if the smallest buddy greater than 70K is a buddy the size of 1M the buddy is split into two buddies the size of 512K. One is kept and the other is split into two buddies the size of 256K, one of which is kept and the other split into two buddies the size of 128K, one of which is kept and the other allocated to the program. When a program terminates, its space is returned to the free partition data structure. However, if its matching buddy (i.e., the buddy that it was originally separated from) is also free, the two will join to form a larger free partition. The process of joining matching buddies continues until no further unions are possible. The state of main memory, in the buddy system, can be represented as a binary tree. The lower level of the three (that is, the level with a lower number) represent larger partitions. Figure 7.1 shows certain state of a main memory which is 512 Mega Bytes (MB) large. In this figure, a black circle represents a partition that has been broken and no longer exists. Dark circles represent a partition that is occupied by a program. An unfilled circle represents a free (available) partition.

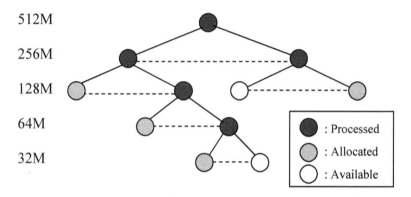

Figure 7.1: The tree representation of partitions in buddy system allocation

Internal fragmentation is usually high in buddy systems. External fragmentation exists when there are free buddies that cannot be combined because they are either not adjacent or not the same size (non-matching buddies), neither of these has enough room for the program to be loaded, but if they were to combine, there would be enough room for the program.

There are other ways to implement buddy system. For example, we could remove the restriction that buddies have to be the same size. A Fibonacci sequence can be used for the size of partitions. In this sequence, the first and the second numbers are both one. From there on, every number in the sequence is the sum of its two previous numbers. The following sequence is a portion of the Fibonacci sequence.

$$34 \quad 55 \quad 89 \quad 144 \quad 233 \quad 377 \quad 610 \quad 987$$

With this sequence, the size of every memory partition is a Fibonacci number. Every partition could be broken into two non-equal (except for the first two Fibonacci numbers) buddies so that their sizes are the two Fibonacci numbers just before the Fibonacci number resenting the size of the partition. For example, if the size of a partition is 610 mega bytes then the size of two buddies that are produced from this partition are 377 mega bytes and 233 mega bytes.

7.1.4 Multiple Partition Memory Management

Multiple partition memory management is an extended version of dynamic partition memory management. With this policy, a program can occupy more than one contiguous partition of main memory. Since a large program is composed of many modules, it is not necessary to load all modules next to each other. Theoretically, every module can have its own memory partition. It is necessary to link all modules of the program in respect to their load area in main memory. When multiple partition policy is used for memory management, **dynamic linking** becomes favorable. We do not need to link all modules of a program together before loading the program. A module could be linked to its calling module the first time it is actually called during run time. Right before linking, a partition is assigned to load the module. This partition need not be adjacent to the partition of its caller. The start address of this partition becomes the base address of the module being linked. As you may figure out, there is one base address for every linked module, including the main program. Therefore, for every program we have a table of base addresses as oppose to only one base address which is used in dynamic partition memory management. **On the fly linking** is another name for dynamic linking methodology.

From your software development experience, you have noticed that, in large software systems, not all the modules will be used every time the software system is executed. Some modules are error handling modules that may seldom be used. Some modules are so that the execution of one excludes the execution of others. The "if" and "case" structures within which different modules are called, are programming structures that incorporate such modules. The cohesiveness of statements within a module is stronger than the cohesiveness of statements within different modules. Statements within a module share many things, especially variables and control of execution. This is the reason for breaking programs from where a new module starts and not breaking so that to fill a memory partition. Multiple partition memory management benefits from the reality of not needing a free partition which is as large as the whole program to be able to run the program.

There are three common techniques for maintaining free partition information. The simplest method is to use a two-dimensional array in which every row stores the information of one free partition. A linked-list in which every node stores the information of one free partition and related link(s) is the next technique. The third technique is called the **bitmap** method. If memory is allocated to processes in multiples of blocks (with each block being an integer multiple of 1K bytes) and the size of main memory is n blocks, an array of n bits is used to show which blocks are free and which ones are allocated. If a bit value is zero, its corresponding block is free. Otherwise, it is allocated. To find a partition of at least mK bytes of free memory, we must find $\dfrac{m\text{K}}{BlockSize}$ of consecutive zeros in

the bit-array. If $\dfrac{m\text{K}}{BlockSize}$ does not reduce to a whole number, the immediate

whole number which is greater than that is chosen.

7.2 Non-virtual Memory Management Policies

A non-virtual memory management policy tries to completely load the program and related procedures and libraries onto main memory, before starting its execution. It does not swap out the modules to secondary memory during execution. Some non-virtual memory management policies adopt the initiative that the loading of every independent module of the program, except for the main program, can be delayed until it is first usage during execution. When such a module is linked with the calling module(s) and is moved to main memory, it will remain in main memory until the program is terminated. The policies that are presented in Section 7.1 are all non-virtual memory management policies. However, they are considered out of date and obsolete policies that are no longer used in contemporary operating systems. Their short introduction in this chapter is just to show the trend of memory management evolution. However, I am not ruling out their usage in special purpose computers that are used for purposes such as control, monitoring, embedded etc. Other non-virtual memory management policies follow in this section. Fundamental methodologies of these policies are still employed in some existing operating systems.

7.2.1 Segmentation Memory Management

Consider a simple program that reads an amount of data, processes it, and produces a result for every datum. The number of results is not known in advance as the amount of data was not known. If instructions, data, and results are interleaved in main memory so that they form one sequential array of information, then, in order to keep all the results together, it is necessary to shift the contents of all memory locations following the first results to get free spaces for new results. This is a time consuming process that decreases system performance. Note that reserving enough storage to accommodate worst-case scenarios is not an efficient solution. **Segmentation** is the solution to this problem. The address space of a program is considered to be a collection of segments. We can think of each segment as a linear array of bytes which can grow to a maximum size. With this methodology, code segment, data segment, and stack of procedure calls and return addresses could each form a separate segment. A logical address is now composed of two parts: (1) the segment number and (2) the offset from the beginning of the segment. See Figure 7.2.

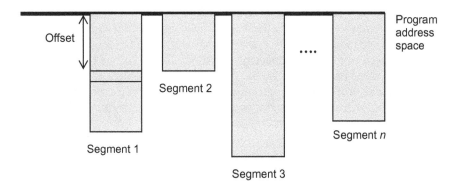

Figure 7.2: The logical addresses as a two-dimensional array

The logical view of program addresses as a two dimensional array of bytes, in that there is segment number for the first dimension and an offset for the second dimension, has to be mapped into main memory, which is (usually) a one dimensional array of bytes. The operating system makes use of a segment table, which could be a simple one dimensional array of base addresses. The ith entry of the array stores the start address of the ith segment. The implicit index of the array serves as segment number. A better solution would be to have a two dimensional array for the base addresses and their sizes. In every row of the table, the base address of a segment and its size are stored.

A logical address is composed of two parts: the segment number and the offset. The system, that is the combination of the hardware and operating system, has to convert every logical address to its corresponding physical address. That is, it has to convert a two-dimensional program address to a one dimensional main memory address. To do so, the segment number will act as an index in a *segment base-table* to find the segment's base address. The offset is then added to this base to produce the corresponding main memory address. The hardware usually provides a register to hold the start address of the segment-base table or **Segment Table Base Register** (STBR). If the size of every row of the segment table is e bytes, then:

$$Content(Content(STBR) + e*(segment\ number)) + offset$$

is the physical address corresponding to the logical address. It is worth mentioning that we have assumed that the index of the segment base-table starts from zero.

This computation has to be done in the most efficient way, because, for almost every address that is generated by the running process, this computation has to be performed. Therefore, a segment-base table is stored in a faster memory than main memory. When the maximum possible number of segments is low, a set of hardware registers is used; otherwise a cache memory has to be utilized.

Segmentation methodology has many disadvantages. The programmer will become involved in memory management matters that should be transparent. It is expected that the programmer should not care whether main memory is one or two dimensional. **Address translation**, or calculating the main memory address from the logical address, reduces the overall system performance. There will still be both external and internal fragmentation.

7.2.2 Relocatable Partition Memory Management

Relocatable partition memory management is an extension of dynamic partition memory management. The difference is that process relocation is allowed in this new policy. When a program is ready to be loaded, if there is no qualified partition (or a free partition which is as large as the size of the program), but the total size of all free partitions combined is as large as the size of program, all processes are moved to one end of main memory. The program is then loaded into the beginning (end) of the newly created partition. From assembly language, we know that process relocation is only possible if address references are computed with respect to a base address value. If a process was stored in main memory starting from location L_1, then the base address of this process would be L_1. Every relocatable address reference is computed as L_1+D, where D could be an operand address or an instruction address or any other relocatable address. The system is careful not to add L_1 to absolute addresses. One example of an absolute address is a memory location that corresponds to data or the status location of an input or output device. This location is fixed for a given device. When a process is moved from location L_1 to location L_2, the base address of the process will become L_2 and future (relocatable) address adjustment is made accordingly, i.e., L_2+D. As in segmentation memory management, the base address of processes is kept in a table called the *partition base-table* which can be similarly used to the segment base-table.

Memory is also broken into interleaved empty and full partitions with relocatable partition memory management. However, because of relocation, there is no possibility for external fragmentation. We may still talk about unusable memory. On the average, **unusable memory** is half the average size of processes. The main disadvantage of this policy is the processing overhead due to process relocation. For a gigantic contemporary main memory, moving all processes to one end of main memory takes an intolerable amount of time. Thus relocation is usually done when it is absolutely necessary, that is when a program has to be loaded and none of the partitions is large enough. By compressing allocated partitions, a large enough free partition will be created to house at least the incoming process. Also, when relocation starts, it is better to move all allocated partitions to one end of main memory in order to create one large single free partition. This way, there will be enough free memory to accept many new processes without restarting the relocation process soon.

Relocatable partition memory management is the most efficient policy amongst non-virtual memory management policies, if its relocation overhead is ignored. Since relocation overhead for contemporary memories is very high this policy is not applicable to user main memory. However, it is an effective policy for small memories of operating system data structures. For example, this is often used for managing memory areas that are assigned to page tables (see page memory management policy in the coming subsection).

7.2.3 Page Memory Management

Relocatable partition memory management has the attractive property of having no external fragmentation. Internal fragmentation is at the lowest possible level, too. In terms of memory alone, relocatable partition memory offers the highest possible utilization amongst non-virtual policies, i.e., one half of the memory allocation unit for every process. Its major drawback is the excessive processing overhead due to frequent relocation of programs. **Page memory management** is another policy with advantages similar to relocatable partition memory management. It does not produce any external fragmentation either and the size of unusable main memory is often equal to that of relocatable partition memory management.

Think of a program which has passed the primary steps of compile and link and the executable code is ready to be loaded in main memory. To load the program, or the executable code, it is chopped up, from the beginning, into small equal sized pieces called *page*. The main memory is also divided into holes of equal sizes with the size of every hole equal to the size of a page. These holes are called *page frames*. The size of a page and, hence, a page frame is a power of two kilo bytes. The smallest page size is 2^0K bytes, or 1K bytes. Figure 7.3 shows a small model of a main memory that is composed of 60 page frames and a program that has 12 pages. Pages of the program are numbered from 0 to 11 and page frames are numbered from 0 to 59. To save space, the main memory is depicted in a two dimensional model, but we know that the main memory is a one dimensional arrays of bytes. The frame number of the top left page frame is zero and consecutive integers are assigned to page frames from row zero to the last row and in every row from left to right.

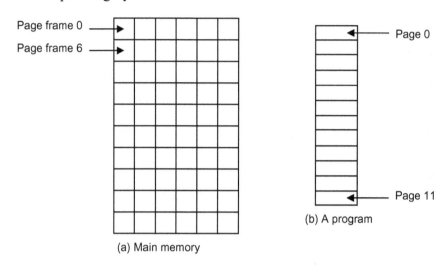

(a) Main memory

(b) A program

Figure 7.3: A main memory with 60 page frames and a program with 12 pages

To load a program, we start from its beginning and pages are picked up one by one. Every page can be loaded into any available page frame. Before starting the loading process, we have to check whether there exists enough available page frames or not. A simple operating system variable is used to show the total number of available page frames at any moment. Every time the computer is started (or restarted) this variable is set to the total number of main memory page fames. With every page that is loaded in main memory, this variable is decremented by one. For every page that is removed from main memory (when a process terminates), the variable is incremented by one. As every page is loaded, its corresponding page frame number is stored in a table called the **page table**. Every page table entry is a two-dimensional structure whose main field is a page frame number. Other fields, such as *protection,* may be included depending on the specific memory management used. Page number is used as an index into this table. Every process has its own page table. Figure 7.4 depicts the page table of a small program that is four pages long.

Page no. Page frame no.

Page no.	Page frame no.
0	4
1	12
2	13
3	46

Figure 7.4: The page table of a four-page program

As shown in the figure, program pages are loaded in page frames 4, 12, 13, and 46, respectively.

An important aspect of page memory management is address translation. To load a program into main memory using page memory management, no address modification is done. Even the address of the first executable instruction is not changed. If, for example, this **logical address** is zero, or the first location of the executable code, the program counter is set at zero to start the execution of the program. It is obvious that the chance of page zero being loaded in page frame zero is very low, if not zilch. The actual location of this instruction depends on the page frame number where this page is loaded. The process of calculating the main memory address of a logical address is called **address translation.**

Address translation is needed for all instruction addresses and all operand addresses that are not absolute. There is at least one address translation for every machine instruction. This is for the instruction's address. The translation is performed before the instruction is fetched. The total number of address translations for every instruction is one plus the number of its non-absolute memory operands. This discussion shows that address translation has to be very fast, otherwise the instruction execution time will be high and overall program execution will be very slow. To fulfill this goal, address translation has to be performed by hardware, whenever possible. The module that does address translation is called **Memory Management Unit** (MMU). The input to MMU is a logical address and its output is a physical address (or real address). This address is then sent to the memory address register

A *logical address* is any address which is generated by a running program. This address could be the address of an instruction or an operand. The program expects to find its required instruction or datum (for storing the information) at the memory location which is expressed by the logical address.

A *physical address*, on the other hand, corresponds to a logical address. It is the actual main memory location that is accessed to load (or store) information. A physical address is not necessarily the same as a logical address.

to read or write the location. For the time being, let's suppose that for the computer under consideration, a logical address is 32 bits long. This means a program could be as large as 2^{32} bytes, or 4 Giga Bytes (GB). Also, suppose a page is 2K bytes. If we assume there is an imaginary vertical line after the eleventh bit of a logical address (counting bits from right to left), then Figure 7.5 shows a model for the logical address.

```
31 30 29       ...           11 10 9  ...   2 1 0
 |       Page number       |      Byte within page |
```

Figure 7.5: A logical address broken into page number and offset

Every logical address from 0 to 2,047 can be represented by 11 bits. For such an address, the left most 21 bits of the 32-bit logical address will be zero. From 2,048 to 4,095 the content of the left most 21 bits of the 32-bit logical address is one and so on. Therefore, it is correct to interpret the left most 21 bits of a logical address as the page number and the right most 11 bits of a logical address as the offset (or byte within the page). When a page is loaded into a page frame, since the order of bytes in the page do not change, the address translation only affects the left most 21 bits of the logical address. As a matter of fact, to translate a logical address to a physical address, it is only necessary to replace the page number with its corresponding page frame number. Recall that every process has its own page table which is filled when the corresponding program is loaded. This data structure can be used within the MMU to translate logical addresses to physical addresses. Figure 7.6 shows a simplified model of a MMU.

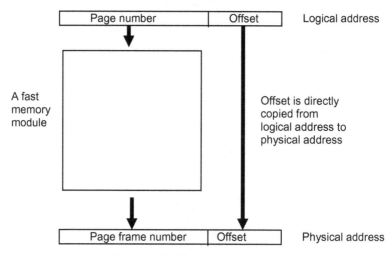

Figure 7.6: The model of a MMU

Details of the MMU design will be discussed later when we talk about page-based virtual memory management. Page memory management (without virtual memory) is no longer used very often. Instead, basic ideas serve as a platform to design a popular virtual memory management policy. We will discuss many problems not presented here when we talk about paged-based virtual memory management.

Page memory management is as efficient as relocatable partition memory management with respect to memory utilization. It does not have the disadvantage of periodically compressing main memory and thus consuming heaps of processing time. Instead, page memory management has the disadvantage of adding per instruction overhead due to address translation. Also, another disadvantage of page memory management is the space that is required to hold the page tables of all processes in the system. Since virtual memory is not available for page memory management, all page tables are kept in the main memory. Page tables are data structures of the operating system itself and are kept within the address space of the operating system. A program the size of 4 giga bytes has a page table the length of:

$$PageTableLength = \frac{4Giga}{2K} = 2Mega$$

If every entry of the table is 4 bytes long, 8 mega bytes is needed for the page table of a program the size of 4 Giga bytes. It is not advisory to reserve the maximum size page table for small processes. Rather, it is better to reserve as much space as is exactly needed by every process. Since we only need space for in-memory programs, the sum of all page tables of all processes (in-memory programs) will require at the most 8 mega bytes of memory, for a main memory the size of 4 giga bytes and page table entries of 4 bytes long. Management of this 8 mega bytes memory for all page tables (that might be hundreds) is a difficult memory management problem, itself. This area could be managed using, for example, relocatable partition memory management policy. Recall that relocatable partition memory management is recommended for small size memories.

Although there is no external fragmentation with paged memory management, we can discuss unusable memory. The average unusable memory is one half the average size of programs. Also, on the average, per every process, one half of a page is lost due to internal fragmentation. The page table is a consequence of using the page memory management policy and not what the program needs it. Therefore, it is also a kind of memory overhead.

Optimal page size

A large page size reduces the size of a page table but it increases the size of internal fragmentation. On the other hand, a small page size increases the size of the page table but decreases internal fragmentation. Based on unused memory, internal fragmentation and page table size, an optimal page size could be selected. To do so, let's suppose the page size is p bytes, program size is r bytes, and page table entry length is e bytes. Total memory waste per process due to internal fragmentation and page table space is:

$$MemoryWaste = p/2 + (r/p)*e. \qquad (7.1)$$

Recall that, memory waste, due to inadequate memory space to load the next program, does not depend on page size and is equal to $r/2$. Thus, it does not affect the optimal page size. If we take the derivative of the equation (7.1), with p as the only variable parameter, and make it equal to zero, the *optimal* value of p is calculated from:

$$1/2 - \frac{re}{p^2} = 0.$$

Or,

$$p = \sqrt{2re} \qquad (7.2)$$

7.3 Virtual Memory

Previous memory management policies all have disadvantages. Because of this, they are seldom used as a general policy in contemporary operating systems of general purpose computers. These disadvantages are:

(1) There is some portion of the main memory that is unused in the form of external fragmentation or the total sum of unallocated memory is not big enough to house the incoming process.

(2) The maximum size of every program and its data is limited to the size of user

Some primitive techniques like *memory overlaying* were able to run programs that are larger than physical memory. The memory overlaying technique was based on having different memory maps for different phases of a program execution. For example, during the Phase one of a program execution, we may use main memory to store the program code and array A. During Phase two we use the main memory to store the program code and array B. The sizes of arrays A and B need not be equal. In this case; we will have two memory overlays. In Phase two of program execution, array B replaces array A in main memory.

main memory. Longer programs are never executed. See side box.

(3) The belief that we could still increase the average number of (live) processes (i.e., in main memory processes) and improve the overall system efficiency, if better main memory management policies are used.

(4) When a program comes into main memory, it remains there until termination even though part of the program, and/or data and results, might be unused for a long time. The space that is occupied by these parts could have been used to load new programs.

The solution to all aforementioned deficiencies is virtual memory.

7.4 Page-Based Virtual Memory Management

All basic ideas that were discussed for page memory management are applicable to **page-based virtual memory management**. Every program is logically sliced into equal size pieces called *pages* (no physical action is taken it is only interpreted so). The main memory is also logically broken into equal size pieces called *page frames*. The size of page frame and page are equal. Any acceptable page size (and, hence, page frame size) is a power of two kilo bytes. Any page of a process can be loaded into any available page frame of main memory. Address translation in page-based virtual memory management is similar to that in page memory management, of which we will provide more details in this section. The only major difference is in loading a program into main memory. In page-based virtual memory management, for a program to start running it is not necessary to completely load the program into main memory, while it is necessary in page memory management.

This and the next section focus on methodologies and techniques for efficient exploitation of both main memory and secondary memory in order to implement the virtual aspect of memory management.

Page-based memory management is customarily called **demand page memory management**. The reason is that, in the early days of virtual memory, a page of the process was only brought to main memory if there was a request for it. In this system, the first executable page, or the first page that encompasses the first executable instruction of the process, is identified by the assembler or compiler and is passed forward to executer. The loader receives this information from the linker and the linker gets it from the compiler (or the assembler or the interpreter). When the execution of the program starts, every instruction that is executed may produce new logical addresses for the operands and a new address for the next instruction to be executed. Any new logical address (or, as we can now say, **virtual address**) may be part of a page that is in main memory, in which case, a new page is not needed. Or, the new logical address may be part of a page that is not in main memory, thus, considered to be a demand for bringing a new page into main memory.

In modern operating systems, some pages may be pre-fetched even though there have not been a request for them, yet. Therefore, as the term *demand-page memory management* does not reflect the state of the art we use *page-based virtual memory*, instead.

When a page is in main memory, it will remain in main memory until a **page removal algorithm** decides to remove it or the corresponding process terminates. There are many page removal algorithms, each with its advantages and disadvantages. These algorithms will be discussed in the next section.

For virtual memory models, main memory is considered to be a temporary place for a process or parts of a process. A page that is brought into main memory may be changed. At a later time, the system may decide to remove it. In order not to lose the changes made, the page has to be copied to its permanent place on the disk. Therefore, a disk is where the complete image of a process is kept and the main memory acts as a temporary location. A page on a disk and its copy in main memory need not be the same at all times; the copy reflects the latest changes in the page content. Since the copy may be removed before the program is terminated, main memory cannot act as the process's main base. In non-virtual memory, the original version of the program is on a secondary storage. However, as soon as it is loaded into main memory, all changes to instructions and/or data are kept in the main memory until the process is terminated. In both cases, a program may produce results that are written on files or it may read input data from files.

There is much interaction between main memory and secondary memory where the permanent place of the process exists due to frequent loading and unloading of process pages. If the secondary memory, which holds the executable program, is slow, the turnaround time of the process will increase tremendously. Compact discs, DVDs, flash memory, and floppy diskettes are types of slow secondary storage. A program that is stored on one of these media has to be moved to a faster secondary storage, like a hard disk, before starting its execution. A special area, called the **virtual memory area**, located on one of the fastest secondary storages is thus reserved for the permanent copy of executable programs for the duration of their execution. Any program on a slow media, like a CD, is copied to this area first and then a process is created for this program to be executed. A program which is in one of the fastest secondary storages need not be copied to the virtual area. However, the decision to make a copy of it or not depends on the specific operating system.

In theory, with a page-based virtual memory, a very small main memory is adequate to run a very large program and to implement a multiprogramming technique. In fact, the size of main memory could be as small as a few page frames. When the system wants to execute an instruction the instruction and its operands have to be present in main memory. Otherwise, a **page fault** occurs and the process is suspended until the page is brought to main memory. If more than one page is needed, that is not present in main memory, more than one successive page fault will occur for that instruction. Every time a page fault occurs, the process is suspended and if the system is multi-programmed a new process may be selected to use the CPU. The state of the suspended process is changed to *blocked* because it has to wait for the I/O operation to execute the instruction in order to bring the page to main memory. An instruction that has k memory operands may need as many as $k+1$ pages if the instruction and its operands are all on different pages. It may even need more than that if the instruction, and/or operand(s) cross page boundaries. Therefore, for every instruction execution, there will be at least zero and at the most $k+1$ page faults, where k is the number of memory operands of the instruction, assuming that neither the instruction nor any of its operands cross a page boundary. Based on this discussion the smallest theoretical main memory size for page-based memory management is computable. Considering even one page fault per every instruction and the fact that, for every page fault, the process has to be suspended and wait for the page to be brought to main memory, we realize that the system is dominated by overhead time and rendered practically inefficient. Page fault reduction is an important topic of page-based virtual memory.

If the processor spends most of its time suspending and resuming processes due to frequent page faults, then a **thrashing** condition occurs. Thrashing is a situation that must be avoided. The chance of thrashing is higher when main memory is not large enough for the number of processes, i.e., active programs. The other extreme is when the main memory is large enough to hold all processes all the time. In such a case, when all pages of a process are loaded into main memory, no further page fault will take place for any process as all page references are successful.

A reference to a logical address which has already been loaded into main memory is referred to as **page success**. On the other hand, if a reference to a logical address is made, and the corresponding page is not in main memory, a **page fault** occurs.

Page-based virtual memory management does not work well for processes that are designed as a single module, or very few modules, having many run-time long distance jumps. Such processes refer to almost all their pages within a short period of time.

Modern programs are written either in a structured, modular manner or by using object oriented tools. In either case, when a block, a module, or a method of a program is being executed, the program refers to a small number of pages. This phenomenon is called **locality of reference** and suggests that not all pages of a process are to be loaded in main memory at all times. The process will keep on working within a small part of the program, with its data and results being limited to a few pages. Many modules and data structures of a large process are never used in one execution of a program. Error handling and exception processing modules, along with their corresponding data structures, belong to this category. The execution of a module may exclude the execution of others. If a module is called in the *then* clause of a *if then else* structure, it is unlikely to appear in the *else* clause of the structure and vice versa. Similar situations arise for different options of the *case* structure. On the other hand, there is no reason to keep portions of the program if it will not be referred to in main memory for a long period of time in the future. These are rationales for a virtual memory management policy.

To make room in main memory for an incoming page, three fundamental techniques are available: (1) swap out a page of a process, (2) swap out a segment of a process, and (3) swap out a complete process. Some operating system designers employ two or all three of these techniques to design a memory management algorithm. In this section, we will concentrate on algorithms with only page swapping possibilities. Later, we will discuss the UNIX virtual memory management case study which exploits both page swapping and process swapping.

Upon creation of a process, the logical address of the process' first executable instruction which is passed from the source to the compiler or assembler and from there to the linker, is stored in the location counter field of the **process control block**. This is the most important piece of data to start the execution of a program.

To start or restart the execution of a process, eventually the content of the process control block's location counter is transferred to the *program counter* register. This is assumed to be a logical address which has to be translated to a physical address by the **Memory Management Unit** (MMU), similar to what is done for page memory management. During the translation, if the page is not present in main memory, a **page fault interrupt** is issued. In response to this interrupt, the process, for which the interrupt is issued, is suspended and its state is changed to "blocked." The process has to wait until the page is moved to main memory and its **page table** and other data structures are updated. Then, the state of the process will change to "ready." The process must then wait again for its turn to be picked for execution resumption. As compared to a page table of a page memory management model, every page table entry in page-based virtual memory management has a new field called *absent/present*. This field could be a bit with either value of zero meaning that the page is absent from main memory or value of one meaning that the page is present in main memory. In order to support page removal algorithms that are discussed in the next section, other fields may be added to every entry of a page table.

Another useful data structure for page-based virtual memory is the **Page Frame Table** (PFT), or in some situations called **Inverted page Table** (IPT), which represents the status of memory page frames. Every entry of this table shows whether the corresponding page frame is available, that is free, or occupied. If it is occupied, which page of what process is stored in the page frame is indicated. For example, row number i $(i=0, 1, 2, ..., n-1)$ of this table represents the state of the page frame number i of main memory. If this page frame is occupied by page number j of process number k, then row i of the table will have the information: k, j, "occupied". The field which represents whether or not the page frame is occupied can be implemented by one bit and is not a character field. The page frame number serves as the index to the table. This index starts from zero and continues up to the number of page frames of the main memory minus one. Depending on the page removal algorithm that is used, for every entry of page frame table there can be other fields. One such field is the protection field. This is a control field that allows some processes to access the information stored in the corresponding page frame of main memory while forbidding other processes from accessing it. The protection field can also allow some kinds of access (like *read*) and restrict some kinds (like *write*). The actual structure of the IPT will be explained when we talk about page removal algorithms. There is only one inverted page table for the whole system and its size is fixed. Recall that there is one page table for every live program, or process. The number of page tables can grow very high when the degree of multiprogramming is very high.

With a main memory the size of say 4 Giga byes and a page frame size of 2K, then

$$number\ of\ page\ frame\ table\ rows\ = \frac{4\text{Giga}}{2\text{K}} = 2Mega\ .$$

If every row of the inverted page table is 4 bytes, then the IPT will occupy 8 mega bytes of main memory. An inverted page table is used to implement some page removal algorithms. It could also be used to find out what page frames of main memory are not occupied, i.e., they are free. This information helps in loading new pages into main memory. It also assists in removing all pages of a process when the process terminates. Without IPT, free page frames are usually threaded together to form a linked list and other information is extracted from the process page tables.

7.4.1 Address Translation

There are three basic schemes for address translation. The first one relies on page tables in the main memory, using the page table, or parts of the page table, of the running process in the core of the **Memory Management Unit** (MMU). The second method relies on an inverted page table in the main memory. Utilizing inverted page table, or parts of inverted page table, in the core of this module. The last method relies on page tables in the main memory. However, this method takes advantage of a structure similar to the inverted page table within the MMU.

Address translation using page table

The address translation method in page-based virtual memory management is very much similar to the address translation method in page memory management. The difference arises when a logical address is not in main memory. The non-existence of the logical address has to be recognized by the MMU module and an interrupt issued. See Figure 7.7.

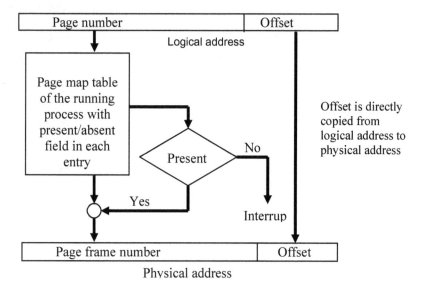

Figure 7.7: The model of MMU using the page table of the running process

As the MMU is part of the CPU, it has to be reasonably small. Based on Figure 7.7, the MMU memory could grow so large that it no longer fits the specification of the CPU. The solution is to have an actual page table in main memory and utilize a cache memory within the MMU. In this case, the main memory acts as a virtual memory for the MMU cache. Although a specific cache memory management method will be discussed later, usual virtual memory management methods could also be used for cache memory management. One characteristic of cache memory is its efficient way of finding out whether a main memory address (or equivalently its content) is in cache or not. There-fore, we can say cache memory is a fast read/ write random access me-mory having the above mentioned quality.

The cache size is usually smaller than the size of the running process's page table. However, it should not be so small that the **hit ratio** becomes very low. It is worth mentioning that the cache hit ratio depends not only on cache size and page table length, but also on the control structure of the program. A program with frequent run-time jumps is likely to refer to a variety of pages and, as a con-sequence, refer to a variety of page table entries. Therefore, new page table entries have to be frequently cached. As a result, the **cache miss ratio** will be high and the hit ratio low.

Address translation using inverted page table

The type of memory that is used within MMU to translate a virtual address to its equivalent real address is **associative memory**. An associative memory, or **content-addressable memory**, is a special purpose memory with the ability of read, write, and simultaneous (or parallel) compare of a given datum with the content of all its words. It is the latter capability that makes associate memory advanta-

The cache hit ratio is defined as the number of successful cache references divided by the total number of successful and unsuccessful cache references. An unsuccessful cache reference occurs when the system tries to access the cache but the corresponding address is not in the cache. The system will then transfer (the content of) that address, plus adjacent addresses, to the cache and then a secondary reference is issued. For the purpose of the cache hit ratio calculation, secondary access is neither counted as a successful nor an unsuccessful reference. The cache hit ratio is only calculated based on primary references.

The cache miss ratio is defined as the number of successful (primary) cache references divided by the total number of successful and unsuccessful (primary) cache references.

A *content addressable memory* is a very fast hardware device for information searching. It can be used in database computers to accelerate information retrieval. The memory address register, the memory data register, the comparand register, which is filled with the information that we would like to find, and a mask register are this memory's interface to the external world. With the mask register, we can exclude some parts of each word of memory from participating in the parallel comparison of the information that we are looking for. For example, we can search for all four-byte data that starts with the character "a." With this query, the first eight bits of every 32-bit word will participate in the comparisons. There may be more than one word that matches the query. Therefore, an array of bits (one per every word) is embedded to keep the results of each comparison. For our applications, at the most, one word can have the data that we are looking for. This is because each page of every program is, at the most, in one page frame of main memory.

geous for address translation. An associative memory that is used in the context of address translation is called a **Translation Lookaside Buffer** (TLB). Due to its simultaneous comparison capability, a content-addressable memory has many more electronic elements than a RAM memory or a cache memory of the same size. Since an associative memory has to be part of every processor, we are unable to use one that is as large as the whole inverted page table. Therefore, only limited parts of an inverted page table are kept in TLB, at any given time. One way to cut the effective size of inverted page table is to load its rows belonging to the currently running process. When translating a virtual address, if the corresponding row of the currently running process' page numbers is in TLB, the parallel comparison mechanism finds the actual page frame number. This is then concatenated with the offset field of the virtual address to produce the physical address. If the corresponding address of the virtual address' page number is not in the TLB, the tuple *(process, page#)* is looked for in the inverted page table in main memory. A hash table is used to reduce the search time in IPT. A TLB miss will cause the system to load the corresponding row of the IPT into the TLB, for future usage. This method does not need the page table data structure for address translation.

Address translation using hybrid structures

Perhaps the most common address translation method utilizes page tables that are kept in the main memory, which can even be swapped out, plus a structure similar to an inverted page table which is produced on the fly, within MMU. This IPT-like structure inside the MMU is produced from the running process's page table. Compared to an actual inverted page table, it lacks the process ID, or number, in every entry. If the row number i of a page table has j as its corresponding page frame number, then a row of the TLB within the MMU can be formed using the tuple *(i, j)*. Other necessary fields are directly copied from the page table. Figure 7.8 shows a sample format of such a TLB's entries.

Virtual page#	Page frame#	Protection	Free/Allocated	Other fields

Figure 7.8: Translation Lookaside buffer format

To translate a logical address, the virtual page number is first looked for in the TLB. If it is present, the page frame number is retrieved and is concatenated with the offset value of the logical address in order to produce the physical address. If the page frame number is not found, a direct page table lookup is performed and the corresponding page frame is taken from the page table of the currently running process. At the same time, for the page table entry that has just been referred to and perhaps some neighboring entries, a TLB entry is built and moved to the TLB. If there are not enough free entries for newly arriving items, a replacement algorithm decides which entries to reallocate. It is possible that a page table may not be completely present in main memory. This may occur when the system also allows the application of virtual memory techniques to page tables. A complete discussion on virtual memory page tables will later be given when we talk about multilevel page tables.

7.4.2 Page Removal Algorithms

The philosophy behind virtual memory is to eliminate the size of main memory as a restricting parameter for the number of processes in the system. With virtual memory, we are able to have more processes in the system than if we were to completely load every process in main memory. Page-based virtual memory is one of the methods for the realization of the virtual memory philosophy. With virtual memory, it is possible for a running process to refer to an address within its address space even though this address is not in main memory and there is also no free page frame available in main memory. What is usually done in such circumstances is to evacuate one of the page frames which are currently occupied by one of the processes in the system. This process is called **page removal** because we are actually removing a page from that page frame to make room for a new page. Some page removal algorithms remove pages even before the appearance of an incoming page which has no place to sit. These algorithms want to ensure that most of the time there is a page frame available for every page coming to main memory. **Page swapping** and **page replacement** are other names for page removal. These names refer to the two actions of removing a page and loading a new page into the evacuated page frame. It is the actually the page removal action that requires an algorithm. We will discuss these algorithms in the rest of this section.

   Before discussing page removal algorithms, some essential concepts are defined as follows. Each of these concepts is used in one or more page removal algorithms.

Working set

The set of pages referred to in the last Δt CPU time of a process is called the **working set** of a process. Recall from mathematics that each element of a set appears only once. The working set can be expressed in terms of the number of pages or in terms of the total storage size of all pages in the set. For example, if a process' working set is calculated as, say, six pages and page size is 2K, then its working set is, obviously, 12K. Δt is a **virtual time** which differs from a real time span because the system is running in a multiprogramming mode and the

CPU time is shared among many processes. The working set is an engineering problem that involves careful selection (by proper selection of Δt) to reduce overall page faults. Therefore, the exact length of Δt is not defined. Sometimes, Δt is expressed in terms of the number of memory references. If so, the working set of a process is defined as the set of pages the process has referred to in the last n memory accesses. Memory references act as a window that slides forward as the program refers to new pages. n is the widow size. Once again, the exact value of n is not defined and is left as implementation dependent. The working set of a process may vary for different intervals of length Δt, but it is a non-decreasing function meaning that, as Δt increases, the working set either stays the same or increases. The working set concept can be used is assigning a certain number of page frames to every process. A process with a higher working set is assigned a higher number of page frames than a process with a lower working set.

Without complementary information about the size and the execution behavior of programs, assignments of page frames to processes are of a **fixed size working set** nature. Every process is given a fixed number of page frames at the time it is created. The process has to execute using no more than its allocated number of frames in main memory. If a page fault occurs, two situations are possible. On the one hand, the process may have not used up its allocated number of frames in which case the system will provide a new frame for the process. On the other hand, the process may have used up its allocated frames, in which case, a **resident page** of the process has to be removed and the coming page takes its place. If the working set size is fixed but it is considered a lower bound of the memory size that a process can use, the system guarantees that each process for sure can use at lease as many page frames as its lower bound whenever it needs them. However, main memory is not reserved for the process. Unless otherwise stated, lower bound case is assumed. The process' lower bound main memory requirement acts as a credit which may or may not be used by the process. However, the unused credit is not put aside for the process. Rather, up to the credit limit, the system guarantees that whenever a process needs more memory space, it will provide it from available memory or by forcefully taking away from other processes. Note that, the sum of working set of all processes is always much less than the total capacity of main memory. Therefore, processes majority of processes use more than their working set of main memory, most of the times.

A **variable size working set** method is devised using the size and the execution behavior information of processes. At first, when the process is created, there is no information about its behavior, thus, a fixed number of frames is allocated to the process. As information is gathered, the process's working set is adjusted to reflect this information. For example, a program may be short but it may reference many of its pages within a short period of time. Therefore, if it is not given more space it will produce many page faults. To prevent this, we better increase its working set to give it the opportunity to use more memory frames.

The same process's behavior may change later according which a smaller working set may suffices to ensure that other needy processes will get enough memory space.

Per process vs. overall page replacement

With the per-process page removal, when a process has used up its working set quota and there is no free page available in the main memory, a newly arriving page has to replace a previously loaded page from the same process. This method is called **per process page replacement**, or **local page replacement**. On the other hand, if the page to be replaced is chosen amongst all pages in the main memory, the method is called **overall page replacement**, or **global page replacement**.

It is simpler to implement the per process page replacement method than the overall page replacement method. The overhead is also lower for per process page replacement. On the other hand, overall page replacement usually produces less page faults than per process page replacement.

Page locking

There are many circumstances that require locking a page into main memory when it is loaded, and forbidding its removal until the process is terminated. When a page fault occurs, the page fault handler will take care of bringing the needed page to main memory. For example, tf parts of the page fault handler are swapped out of main memory, a new page fault will occur during the execution of the handler which will cause re-entry into the handler. An infinite re-entry cycle will be formed and the needed page will not be loaded into main memory. To prevent this cycle, the pages occupied by the page fault handler are locked into main memory and are never removed. Another scenario is for I/O processors that lack a memory management unit. In other words, they do not have the circuitry for address translation. Physical addresses are used for the source and/or the destination of I/O operations that are performed by this kind of processor. I/O processors transfer data on behalf of processes, thus, the source and/or destination of data transfer is one or more pages of a process. These pages have to be locked into main memory until the I/O operation is complete. Otherwise, the data will be transferred from or to a place which does not belong to the address space of the correct process.

It is desirable to lock into main memory pages that are very frequently used. Usually, instruction pages of a short program that manipulate a large set of data are heavily used. A matrix multiplication program that is used to multiply large matrices and a program to numerically solve a set of linear equations are examples of such programs. A heavily used routine in an application program has a similar property. As most operating system kernel routines are very heavily used, most pages of the kernel are locked into main memory.

What to do with removed pages?

Recall that a program, as a whole, is kept in secondary storage and only temporary copies of some pages are brought to main memory. A page in main memory may contain instructions and/or data, either of which could change while in main memory. A page which has changed is no longer an exact copy of the corresponding page in secondary storage. Therefore, if it is removed from main memory, such a page has to be copied back to its original place in secondary storage. Otherwise some execution results will not be reflected in the original transcript of the program. A page that has not been modified since coming to main memory need not be copied back to its original place. Due to the extra overhead and transfer time, we prefer not to copy a page back to its original place, if it has not changed.

To distinguish between modified and non-modified pages a flag bit called a **modified bit**, represented by M (or C for a changed bit) is used. This is added to every entry of every page table, every entry of an inverted page table, or even every physical memory page frame, depending on the hardware architecture of the computer and the removal algorithm used. The M bit of a page is set whenever something is stored in the corresponding page frame. It is initialized to zero when the page is brought to main memory from secondary memory. A page whose M bit is set to one is copied back to its original place whenever it is removed from main memory. If the M bit is zero, this page will not be copied.

First-In-First-Out policy

One of the simplest page removal methods is the **First-In-First-Out** (FIFO). As the name suggests, when we want to remove a page from main memory, the page that has been in main memory for the longest duration of time is removed. Assume that, a **time stamp** is attached to each page whenever the page is loaded in main memory. The time stamp can either represent the exact time that the page was loaded or a **logical time**. The logical time does not represent an exact physical time. Rather, it is a number that is designed to show the order in which pages are loaded. To remove a page, the page with lowest time stamp is chosen. From a practical view point, it is not possible to search all page frames for the one with the lowest time stamp as it would take an unacceptable amount of time. However, to save processing time, a FIFO data structure could be organized using a single-linked list. In such a list, each link points from each node to the node corresponding to the immediately older page. In addition, one pointer points to the front of the list and another pointer points to the rear of the list. As a page is loaded into main memory, a node for the list is build with some of the page information (for example, the page's corresponding page frame number). The node is then added to the rear of the list. To remove a page, the page pointed by the front of the list is chosen. This node is then deleted from the list and the front pointer is updated. To prevent too many data structures, the list can be built within the inverted page table and even within the page tables. The fields comprising the structure of the node are added to the page table or inverted page table's entries. The pointers to the front and the rear of the list are then kept as new variables of the memory management algorithm. One disadvantage is extra space that is needed for the list to practically implement the FIFO algorithm. Another FIFO algorithm disadvantage is that a newly removed page might be needed in the near future. In other words, there is no reason to think an old page will not be referred to in the near future.

The main disadvantage of the FIFO algorithm is its Belady's anomaly. For any **page trace**, a rational page removal algorithm does not produce more page faults if the number of memory page frames increases. An algorithm exhibits abnormal behavior if there exists a page trace (or **page reference string**) for which it produces more page faults when the number of memory page frames is increased. This anomaly is called **Belady's anomaly**, or, in the case of FIFO, **FIFO anomaly**. An example of a page trace is shown in Figure 7.9. Part (a) of the figure represents the performance of FIFO for a three-page frame memory. The first row of each table is the page trace. The next three lines represent

> A *page trace* or *page reference string* is an ordered set of page numbers that is generated when a program is executed (or a set of programs are executed in a multiprogramming and/or multiprocessing fashion). As the execution of program(s) proceeds, this string of page numbers is dynamically generated. For the purpose of showing the behavior of different page replacement algorithms, we have no choice but to assume the page trace is known in advance. Except for a theoretical algorithm called *optimal*, all page replacement algorithms studied in this chapter make their page removal decision based on the set of pages that have been references up to this time.

three page frames of main memory, one for every page frame. Each column shows an instant of main memory. In every instant, the requested page is on top of the column and next three items are pages occupying three page frames, with the older pages closer to the bottom of the column. The last item shows whether the required page was already in main memory or not. A plus (+) sign represents a hit, meaning the required page was in main memory, while a minus (-) sign indicates a miss. This is a simple graphic representation of FIFO's behavior. Note that, in reality, pages in main memory do not move from one page frame to another as new page arrives. This figure is for us to comprehend how FIFO works. Its implementation for computer is based on the list that was explained earlier. will follow. In this figure, H represents the number of hits and M represents the number of misses, h indicates **hit ratio** (the number of hits divided by the number of pages in the page trace), and m shows **miss ratio**, that is, the number of misses divided by the number of pages in the page trace.

Page trace	1	2	3	4	1	2	5	1	2	3	4	5
Page frame 0	1	2	3	4	1	2	5	5	5	3	4	4
Page frame 1		1	2	3	4	1	2	2	2	5	3	3
Page frame 2			1	2	3	4	1	1	1	2	5	5
Hit?	-	-	-	-	-	-	-	+	+	-	-	+

(a) FIFO behavior with three page frames, $H=3$, $M=9$, $h=3/12$, and $m=9/12$.

Page trace	1	2	3	4	1	2	5	1	2	3	4	5
Page frame 0	1	2	3	4	4	4	5	1	2	3	4	5
Page frame 1		1	2	3	3	3	4	5	1	2	3	4
Page frame 2			1	2	2	2	3	4	5	1	2	3
Page frame 3				1	1	1	2	3	4	5	1	2
Hit?	-	-	-	-	+	+	-	-	-	-	-	-

(b) FIFO behavior with four page frames, $H=2$, $M=10$, $h=2/12$, and $m=10/12$.

Figure 7.9: A sample page trace that shows FIFO anomaly

An algorithm not having Belady's anomaly is said to have **stack property**. In other words, for such an algorithm there does not exists a page trace for which if the number of page frames is increased then the number of page faults is also increased. FIFO does not have stack property.

Clock policy

This algorithm makes use of the **reference bit**, R. The R bit shows whether or not a successful reference was made to the corresponding page after the bit was reset. For the clock algorithm, when a page is first moved to main memory, its reference bit is set to one. It may seem unnecessary to set the reference bit to one when a page is moved to main memory, as any successful reference to the page in main memory will automatically set the reference bit to one. However, if the reference bit is not set, it is possible for a page that has just moved to main memory to be removed before being actually used. Every page (or page frame, depending on the implementation) has a reference bit of its own. The **clock algorithm** assumes that all pages in main memory form a circle and a pointer, similar to a clock hand, points to one of the pages. To remove a page, the algorithm examines the page that the pointer is pointing to. If its reference bit is one then the reference bit is reset to zero and the pointer moves clockwise to the next page. If the reference bit is zero, the page is removed from main memory, the corresponding page frame is chosen to load the incoming page and the pointer is moved to the next page. A reference bit with a value of one means that either the page has recently moved to main memory or a successful reference has been made to the page as the page reference bit was reset by the algorithm. When a page has just been loaded to main memory, its R bit is set to one to prevent its removal before use. In the worst case, when all reference bits are one, the pointer will make a complete cycle setting all reference bits to zero, stopping at the point where it started. The corresponding page is then chosen for removal. Therefore, the clock algorithm scans all pages in a circular fashion and leaves pages whose reference bits are one to stay in main memory for the next round. The clock algorithm favors pages that are recently referenced and removes the first encountered page whose R bit equal to zero.

Second Chance policy

Another page removal algorithm which uses the reference bit, R, in its core decision making is the **second chance** algorithm. It is generally similar to the FIFO algorithm, with the exception of the candidate page for removed whose R bit is one. In this case, the page is not removed and both its timer and R bit are reset to zero. Afterwards, the next candidate is looked for. In the worst case, when the reference bit of all pages is one, the algorithm will make a complete cycle, examining all pages, setting all reference bits to zero, resetting all timers to zero and stopping at the point where it started. The first page is then chosen for removal. In this situation, the second chance algorithm acts like a simple FIFO algorithm, in that it degenerates into FIFO. As discussed earlier, working with timers is not practical. A practical approach to the design of a second chance algorithm is to make use of a linked list with two pointers similar to what was discussed for the FIFO algorithm. If the R bit of the page to be removed (at the front of the list) is one, then the page is not removed. Instead, its R bit is reset to zero. With the page itself, being removed from the front of the list and inserted at the rear of the list. Otherwise, the algorithm works like FIFO. Figure 7.10 shows a graphic example of a second chance algorithm. In this figure, the subscript next to page number is the R bit.

Page trace	4	0	2	3				0	4		3	2		4
Page frame 0	4_1	0_1	2_1	4_0	0_0	2_0	3_1	3_1	0_0	4_1	4_1	3_0	2_1	2_1
Page frame 1		4_1	0_1	2_1	4_0	0_0	2_0	2_0	3_1	0_0	0_0	4_1	3_0	3_0
Page frame 2			4_1	0_1	2_1	4_0	0_0	0_1	2_0	3_1	3_1	0_0	4_1	4_1
Hit?	-	-	-	-				+	-		+	-		+

Figure 7.10: Second chance behavior with three page frame, $H=3$, $M=6$, $h=3/9$, and $m=6/9$

Second chance and clock algorithms are conceptually the same. The difference is in implementation. In the former, we can assume a pointer is moving (clockwise) from one node to the next in a circular list to find the proper page to remove. In the latter, we can assume that a circular list is being moved (clockwise) under a fixed pointer so that the pointer can find the proper page to remove.

Least Recently Used policy

Imagine a timer that is attached to each page being transferred to main memory. The timer is reset to zero when either the page is first transferred to main memory or whenever it is referred to in main memory. The timer keeps track of the time length passed since it was last reset. To remove a page, the LRU picks the page with the largest timer value. In other words, the page that has not been referred to for the longest period of time is always removed. Attaching an actual timer, or even a virtual timer, to every page and keeping it constantly updated is a time consuming process which makes the **Least Recently Used** (LRU) algorithm impractical. A more efficient approach is to organize a doubly-linked list with two pointers pointing to its front and rear, similar to what was designed for the FIFO algorithm. The difference is that the list must always be organized so that the page referred to later is closer to the front of the list. The algorithm always removes the page pointed to by the front pointer of the list. Even this approach requires an unacceptable amount of overhead, thus making the LRU algorithm impractical. To keep the list in order, every time a page is successfully referred to, the algorithm has to find the page in the list. If the page is not already at the rear of the list, it is moved there. Figure 7.11 shows the behavior of LRU for Figure 7.9's page trace and a main memory with three page frames.

Page trace	1	2	3	4	1	2	5	1	2	3	4	5
Page frame 0	1	2	3	4	1	2	5	1	2	3	4	5
Page frame 1		1	2	3	4	1	2	5	1	2	3	4
Page frame 2			1	2	3	4	1	2	5	1	2	3
Hit?	-	-	-	-	-	-	-	+	+	-	-	+

Figure 7.11: LRU with a main memory of three frames, $H=2$, $M=10$, $h=2/12$, and $m=10/12$

LRU does not have Belady's anomaly as LRU is a **stack algorithm**. To get a feeling of this, see Figure 7.12 for the LRU performance of Figure 7.11's page trace on a main memory of four page frames.

Page trace	1	2	3	4	1	2	5	1	2	3	4	5
Page frame 0	1	2	3	4	1	2	5	1	2	3	4	5
Page frame 1		1	2	3	4	1	2	5	1	2	3	4
Page frame 2			1	2	3	4	1	2	5	1	2	3
Page frame 3				1	2	3	4	4	4	5	1	2
Hit?	-	-	-	-	+	+	-	+	+	-	-	-

Figure 7.12: LRU behavior with four page frames, $H=4$, $M=8$, $h=4/12$, and $m=8/12$

By comparing Figures 7.11 and 7.12, we realize that their first three rows (below the page trace) are exactly the same. It is clear that at any instant, the last three pages referred to do not change whether or not there are three or four frames in main memory. Both figures show exactly the same pages in the first three rows. Actually, at any instant, the last m pages referred to (for example the first three rows of the LRU visualization) do not change whether or not there are m or n ($n>m$) frames in main memory. In the case of n page frames, there are extra opportunities to encounter a page hit for the next page reference. This is the reason why LRU has stack property. Because of LRU's impracticality, on the one hand, and its attractive stack property, on the other hand, many LRU-approximate algorithms are developed. *Not recently used*, *least frequently used*, *most frequently used*, *not frequently used*, and *aging* algorithms are all approximations to the LRU algorithm.

Not Recently Used policy

This algorithm makes use of both referenced, R, and modified, M, bits. The combination of these two bits makes up the following four classes:

Class 1: (0, 0): not referenced and not modified

Class 2: (0, 1): not referenced but modified

Class 3: (1, 0): referenced but not modified

Class 4: (1, 1): referenced and modified

Periodically, the R bit of all pages is reset to zero. The R bit of every page that has been successfully accessed is set to one. When a page is moved to main memory its M bit is reset to zero. This bit is set to one whenever something has been stored in its corresponding page, as it is not worth it to check whether the page was actually changed or not. A one value for R indicates that the corresponding page has been successfully accessed in the current period. A one value for M means that the page was "changed" since it was loaded into main memory. Pages are always removed from the lowest numbered nonempty class. When there are more than one candidate pages to remove, any one of the candidates may be chosen. The R bit of a page that has just been moved to main memory is set to one to prevent it from being removed before actually being used.

This classification is made so that the R bit has a preference over the M bit. The **Not Recently Used** (NRU) algorithm tries to leave the most recently accessed pages in main memory. Yet, this policy has to be approximates to become practical.

Least Frequently Used policy

In this policy, a counter field is added to every page table entry (or inverted page table, depending on the memory management policy in effect.) When a page is transferred to main memory, its counter is reset to zero. Every time a page is referenced, its counter is incremented. To remove a page, the **Least Frequently Used** (LFU) algorithm selects the page (or one of the pages) with the smallest count. There are few disadvantages to this algorithm. A counter may soon reach its limit where a further increment is not possible. If a page is heavily used during a period of time, its counter will show a high number. This will prevent the page from being removed even though it has not been used lately. Due to the high overhead of choosing the page with the smallest count, it is not possible to use this algorithm within a real operating system. A possible approximate LFU exists if a threshold is used to remove a page. The threshold, in this case, is a value which is much more than zero. A pointer moves around the circular page list like a clock algorithm. The first page whose counter value is less than the threshold is removed.

Most Frequently Used policy

This algorithm is the exact opposite of the LFU algorithm. **Most Frequently Used** (MFU) selects the page with the largest count for removal. The rationale for this approach is the likelihood that pages with smaller counts have been brought in recently and will, therefore, be needed in the future.

Not Frequently Used policy

Counters are often implemented in software. With this kind of counter, it is very time consuming to count the exact number of times every page in main memory was successfully accessed. A more relaxed approach is to count the number of intervals in which every page in main memory was successfully accessed. The interval length is implementation dependent. This interval is called the **reference counter update interval**. At the beginning of every reference counter update interval, which is announced by an interval timer interrupt, the R bit of every page in main memory is added to its corresponding counter and the R bit is reset to zero. If the R bit of a page is one, it means that the page was successfully accesses in the previous interval. The number of times the page was successfully accessed within the interval does not matter. To remove a page, the **Not Frequently Used** (NFU) algorithm selects the page (or one of the pages) with the smallest count. Like least frequently used algorithm, NFU does not forget the history of references to pages. This is a disadvantage that is eradicated in the *aging* algorithm.

Aging policy

The fundamental requirements of the **aging** algorithm are similar to the NFU algorithm. *Aging* utilizes the R bit and a counter for every page, plus an interrupting interval timer for reference-count updates. Also, to remove a page, the *aging* algorithm selects the page (or one of the pages) with the smallest count. Instead of adding all R bits to their corresponding counter, at the beginning of every interval, the *aging* algorithm shifts every R bit to its corresponding shift counter. The shift moves all the bits of the counter one place to the right and the corresponding R bit is inserted into the leftmost bit of the counter. The rightmost bit of the counter is lost in every shift. If counters are n bits long, the history of references to pages are kept only for n intervals. Consider two counter values: 0100 and 0010. Both counters show that their corresponding pages have been successfully accessed one time (to be correct, in one interval) during the last four intervals. However, the decimal equivalent of 0100 is four while the decimal value of 0010 is two. In other words, the value of the first counter is larger that the value of the second counter. One more point is that the page corresponding to the first counter was referenced later than the page corresponding to the second counter. The page whose counter value is smaller has a higher possibility to be removed from main memory. The conclusion is that the algorithm favors later references. Figure 7.13 shows how the *aging* algorithm works for a given page trace and a main memory with three frames. It is assumed that for every three memory references, the clock will interrupt to perform "counters" to update operations. In this figure, subscripts to page numbers are their R value and the binary number beneath the page numbers are their corresponding counters. Every counter is four bits long. The disadvantage of *aging* is that a newly loaded page may be removed before its corresponding counter becomes nonzero.

Page trace	1	2	3		2	5	3		4	2	4		5
Page frame 0	1^0_{000}	1^0_{000}	1^0_{000}	1^0_{000}	1^0_{000}	5^0_{000}	5^0_{000}	5^0_{000}	4^0_{000}	4^0_{000}	4^1_{000}	4^0_{100}	4^0_{100}
Page frame 1		2^0_{000}	2^0_{000}	2^0_{000}	2^1_{000}	2^1_{000}	2^1_{000}	2^0_{100}	2^0_{100}	2^1_{100}	2^1_{100}	2^0_{110}	2^0_{110}
Page frame 2			3^0_{000}	3^0_{000}	3^0_{000}	3^0_{000}	3^1_{000}	3^0_{100}	3^0_{100}	3^0_{100}	3^0_{100}	3^0_{010}	5^0_{000}
Hit?	.	-	-		+	-	+		-	+	+		-

Figure 7.13: Aging algorithm for counters of four bits long

Optimal page replacement policy

There is no realistic algorithm that is always optimal. A theoretical and non-practical optimal algorithm is defined as one which assumes that the whole page trace is known in advance. This algorithm removes the page which will be referred to in the farthest future. Belady showed that this algorithm leads to the fewest number of page faults. For a visual demonstration of how this algorithm works, we can count the number of memory references to the next reference of every page in main memory and then remove the page with the largest count. Figure 7.14 shows a sample example of a page trace and the behavior of the **optimal page replacement** algorithm for a memory the size of three frames. The "optimal" algorithm does not have Belady's anomaly.

Page trace	2	3	4	1	5	2	3	5	4	2	1
Page frame 1	2	2	2_3	2_2	2_1	2	2_3	2	2	2_i	1
Page frame 2		3	3_4	3_3	3_2	3	3_i	5	5	5_i	5
Page frame 3			4_6	1_7	5_3	4	4_2	4	4	4_i	4
Hit?	-	-	-	-	-	+	+	-	+	+	-

The letter "i" stands for infinity, in this table.

Figure 7.14: "Optimal" algorithm for memory size of three frames

7.4.3 Optimal Page Size

A large page size reduces the size of a page table, but it increases internal fragmentation. On the other hand, a small page size increases the size of a page table but decreases internal fragmentation. For page-based memory management (without virtual memory) we compute the optimal page size based on internal fragmentation and page table size. This is not so for page-based virtual memory which will be explained, the reason being that the last page of a live process may or may not be in main memory. In addition, parts of page tables may be swapped out of main memory. Let's assume that all page tables are memory resident and the probability of being in main memory is the same for all pages of a process. Let's also assume that the total size of main memory is m and there are n live processes. Besides, assume that the average process size is r bytes. The probability of a page of a process being in the main memory will approximately be

$$\frac{m}{nr}$$

However, the last page of each process is approximately half full, thus the need for its content is half the need for the content of a full page. The probability of a half-full page being in the main memory is:

$$\frac{m}{2nr}$$

If the size of each page table entry is e bytes, then the total memory waste per process is:

$$MemoryWaste = \frac{m}{2nr} * \frac{p}{2} + \frac{r}{p} * e = \frac{mp}{4nr} + \frac{re}{p}. \qquad (7.3)$$

If we take the derivative of the equation (7.3) with p as the only variable parameter and make it equal to zero, the optimal value of p is calculated using:

$$\frac{m}{4nr} - \frac{re}{p^2} = 0.$$

Or,

$$p = 2r\sqrt{\frac{ne}{m}} \qquad (7.4)$$

Equation 7.4 is applicable if the sum of the sizes of all processes is at least equal to m (the size of main memory).

7.4.4 Multilevel Page-Table Page-Based Virtual Memory

The page table of a running process is an essential part of many address translation methods. If the required page number is not in the memory management unit, that is, the page number is not in the internal cache or the translation look-aside buffer of the MMU (depending on the technique used), then the page number is directly looked up from the page table of the running process. So far, every page table is assumed to be a linear array for which the page number is the index. Also, up until now, we have assumed that the page table of every process is completely in the memory. In other words, without adding new data structures and extending address translation methods, it is not possible to apply the virtual memory technique to page tables. The page table of the running process has to be locked in main memory in order to translate logical addresses into physical addresses. A **multilevel page table** is a methodology which makes it possible to apply the virtual memory technique to page tables. For an n-level page table every logical address is divided into $n+1$ parts. Part one (counting from left to right) is the highest level of page table directory. Part number $n+1$ is the offset from the beginning of a logical page. Part one of a logical address points to a directory, with every entry of this directory pointing to another directory and so on. The nth part of a logical address points to a page frame of main memory. The whole superstructure is called a **multilevel page table structure** or page table structure, for short. Towards the end of this chapter, a detailed implementation of multilevel page table methodology for **Windows NT** and its descendents is presented. It uses a two-level page table structure. The reader is urged to study this case study on memory management policy. Should we ignore this section, the discussion of multilevel page table methodology would not complete.

7.5 Segmentation with Paged Virtual Memory

Segmentation (without paged) memory management is very much similar to multiple partition memory management, but there are some differences. These methods are similar in that every program portion (that is, the main program, every procedure, and every data structure) is considered a logical entity that requires physical memory space during execution. A program (or data) portion, called a segment, can be loaded into a physical partition of main memory. A partition can hold more than one program portion. The difference is that multiple partition memory management is an operating system process which is performed without the knowledge of the programmer. The programmer does not know what program portion is loaded into what partition of main memory. On the other hand, with segmentation memory management, the programmer has explicit information on what portion of the program is in what segment. With multiple partition memory management, the programmer's view of a program is a sequential array of instructions and data. With segmentation memory management, the programmer's view of a program is a collection of sequential arrays of instructions and data. This view enables the programmer to explicitly work with every segment within its program. Some processors, such as the Intel family, provide special hardware to materialize the programmer's view and provide special hardware for address translation.

Segmentation memory management, similar to multiple partition memory management, suffers from external fragmentation. The combined segmentation and paged virtual memory method has the benefits of segmentation and at the same time, eliminates external fragmentation.

Segmentation with paged virtual memory management greatly increases the complexity of memory management, but in return, offers many advantages that make this method worthwhile.

(1) Every program portion can dynamically grow. The programmer need not know in advance the size of program portions. Segment size is an attribute of segments and is kept in the segment table. It is updated as the size changes.

(2) Protection can be defined for individual segments. One segment could be read only while the other may be read/update.

(3) Segment sharing between processes becomes possible. Therefore, simultaneously executing processes can then define shared data areas.

(4) Every module can independently be compiled and linked, without any side effects on other modules' start address.

Segmentation, in the segmentation with paged virtual memory, is a logical concept. Physical memory is a collection of page frames, as in page-based virtual memory. Every memory page frame can be assigned to any page of any segment of any process. In other words, pages of one segment need not be loaded into contiguous page frames of main memory. As a matter of fact, it is not necessary to load all pages of a segment into main memory before needed. Logically speaking, every process is composed of one or more segments and every segment is composed of one or more pages.

In segmentation with paged virtual memory, the format of a logical address is shown in Figure 7.15.

Segment number	Page number	Offset

Figure 7.15: Logical address format in segmentation with page policy

Every process has its own **segment table**, in that there is one segment table per process and every segment has a corresponding page table. The main function of a segment table entry is to register the base address of its corresponding page table. It may also include protection, sharing, and present/absent. See Figure 7.16.

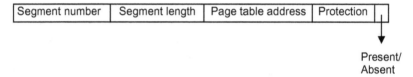

Present/
Absent

Figure 7.16: Format of each row of segment table

Schematically, address translation is similar to two-level page table page-based virtual memory with the segment number replacing the *partial page table number*, which is discussed towards the end of this chapter.

7.6 Cache Memory

Computer architects and producers are in continuous demand to increase the processing speed of computers. They have to constantly exploit novel ideas and new technologies to fulfill computer user demands. Memory access time is one target to focus on, because instructions and data are fetched from main memory, which is, thus, continuously in use. Not only

Two or more data that express exactly the same phenomenon and must, therefore, be the same at all times may be stored as different values in computer memories (or storages). For example, suppose you have received a promotion at work and your job title has changed as a result. The company's web-site is modified accordingly, but the payroll system has not yet updated. This discrepancy in data reflects an inconsistency. We cannot avoid inconsistency among redundant information in secondary storage, main memory, and cache memory, all the time. The focus should be on producing correct results even though there may be *information inconsistency*.

general purpose processor(s) use main memory, I/O processors usually utilize each memory cycle that is not being used by the processor(s). Reducing main memory access time directly improves overall system perfor-mance. Integrating **cache memory** into storage superstructures is one way to improve effective memory access time. As a result, a new level is thus added to the hierarchy of memory. Cache memory is a special **read/write memory** with extra hardware to recognize whether a copy of the content of a given address of main memory is in cache or not. It actually checks for the address not the content.

The content of every location in cache is a copy of a content of a location in main memory. There is the possibility that this copy may have been modified since it moved to cache. If this copy is changed, it must be written back to its corresponding location in main memory in order to eliminate cache and main memory inconsistencies. In the presence of a cache memory, the memory hierarchy is illustrated in Figure 7.17. In this model, the CPU is shown in the top level because it is the main user of memory information. The CPU has registers to which information is moved, from either cache or main memory and vice versa.

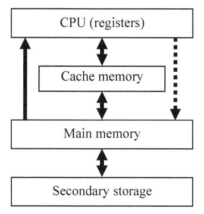

Figure 7.17: Memory hierarchy of contemporary computers

Information transfer for main memory to cache is in units of **blocks**. A block is different from a page or a page frame. It is an independent unit that is specifically used for cache memory management. A block is usually smaller than a page, in size, and has a power of two bytes, e.g., 128 bytes. When the CPU needs to access a main memory location, the cache memory hardware will immediately inform it whether the corresponding block is in cache or not. If it is, the desired word is fetched from cache. If not, the needed word is directly transferred from main memory to the CPU and, at the same time, it is ordered to the cache processor to bring the block that contains the desired word from main memory to the cache memory. The arrow from main memory to the CPU shows it is possible to transfer information to the CPU directly, when the information is not in cache. If a structure does not have this line, the needed data must be transferred to cache and from there to the CPU. Any store operation in cache memory, by the CPU, may change the content of the corresponding word in cache. In this case, if the data is simultaneously stored in main memory, to prevent cache and main memory inconsistencies, a technique called **write-through cache** is utilized. For this, the dotted line from the CPU to the main memory is required. Otherwise, the modified block will be copied into its permanent place in main memory at a later time and the dotted line from the CPU to main memory is not necessary.

There are many **cache management** methodologies and techniques, most of which are similar to main memory management methodologies and techniques. We will discuss a simple method which is not derived from any main memory management method.

Let's assume we have 1Mega bytes of cache memory and the **block frame** size is 128 bytes. In addition, an address (this time we are talking about physical or real addresses) is 32 bits wide, meaning main memory could be 4 giga bytes large. Think of main memory as a two dimensional array of blocks. For our hypothetical sizes, there will be 2^{13} columns in every row, if we consider the total size of every row of main memory to be equal to the total size of cache memory (i.e., 1 mega bytes, in this case.) If every block frame is 2^7 bytes, then $2^{13} * 2^7 = 2^{20} = 1$Mega. There could be 2^{12} rows in the main memory array because $2^{12} * 2^{20} = 2^{32}$. Let's also assume that a physical address has three parts: (1) the right most 7 bits (i.e., $2^7 = 128$) defines the offset (that is, the displacement from the beginning of a block), (2) the middle 13 bits identifies the column number of the main memory block that corresponds to this address, and (3) the leftmost 12 bits indicating the row number of the main memory block that corresponds to this address. See Figure 7.18.

12 bits	13 bits	7 bits
Row number	Column number	Offset

Figure 7.18: Structure of a physical address with respect to cache memory

How does cache hardware know whether or not a given main memory address is in cache? A hardware array of 2^{13} registers (i.e., the number of columns in main memory) keeps track of what blocks of main memory are in cache at any given time. In the simplest method, at any given time, only one block of every column of main memory can be in cache and a block of column i, $i=0, 1, ..., 2^{13}$-

1, of main memory may only be loaded in block frame *i* of cache. The register number *i* will contain the row number of that block of main memory. See Figure 7.19.

To summarize, if a **cache miss** occurs when accessing an address that is in the block of row *r* and column *c* of main memory, the block is transferred to block frame *c* of cache memory, that is after the previously occupying block is removed, and register *c* is filled with *r*. An address composed of row *r*, column *c* and offset *f* is in cache if and only if the content of register *c* is equal to *r*. This comparison is done automatically by cache hardware. There are two more points. First, when the computer is first started (or at every restart) if the content of all cache registers is reset to zero, the interpretation is that all blocks of row zero of main memory are in cache. On the other hand, upon every start (or restart) of the computer if the content of all cache registers are set to one, the interpretation is that all blocks of the last row of main memory are in cache. Neither of these interpretations is true, unless an actual transfer is performed during the start (or restart). This is not recommended because in most cases it may not be necessary to do so. To fix this problem, registers are assumed to be 13 bits long and the extra bit of every register is for the purpose of showing whether the content of the register is valid or not (zero for not valid and one for valid). The extra bit of all registers is reset to zero whenever the system starts or restarts. It is set to one whenever a block is transferred to a corresponding block frame of cache. Second, we may decide to remove all blocks of a process from cache memory when it terminates. In this case, for every block frame that is emptied, the extra bit of its corresponding register is reset to zero.

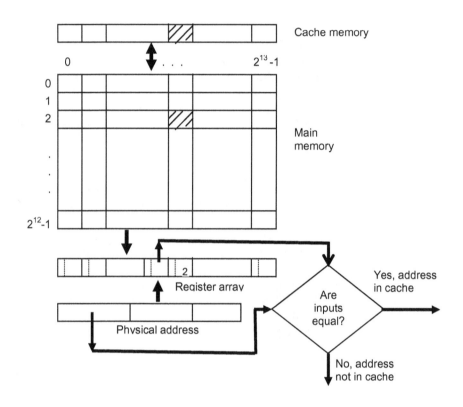

Figure 7.19: The structure to check whether a physical address is in cache

A simple example showing how cache memory can improve the **effective access time** of main memory follows.

Example 7.1: Cache success rate is given to be 0.9 for reading from main memory or writing to it. This means, on the average, 90% of the time that we need something from main memory we can actually find it in the cache memory. With this **cache hit** ratio, on the average, in only 10% of the times processes want to read something from main memory of want to write something to main memory an actual access to main memory will take place. If cache access time is say 20 nanoseconds and main memory access time is 50 nanoseconds, on the average, it will take

$$0.9*20 + 0.1*(x + 50)$$

nanoseconds to read a data or instruction from main memory or write a result in it. In this expression x is the time that takes to fine out what we need to access is in the cache or not. If we take this value to be five nanoseconds then effective main memory access time will become

$$0.9*20 + 0.1*(5 + 50) = 23.5 \; nanoseconds$$

As we can see, the access time which is 50 nanoseconds when there is no cache memory is reduced to 23.5 nanoseconds where we use this type of cache memory. This means we read/write more than twice as fast as we used to read/write.

7.7 Windows Two-Level Page-Table Structure

The address register of Pentium processors is supposed to be 32 bits wide and the address bus is also 32 bits wide. A logical address is thus at most 32 bits, which allows the address space of a program to grow to 4 Giga (or 2^{32}) bytes. Windows NT and later versions (e.g., Windows 2000, Window 2003, and Windows 7) utilize all 4 giga bytes of address space. The page size and therefore page frame size for these Windows are 4K bytes, making the offset part

> *Windows NT* was designed to fulfill the needs of its era. It is not a new version of older Windows, but rather a new design with novel ideas. Later versions of Windows are all based on Windows NT with additions and improvements.

of a logical address 12 bits. If a one-level page table is used, the page table will have 1Mega (or 2^{20}) entries. If every entry is 4 bytes long, the page table of a 4Giga byte program will require 4 mega bytes of main memory to reside in. This is quite a large real memory to spare for a process's page table, especially being part of an operating system's address space, which would increase the run-time size of the operating system.

The two-level superstructure of a page table in Windows divides a logical address into three parts. Parts one (counting from left to right) and two are each 10 bits long. Part three is the offset and is 12 bits long. Every value of part one (if used) refers to one entry of a table called "directory" by Windows. Therefore, the *directory* is a table of 1,024 (or 2^{10}) entries. Each entry of the *directory* points to a table of 1,024 entries, if used. Each one of these tables is called a **partial page table**. There are 1,024 *partial page tables* for the largest possible program. Every entry of a partial page table points to a page frame of the main memory. Figure 7.20 shows the three parts of a logical address.

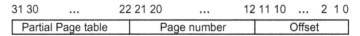

31 30   ...   22 21 20   ...   12 11 10 ... 2 1 0

| Partial Page table | Page number | Offset |

Figure 7.20: A schematic address structure

Any unsuccessful access to the *directory*, or partial page tables, will cause an interrupt. In response to this, an I/O operation for bringing the required page to main memory is performed. Figure 7.21 depicts a structural view of the address translation schema in Windows.

If the page table superstructure is fully exploited and every entry of the *directory* and partial page tables uses four bytes, then the total page table superstructure will need:

$$1024 * 4 + 1024 * 1024 * 4 \quad \text{bytes}$$

Or,

$$4\text{Mega} + 4\text{K} \quad \text{bytes}$$

For such a program, if one-level page table is used and the size of each entry of the page table is four bytes then we would need $2^{20}*4 = 4$ mega bytes of memory for the page table. If we compare the total size of a one-level page table and a two-level page table for the largest possible program, with equal entry lengths, the result is that the one-level page table will need 4K less storage area. Therefore, we do not save storage space by using a two-level page table structure. Instead, the benefit is in making use of the virtual memory concept for page tables. The *directory* of the running process is kept in main memory, but partial page tables can be in secondary storage. How does the system know whether the wanted partial page table is in main memory or secondary storage? A field in every *directory* entry shows whether the corresponding partial page table is present (in main memory) or absent.

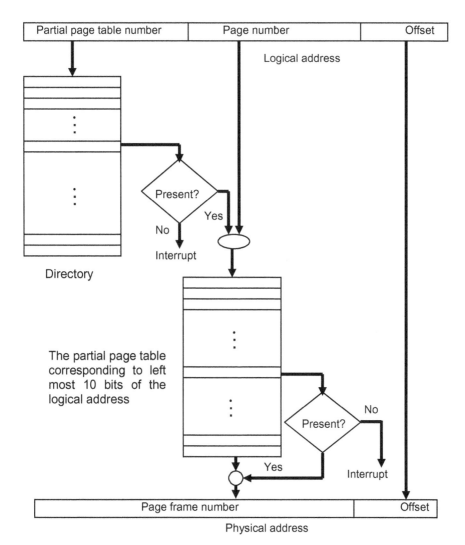

Figure 7.21: Address translation schematic in Windows

In order to complete the memory management policy of contemporary Windows operating system, we have to clarify a few other guidelines.

Windows uses the concept of "working set". It assigns a default fixed number of pages as a minimum working set to every new process. This working set is adjusted as the execution of the process continues. It makes use of **per process page removal**. When a page has to come to main memory, if the list of free page frames is empty, pages are removed from processes that are using more page frames than their minimum working set size. FIFO is the page removal algorithm. It uses the page frame table structure to keep track of the status of all page frames of main memory. Free page frames are linked together to form a list of free frames. Many other lists are formed within the page frame table. The page frame table is called the **page frame dataset** in Windows. It makes use of the locality of reference concept. If a page fault occurs, the memory manager intentionally generates page faults for neighboring pages in order to force the system to **pre-fetch** these pages. According to the locality of the reference concept, if a page is referred to now, there is a great possibility that neighboring pages will be referred to in the near future. By pre-fetching adjacent pages, *miss ratio* is usually decreased.

7.8 The UNIX Memory Management Policy

Many versions of the UNIX operating system have been developed since the first version was announced in 1969 by Bell laboratories. The UNIX System V Release 4 (SVR4, by the UNIX support group for distribution within AT&T), BSD4.4 (by the University of California-Berkeley), OSF/1 (Open System Foundation/1 by DEC Company), and Solaris 2 (by SUN Microsystems) are some newer versions of UNIX. UNIX versions vary and memory management policies are not exactly the same in all versions. In this section, we will discuss general methods that are used for memory management. For any specific algorithm explained, the UNIX version which uses it is introduced.

The most important data structure for memory management is the *page table*. As usual, there is one page table for every process. This table is indexed by page number, with the page frame number being the most important piece of information in every entry. Another important structure is the *page frame table*, called the **page frame dataset** in UNIX. Every entry of this table describes the state of its corresponding page frame in physical memory. Entries with similar states are linked together to form a list. For example, entries that correspond to free memory frames are linked together to form a list of free frames. This list is also used to assign frames to incoming pages.

UNIX likes to have a certain number of free (or unallocated) page frames available all the times. This does not mean that violations cannot occur. However, if they do, the memory manager will take proper actions. The desired minimum number of page frames is called *minfree* (sometimes called *low water level*). The exact value of this parameter is calculated based on the main memory size upon system boot time. If the number of free page frames becomes lower than *minfree*, memory manager will try to free page frames until the number of page frames reaches *lotsfree* (sometimes called *high water level*). It is clear that *lotsfree* is grater than *minfree*. The page replacement algorithm decides which pages are to be removed from main memory. To get a feeling of what *minfree* and *lotsfree* are, think of a control system that monitors the temperature of an office during winter. The system may turn the heating device on when the temperature goes lower than 20 degrees (Celsius). The heating device may run until the temperature reaches 25 degrees before being turned off. In this analogy, number 20 corresponds to *minfree* and number 25 corresponds to *lotsfree*. It is clear that if the difference between these two numbers is high the heating system will be turned on and off less frequently. However, when the heating is turned back on, it has to work for a long time to reach the desired temperature. On the other hand, if the difference between these two numbers is low, the heating system will be turned on and off more frequently. When it is turned on again, the heating will work for a short time before being turned off.

When the number of free page frames fall below *minfree*, the **page removal process** (called *pagedaemon* in the 4.3BSD version) is activated. This process uses a modified version of the clock algorithm to decide which pages to remove. Recall that the original clock algorithm removes one page at a time. However, its modified version, which is discussed here, removes many pages every time it is activated. It begins sweeping the page frame data set starting from where the clock hand is pointing. If the reference, R, bit of the frame that is pointed to is zero, this frame is evacuated and added to the free list. The modified (or dirty) bit of the outgoing page has to be checked. If it is dirty, it must be copied back to its permanent place in virtual memory. Note that, the page removal process cannot remove locked-in-memory pages. The clock hand then moves to the next frame. If the reference, R, bit is one, it is changed to zero and the clock hand moves on to the next frame. The page removal process continues until the number of free frames reaches *lotsfree*, or until enough frames are scanned, as defined by the memory manager.

When enough frames are scanned by page removal process, but the number of free frames have not reached *lotsfree* the **process swapper** complements the page removal process. This may be because most in-memory pages are frequently being used and if the page swapper swaps them out they will have to be swapped in, again. In such a situation, we better stop page swapping to prevent efficiency degradation. Using process swapper, some of the processes will temporary be swapped out of memory. A swapped-out process will be swapped back in when the situation changes and the memory shortage pressure has lessened.

7.9 Summary

There are variety of memory management methods ranging from single contiguous memory management to multilevel page table page-based virtual memory with segmentation and cache memory. Contemporary computers use virtual memory methods while special purpose computers for sensitive environments use non-virtual memory management methods. With virtual memory it is possible to lock some pages in main memory to prevent their removal. This may be thought of as a combined virtual-nonvirtual memory management method. With virtual memory management, comes a variety of page removal methods with different complexity and efficiency. It is not possible to devise an optimal page removal algorithm which, at the same time, is also practical. Although cache memory is not part of main memory, contemporary computers use it to improve overall main memory access time. A short discussion on cache memory was also presented in this chapter. Two case studies, UNIX and Windows memory management, were presented in this chapter and fit in very well into our discussions.

7.10 Problems

1. Suppose we use a singly-linked list for implementing each of the following placement algorithms in a dynamic partition memory management policy. If we want to look for a certain sized partition and we know that such a partition exists, what is the average search length for each one of the following algorithms?

    (1) first-fit

    (2) next-fit

    (3) best-fit

    (4) worst-fit

2. If a double-linked list is used to implement the FIFO page replacement algorithm and the list is built within every process' page-table, is it possible to implement an overall page replacement algorithm? Explain.

3. With the *buddy system*, when a program terminates, its occupied space is returned to the free partition data structure. However, if its matching buddy (the buddy that it was originally separated from) is also free, the two join to form a larger partition. In buddy system, why can't any two adjacent partitions the size of $2^i \cdot K$, join to form a partition the size of $2^{i+1} \cdot K$ partition?

4. Consider a system that uses relocation partition memory management for the page table area within the operating system. The size of memory that is managed is 512K. Every time the memory is 90% full, the relocation process is activated. If moving one word of main memory from one location to another takes 100 nanoseconds, how long does it take to relocate all allocated memory, every time the relocating process is activated?

5. For page-based (non-virtual) memory management, (a) clearly explain the difference between a logical and a physical address. And (b) when a program runs, does it produce a logical address or a physical address? Explain.

6. Can you imagine the page size that is not of the power of 2? What are the disadvantages of such a page size?

7 For page-based (non-virtual) memory management, we can think of two techniques to keep track of available memory frames: (1) Using a link list that has one node per every free block and (2) using a bit map technique with one bit for every block of main memory. If main memory is one giga bytes, page size is 2K bytes, and every node of the free block list is four bytes long, for what number of free blocks is the space overhead of these two techniques (approximately) the same?

8. For some machine instructions, the operand(s) could be very long. For example, the operands of the move character (MVC) instruction could be as long as 256 characters. If the system starts to execute this instruction and either of the operands straddles a page boundary midway through the execution of the instruction, we may find out that the rest of the operand is not available. As a result, a page fault is generated. When the page comes to the main memory, we have to restart the execution of the instruction. How can we avoid this situation of restarting the execution of partially executed instruction?

9. For page-based virtual memory management, with the average program size of two mega bytes and a page-table entry size of 4 bytes, what is the optimal page size with respect to memory waste due to page tables and internal fragmentation?

10. For a page-based memory management system that can run programs as large as one giga bytes, if the size of pages is 2K:
   a.   Illustrate the format of the logical addresses
   b.   Illustrate the format of the physical address
   c.   Illustrate the format of the page table entries
   d.   What is the maximum possible length of a page table?

11. For page-based virtual memory management, with an average program size of two mega bytes and a page-table entry size of 4 bytes, what is the optimal page size with respect to memory waste due to the page table and internal fragmentation?

12. A binary search program for an array of 2^{20} elements, indexed from zero to $2^{20}-1$, is supposed to be executed under page-based virtual memory management. Every element of the array is four bytes long. Every page is 1K bytes. In addition, the whole program, without the data array, is 1K bytes, or

one page. When moved to main memory, the page is locked so it will not be removed until the execution of the program finishes. The main memory has only three page frames and there will not be any other process in the system when this process is executing. If the process searches for data that does not exist in the array:

    a. How many page faults will the process generate, if the page removal algorithm is LRU?

    b. Will the number of page faults differ if the page removal algorithm is FIFO? Why?

13. A system with page-based virtual memory management has only six page frames. This system is running two processes in a multiprogramming manner. At the beginning, every process's quota is three page frames, which has to be observed at all times. A process quota may change under certain conditions. If the number of page faults of one process becomes twice the number of page faults of the other process, its page frame quota is increased by one. The page frame quota of the other process is decreased by one. These quotas remain intact until the current page fault ratio once again changes. The page removal algorithm is per process LRU. The following page trace is generated during the execution of these processes. The pages of process two are underlined. How many page faults are generated?

    2 5 5 4 4 2 3 2 6 5 4 4 5 4 7 5 3 3 2 3 5 4

14. The following procedure calculates the sum of two arrays, A and B, and stores the results in array C. The code size of this program together with the size of the variable *i* are exactly 1K bytes. Every element of the arrays is four bytes. Page-based virtual memory management, with a memory size of four page frames is used to run this procedure.

    a. How many page faults will the FIFO page replacement algorithm generate?

    b. How many page faults will the second chance page replacement algorithm generate?

```
void summat(int A[ ], int B[ ], int C[ ])
{
    for (int i =0; i<512; i++)
        C[i] = A[i] + B[i];
}
```

15. For the following page trace and a main memory of five page frames, the main memory management policy is page-based virtual memory. The page

replacement algorithm is NFU. Two processes, P1 and P2, are running concurrently and neither is allowed to use more than three page frames at any time. How many page faults will be generated for the following page trace? The notation P_k stands for page P of process k. A clock tick is supposed to be issued per every three memory references, in order to process the R bits.

$$1_1 \quad 2_1 \quad 3_2 \quad 2_2 \quad 4_2 \quad 1_2 \quad 3_1 \quad 2_1 \quad 4_2 \quad 3_1 \quad 2_1 \quad 4_1 \quad 1_1 \quad 5_1 \quad 1_2$$

16. Consider a three-level page table organization as shown in the figure below. If a program is 4 giga bytes, what is the total space needed for its page table (that is, the total space needed by directories and partial page tables)?

4 bits	8 bits	8 bits	12 bits

17. The main memory management policy is a page-based virtual memory and the replacement algorithm is *clock* algorithm. If the R bit of a page that has just been moved to main memory is not set to one, provide an example in which this page is removed from main memory before being actually accessed.

18. For the problem at hand, the main memory management policy is a page-based virtual memory and the replacement algorithm is NFU. Page reference counters are two bits. If a counter reaches its maximum, it will no longer be incremented. If the number of page frames is three, how many page faults are generated for the following page trace?

$$2 \ 1 \ 1 \ 2 \ 2 \ 3 \ 0 \ 3 \ 1 \ 2 \ 0 \ 2 \ 4$$

19. The page replacement algorithm in page-based memory management is per-process second chance. Main memory consists of four frames and there are two processes in the system. Initially, all memory frames are free. The set of frames, which each process seizes from the initial free frames of main memory, belongs to the process for its lifetime. Each process is allowed to replace the content of its own frames with new pages, if there is a page fault for that process. What is the page fault ratio for the following page trace? The pages of process two are underlined.

$$2 \ \underline{7} \ 1 \ \underline{0} \ 5 \ \underline{1} \ \underline{0} \ 2 \ \underline{7} \ 0 \ 1 \ \underline{3} \ \underline{0} \ 3 \ 0 \ \underline{2} \ 4 \ \underline{1} \ 2 \ \underline{6} \ 3 \ 1 \ \underline{5} \ 2 \ \underline{3}$$

20. A program two giga bytes long is going to run under a page-based virtual memory management policy. The page frame size of main memory is 4K bytes. How many entries does the program's page table have?

21. We presented the optimal page replacement algorithm in this chapter. Can you develop a page replacement algorithm which always gives the highest number of page faults?

22. To translate a logical address into a physical address, the memory management unit (MMU) may utilize a TLB memory. If it does so suppose the TLB access time is 20 nanoseconds and its hit ration is .95. If a TLB miss occurs, the system directly uses the page table that resides in main memory. If main memory access time is 60 nanoseconds:

    a. What is the effective time for translating a logical address to a physical address?

    b. What is the effective time to access a memory location through the MMU?

23. To translate a logical address into a physical address, the memory management unit utilizes a cache memory. Cache access time is 20 nanoseconds and its hit ratio is .95. If a cache miss occurs, the requested page table entry is moved to the cache memory. For this, one extra main memory access and one extra cache memory access is needed.

    a. What is the effective time for translating a logical address to a physical address?

    b. What is the effective time to access a memory location?

24. The system under investigation uses a page-based virtual memory policy. Main memory consists of only 5 page frames that are currently empty. For a size 10 page reference string in which there are only 7 different pages:

    a. What is the upper bound for the number of page faults?

    b. What is the lower bound for the number of page faults?

25. The average instruction execution time is 100 nanoseconds and every fault imposes n extra nanoseconds on the system. If, on the average, for every k instructions, there is one page fault, what is the effective average instruction execution time?

26. In the memory management method of the UNIX operating system, what are the rationales for stopping the page removal procedure when "enough" frames are scanned and activating the process swapper procedure?

27. The page replacement algorithm of an operating system is a modified version of FIFO. The modification is namely that, if within a time interval, a page is referred to k times, for k greater than two, and the page still exists at the end of the time interval then this page is locked for the next $k-1$ time intervals. If a locked page is referred to more than once in a time interval, it will remain

locked for the maximum number of intervals that it supposed to be locked after this interval and one minus the number of times this page was referred to in this interval. A locked page will retain its position in the FIFO queue for the locked duration even if it is not referred to. The length of each time interval is equivalent to five memory references. The first interval starts just before the first memory reference. What is the number of page faults for the following page trace?

3 1 2 3 4 2 3 5 2 6 7 1 7 3 1 4 1 5 6 3

Recommended References

For Virtual memory management see references [Mad74, Jac98, Sta05, Sil08, and Tan07]. For detailed treatment of the FIFO anomaly, refer to Belady, Nelson, and Shedler [Bel69]. For the optimality proof of the "optimal" page replacement algorithm, refer to [Bel66]. The concept of a working set is discussed in [Den68]. For the history of the UNIX operating system, refer to operating system concepts (Fifth edition) by A. Silberschatz and P. Galvin [Sil08]. For a detailed treatment of memory management in the UNIX operating system, however, see [Vah07]. A discussion on a memory manager subsystem of the Linux operating system is covered   in   [Ogo01].

Chapter 8

Interprocess Communication/ Synchronization

Communication is essential among all societies, be they human, bees, ants, etc. Not all entities of all societies have the same level of intelligence nor do they all communicate the same way. Humans are the most intelligent species, communicating essentially through languages. Ants, on the other hand, communicate using pheromone. One can say that processes (or threads) form a society in the world inside computers. Processes inhabit the computer environment along with the CPU, main memory, secondary memory, peripheral devices, software modules, etc. They communicate by using a variety of techniques, such as shared memory and message passing. Dependent processes have to synchronize their activities. We even have to synchronize independent processes for using shared resources in order not to interfere with one another. Improper synchronization of processes may lead to deadlock. Deadlock is a situation in which two or more processes are stuck in a circular wait. Each process is waiting for something (or some action) from the next process in the circular-wait without in order to proceed. In this chapter, methodologies and tools for safe and efficient communication between processes (or threads) are discussed.

8.1 Why Process Communication/Synchronization?

If there were enough (hardware and software) resources and if the operating system assigned all the required resources of for every newly generated process at the time of generation, perhaps there would be no need for independent processes to synchronize their use of resources. Because there are not enough resources to fulfill the needs of all processes all the time, we have to consider sharing resources. Process communication/synchronization is necessary for two types of processes. The first is dependent processes, or processes that are part of one application. These are each given a specific responsibility, which includes the sharing of processing results or synchronization at certain points. This kind of communication/synchronization is a part of the application's specifications and must be designed and implemented. The second type of processes, i.e., independent processes, also requires communication/synchronization. Whether processes are parts of one application or otherwise, they have to share computer resources during execution. The most essential assertion which must hold for these processes is conflict-free resource usage. This dictates the existence of a correct and reliable mechanism for acquiring and releasing resources. With contemporary operating systems, all simultaneously running processes have to share computer resources. Thus, process communication/synchronization is inevitable.

8.1.1 Race Condition

Failure to correctly share resources among processes can lead to incorrect and even unexpected results from processes. For clarification, a simple example is discussed in the following.

The lost update problem

Suppose two transactions are issued against a single bank account. Transaction one wants to clear a check for the amount of $1,000 against account number 123 and transaction two wants to clear a check for the amount of $2,000 against the same account. Suppose the account balance is $10,000 right before receiving the transactions. The bodies of transactions are as follows:

Transaction 1:	*Transaction 2:*
1-1 Read account 123's record	*2-1 Read account 123's record*
1-2 Subtract $1000 from balance	*2-2 Subtract $2000 from balance*
1-3 Write account 123's record	*2-3 Write account 123's record*

Without any form of process (transaction) synchronization to use the shared resource (the account 123's record, in this case), we cannot be sure that transactions statements are properly ordered to produce the correct results. Suppose the execution of statements is interleaved as follows:

1-1 Read account 123's record   //Balance is $10000
1-2 Subtract $1000 from balance   //Balance is $9000 but not saved
2-1 Read account 123's record   //Balance is $10,000

2-2 Subtract $2000 from balance   //Balance is $8,000 but not saved
2-3 Write account 123's record   //Balance is $8,000
1-3 Write account 123's record   //Balance is $9,000

The net result is that the transaction two's update is lost. Another arrangement of the execution of statements would have led to a correct execution of the transactions, making the final balance of the account $7,000. Nowadays, **Database Management Systems** (DBMS) take care of correct transaction processing by using proper transaction management mechanisms. In the absence of correct synchronization mechanisms similar errors may occur within the operating system.

Suppose that a client-server system is set up to save the picture of all people that enter or leave a museum having highly valuable objects. The museum has one entry and one exit. There are two cameras, one for the entrance and one for the exit, which photographs every person entering or leaving the museum. There are two processes (clients), one controlling the entrance camera and the other controlling the exit camera. These processes communicate with another process (the server) that is mainly responsible for saving pictures in archive files and keeping track of the exact number of people in the museum at all times. Communication from clients to the server is done by sending messages. A message has at least three parts: a sender, a receiver, and data (i.e., a picture). A server subsystem will put all received messages in a queue to be processed in a first-in first-out fashion. This is because matching pictures against a database of suspected people and saving pictures in secondary storage is a slow process, in which the system may fall behind during busy hours. A *count* variable in the server process keeps track of the number of people inside the museum at any given time. This is updated every time a message is removed from the queue and it is processed. Just before closing the museum at the end of working hours, the queue must be empty (that is, all messages must have been processed) and the counter should be exactly equal to five (the number of after hour security personnel). The queue is (supposedly) an infinite array of message frames and client and server processes are running in a multiprogramming manner.

Suppose the pointer to the rear of the queue is the variable *r* which is actually an index to the array of message frames. If it is, say 10, this means there are 10 unprocessed messages in the queue. Each one of these messages is either from the entrance or exit door. To enter a message in the queue, the following steps are taken in that order:

1. Transfer *r* to register R_1
2. Increment R_1
3. Store message in frame number R_1
4. Store R_1 in variable *r*

Now, suppose that r is equal to 10 and the execution of two client processes (P1 for the entry process and P2 for the exit process) is interleaved in the following way:

P2-1. Transfer r to register R_1, //Every process has its own set of registers
P1-1. Transfer r to register R_1, //Every process has its own set of registers
P2-2. Increment R_1, //R_1 becomes 11
P2-3. Store message in frame number R_1, //Pic. from P_2 stored in frame 11
P2-4. Store R_1 in variable r. // r = 11
P1-2. Increment R_1, // R_1 for process P1 becomes 11
P1-3. Store message in frame number R_1, //Pic. from P_1 stored in frame 11
P1-4. Store R_1 in variable r. // r = 11

It is clear that, a message from P2 is lost. This means one person has left the museum, but the system failed to respond correctly. As a result, at the end of the working hours, the system will show 6 people in the museum although the correct number is 5. Security will keep looking for a person who does not really exist. The system has produced an incorrect and misleading result or a **race condition** has occurred. This is a situation in which more than one parallel (or multiprogrammed) processes work with one or more shared resources and the result depending on how instructions that manipulate the shared resource(s) are interleaved. In our case, if process P2 had completely finished its operations before process P1 started, both messages would have been properly inserted in the queue.

What is the role of the operating system? It seems that the above scenario is part of an application program and has nothing to do with the operating system. This may be the way it looks.

In contemporary operating systems, processes can communicate using message passing methodology. A message is roughly composed of three parts (*sender, receiver, load*). The *load* is what the *sender* wants to pass on to the *receiver*. To do so, the sender calls on an operating system procedure (or method) called "send", providing the aforementioned arguments. On the other end, the receiver calls on an operating system procedure (or method) called "receive". It is the responsibility of the operating system to correctly transfer every message from the source to the destination. The details of message passing implementation are application transparent. Therefore, for our example, manipulation of the message queue is performed by the operating system.

A major difficulty in designing an InterProcess Communication (IPC) technique is that, in a multiprocessor and/or multiprogramming environment, instructions for different processes may interleave in numerous ways at a machine instruction level. A simple increment operation on a shared variable (or resource) by two processes may lead to unacceptable results, as seen earlier. A simple increment in the C++ programming language for a variable *k* is written as *k*++, but this is translated to three assembly language instructions (or machine instructions) roughly as follows:

```
Load        R1, k   // load the content of k into register R1
Inc   R1
Store       R1, k   // Store R1 to k
```

The system only guarantees that when a machine instruction is started by one processor, the processor will not be interrupted before completing this instruction. In other words, when the execution of a machine instruction is started, the processing of any incoming interrupt to this processor is suspended until this instruction is completed. That is, every processor looks at the interrupt vector right before starting every machine instruction, not during its execution. This is exactly one lessen we have learned from the fetch-execute cycle explained in Chapter One. The actual purpose of explaining the cycle was to be useful though out the current chapter. There are some limited exceptions to this rule. For example, a *move* instruction, that moves large chunks of information from one location of main memory to another location, may be interrupted in some systems. We will not consider this limited number of exceptions in our discussion. With this in mind, two increments of one variable by two processes can lead to either a correct result or an incorrect result depending on how the increment instructions of the two processes are interleaved.

8.1.2 Critical Region

In the previous section, we encountered a situation that led to a race condition, which, in turn, caused the processes to produce incorrect overall results. Although, one process was not finished using a shared resource (the message queue), another process started to use the same resource. The update of the queue by the former process was not completed before the latter process attempted to access the queue. The former process was in a "critical" situation, in which the intervention of another process could affect the outcome of the process. In our example, the message queue is a **critical resource**. If it is not used in a controlled way, incorrect results could result. A critical resource is thus a **long-term shared resource** that has to be used exclusively in the short term. When a process takes over this kind of resource, no other process is allowed to use it until the first process frees the resource. The **critical region** (or **critical section**) is therefore the portion of a program that uses a critical resource. We have to devise methods for the operating system to ensure that, when a program is executing its critical section, no other program can enter that critical section. To enter a critical region, every process must first get the permission. It can then enter the critical region and use the resource. To leave a critical region, the process must inform the system that it has freed the resource. These three steps for the proper running of every critical section are listed in order as follows:

Get permission to enter critical region

Enter critical region and use the resource

Leave the critical region and free the resource

8.1.3 Mutual Exclusion

Different processes within the operating system ought to use **short-term exclusive** devices in such a way that no more than one process, at any given time, uses any such device. A process is said to be using a device if that device has been assigned to the process and has not yet been freed by the process. For example, it is customary to introduce printers as short-term exclusive devices. It is not correct to send outputs of more than one simultaneously (parallel or multiprogrammed) executing processes to a unique printer. If done, the outputs of the processes would be mixed-up and incorrect printouts produced, that is, the outputs does not match any process's requests. The concept of **mutual exclusion** is not well describable using printers, because, in reality, mutual exclusion is not applicable to printers. These days, printing problems are solved using a special approach. During the execution of a process, if a printer is needed, a real printer is not assigned to the process. Instead, one or more virtual printers are assigned to the process, with the outputs written on the virtual printers. Files or datasets are virtual printers and different processes are given different files. In this way, the outputs of different processes are not interleaved. When a process completes, its output file(s) is closed and sent to a print queue to be printed one at a time. The print-queue is a perfect example of where mutual exclusion must be enforced. Otherwise, race conditions may occur and problems such as *lost update* are likely to happen. Therefore, processes must exclude each other in using print-queue through the enforcement of mutual exclusion.

The concept of mutual exclusion may be extended to be applicable to all devices that can be used by more than one process at any given time, but with the number of processes bounded by a fixed number. For example, a 1/16 demultiplexing device can have one output line and 16 input lines. The system must ensure that no more than 16 users (processes) are simultaneously making use of this device.

The operating system has the responsibility to ensure that application programs use their resources mutually exclusive. There are many methods of this, each better applicable to one or more resources. Mutual exclusion enforcement of computer resources that are directly managed by the operating system is thus transparent to computer users.

One way to enforce mutual exclusion is to have only one process at any given time, thus preventing the creation of other processes (or child processes) before process termination. The process does not have to compete with any other process to grab a desired resource. Nor are resources used by more than one process at any given time. This method guarantees mutual exclusion but it provides a single-programming environment that is inefficient and impractical for contemporary operating systems. Therefore, not all methods of enforcing mutual exclusion are acceptable. For a method to be acceptable, it must have four properties:

1. The number of processes that are inside a critical region (for a critical resource usage) must be, at the most, equal to the maximum number of allowable processes (that is, one for a majority of resources).
2. Mutual exclusion must be upheld disrespectful of relative execution speed of processes and the number of processors.
3. A process may only block other processes from using a resource when it is inside its critical region using the resource.
4. A process does not have to wait forever to get its chance to use a needed critical resource.

8.2 IPC and Synchronization Techniques

In this section, race-free **InterProcess Communication** (IPC) techniques are presented in three categories. A **busy-wait-based technique** keeps checking some parameters to make sure it is safe to enter the critical region. This parameter is shared among all processes that want to use the same resource and is usually updatable by all these processes. This technique is called busy-wait because it consumes processing time by continuously checking the state of the parameter. No progress can be made until the parameter indicates it is safe for the process in the busy-wait state to use the corresponding resource.

A **semaphore-based technique** uses an abstract data type composed of a counter and two operations. These can be used for obtaining permission to use a shared resource and for freeing the resource once it has been used. This technique checks if the resource is safe to use. If it is not, the process is blocked until the resource is available and a wakeup message is received by the process. Therefore, by using this method, busy-waiting is prevented.

The third technique for interprocess communication/synchronization is **message-based**. To use a resource, the resource-seeking process must grab a message which acts as a permission to use a resource. When grabbed, the seeking process can go ahead and use the resource; otherwise it has to wait.

An important point about interprocess communication and synchronization tools is that just using them does not guarantee correct and race-free implementation of interprocess communication and synchronization of competing processes, like any other tool which has to be used properly. Rather, only proper usage of these techniques can result in correct and race-free solutions.

8.2.1 Disabling Interrupt Method

A running process (or thread) keeps running until it is terminated or an unmask interrupt is received by the processor running the process. In a multiprogramming environment, when a process is running, if it disables the whole interrupt system, the process can keep running until it is either completed or an internal event causes its termination. This fact suggests a method for enforcing mutual exclusion. Right before using a critical resource, the "disable interrupt" operation is executed. The successful execution of this operation guarantees that the process will be the only running process. Therefore, the process can safely use a shared resource (that is a resource shared over a long time span but must be used exclusively by the process or thread that gains control of it until the resource is freed by the process.) When finished with this resource, the process enables the interrupt system. Every processor in a multiprocessor system has its own interrupt system. Disabling the interrupt system will only disable the interrupt system of the processor which executed the "disable interrupt" operation. Thus disabling interrupt cannot be used to enforce mutual exclusion in a multiprocessor environment. The steps to insure exclusive usage of a critical resource in a single-processor multiprogramming environment are:

1. Disable interrupt
2. Use the critical resource
3. Enable interrupt

This technique has two problems:

I. It is not applicable in multiprocessor environments.
II. During the time span in which the interrupt is disabled, the system works in single programming manner.

Because of the second disadvantage, overall system performance may drop very low. This is the reason for restricting its usage. As a result, its usage is not permitted by application programmers. To enforce this, the disable interrupt is made privileged. Its usage within the operating system is also restricted to the kernel. Even there, its usage is restricted to critical regions with very few machine instructions.

8.2.2 Busy-Wait-Based IPC

A **busy-wait-based technique** allows a process which needs a long-term shared resource to keep checking until it is safe to use it. If it is in a busy-wait state the processor time that is assigned to this process is, therefore, wasted in doing unproductive operations. This is the major disadvantage of the method. The first simple method is two-process strict alternation. Suppose two processes are competing for a resource. One will succeed and the other will fall into a busy wait cycle. This does not mean, with say a round robin CPU scheduler, 50% of the CPU time is wasted as there might be many more processes that are properly using their shares of CPU time.

Strict alternation method

This technique is designed only for two processes. It makes use of a global variable for the two processes which takes one of two values, zero and one or any other two distinct values. Each value is reserved for one of the processes. The global variable is given an initial value in accordance with the nature of the synchronization that defines which process has to first take hold of the resource. The processes are presumably continuously alternately using the shared resource. The **strict alternation** method is best described if we suppose there are two processes, one to input data and the other to process data and print results. Every time a datum is read, it is put in a buffer of size one (i.e., the shared resource). Before the first process can put a new datum, the previous datum must be picked up by the second process. If the global variable's name is *turn*, it must be globally initialized to define which process must use its turn first. Suppose it is set to zero, as follows:

$$turn = 0;$$

To get permission to use the shared resource, the inline code (a set of instructions not in the form of a procedure call within a program) for the process zero (the process that corresponds to *turn=0*) could be:

GetPermission: If (turn != 0) goto GetPermission;

Although the goto statement is not well accepted within application programs, structures such as *while* and *do...until* are implemented using *branch* machine instruction. The direct equivalent of this instruction in high level languages is the *goto* statement. To implement operating system primitives as a short inline piece of code, we do not hesitate to use the *goto* statement. An equivalent of a goto-free piece of program would be:

GetPermission: while (turn != 0);

For this statement, the semicolon symbol signifies a null statement. To free the resource, process 0 could utilize the following inline code

$$turn = 1;$$

A similar code is used by process 1.

Suppose processes 0 and 1 want to indefinitely use a resource in an alternating mode. The following would be the body of the processes. For the rest of this chapter, it is assumed that variable *true* is a Boolean variable which represents the logical value "true".

```
// Process 0
while (true) {
    GetPermission: if (turn != 0) goto GetPermission;
        /* Critical section where the resource is used by this process */
    turn = 1;  //Set turn to process 1 to get permission and use the resource
}
```

```
// Process 1
while (true) {
    GetPermission: if (turn != 1) goto GetPermission;
        /* Critical section where the resource is used by this process */
    turn = 0;  // Set turn to process 0 to get permission and use the resource
}
```

This solution has three essential disadvantages: (1) it suffers from busy-waiting; (2) it is only good for two processes; (3) processes must alternate to use the resource. It is not possible to design two communicating processes for which one process is able to use the shared resource for more than one consecutive round when the other process is not interested in using it for the time being. However, having in mind its restriction, this solution is a practical technique for the design of safe interprocess communication for two processes.

Peterson's method

The alternation property of the aforementioned technique is removed by a technique that was invented by Peterson. His initiative was to use a local variable in each process that shows the process' intent to use or not use the shared resource, for the time being. If the value of this variable is *true*, the process will want, or desire, to use the resource; otherwise, it does not want to. When one process intends to use the resource and the other does not, the former process can keep using the shared resource over and over again. The difficulty arises when both processes want to use the shared resource. In such a situation, one process enters a busy-waiting loop until the other process leaves its critical region. To make this possible, the global variable *turn* is utilized. Based on that the system decides who can use the resource. It is worth mentioning that for every round a resource is used, the using process has to free the resource. If it is interested in using the resource again, the process must go through the procedure of getting the resource again. This is because while this process is using the resource the other may have generate a request. The "get permission" and "free resource" actions are designed as standalone procedures with one argument "process." The argument *process* is either zero or one, in that one process is identified by the number zero and the other by the number one. The variable *turn* is an integer and the array *desire* is a Boolean array, both are declared globally as follows:

```
int turn;
int desire [2];    //whether or not process wants to use the resource
```

The following is the "get permission" procedure. When there are two processes who want to use the resource simultaneously, the *while* statement will cause one of the processes to keep executing the loop over and over again until the loop condition becomes *false*. The semicolon symbol indicates that there is no explicit operation within the loop.

```
void GetPermission (int  process)
{
    int other;          // Variable Other defines other process's number
    other = 1-process;
    desire [process] = true;  //This process wants to use the resource
    turn = process;
    while (turn== process && desire [other] == true) ; //Busy-wait
}
```

To relinquish the resource, the process who owns the resource calls the following procedure.

```
void FreePermission (int process)
{
    desire [process] = false;
}
```

For process zero to use the resource, it has to execute the following statements. Similar statements have to be executed within process one. If the resource is not available (because it is being used by the other process) the requesting process will remain in "*GetPermission*" procedure.

```
...
GetPermission(0);
// Use the resource
FreePermission (0);
...
```

The **Peterson's method** is restricted to two users and has the disadvantage of busy-waiting.

Dekker's method

A very similar solution to the Peterson' solution is given by Dekker. It makes use of a global array of type Boolean and the global variable *turn* of type integer that are defined as follows:

```
int desire[2]= {0,0};
int turn =0;
```

Because of its similarity to Peterson's solution, without discussing the details of this procedure **Dekker's method** is presented in the following. *GetPermission and FreePermission* are the procedures for obtaining permission to use the resource and for freeing this permission to let other processes use the resource. The statement *1-process* identifies the other process in these procedures.

```
void GetPermission( int process)
{
    desire[process] = true;
    while ( desire[1-process] == true) {
        if ( turn != process) desire[process] = false;
        while (turn != process);
        desire [process] =true;
    }
}

void FreePermission(int process)
{
    turn =1-process;
    desire [process] = false;
}
```

The deficiencies of Dekker's solution are the same as the deficiencies of Peterson's solutions. However, with Dekker's algorithm if both processes want to enter their critical region one of them will set its desire to false to let the other enter its critical region. This will have a positive effect on reducing the overall CPU waste. Recall that the *GetPermission* and the *FreePermission* routines are for the permission to use the resource and the release of this permission, respectively, in order for the other to have the chance of using the resource. To do a repetitive job a proper loop of actions must be designed. In the following, a hypothetical body for process zero is provided. Process one may have a similar structure.

```
void ProcessZero(void)
{
    int  zero = 0;
    while (1){
        GetPermission(zero);
            // Permission is granted; use the resource
        FreePermission (zero);
    }
}
```

Test and set lock method

The techniques presented up to now, in this section, are all limited to two-process synchronization and communication. This does not mean we cannot modify them to handle more that two processes. The **Test and Set Lock** (TSL) method does not have this limitation, but relies on a specific machine instruction that is included in contemporary processors mainly for the purpose of implementing this kind of IPC technique. In one machine instruction, the *test and set lock* instruction does the equivalent of two (or more) machine instructions. Although the details of the operations are machine dependent, the contents of a memory location is loaded in a processor register. If the content of the memory location is zero it is changed to one. Therefore, the effect of the *tsl* instruction shown below is the same as the two instructions in front of it. It is assumed that the storage location tested will be either zero or one. After the execution of the *tsl* instruction, the contents of the variable being tested will be one and the contents of the register used will be the previous value of the variable.

$$tsl \quad register, x \quad \longrightarrow \quad \begin{cases} load \quad register, x \\ store \quad \#1, x \quad // Store \; integer \; 1 \; into \; x \end{cases}$$

The following is a sample implementation of the inline version of the "get permission" and "free resource" operations.

```
GetPermission:  tsl  register, x
                cmp  register, #0
                jnz  GetPermission


FreePermission:  store  #0, x
```

The procedure-based implementation of these two operations will look like:

```
void GetPermission (void)
{
```

```
            ASM;
            top: tsl  register, x
                 cmp  register, #0
                 jnz  top
            ENDASM;
    }

    void FreePermission (void)
    {
        x = 0;
    }
```

Like other solutions in this section, the *tsl* solution suffers from busy-wait. The hardware must support a *tsl*-like machine instruction for us to be able to implement this technique. For example, some IBM processors have the *TS* (test and set) instruction which checks a byte of main memory and (if the content is zero) stores the value *one* in the byte. This instruction sets the **Condition Code** (CC) flags of the processor based on the previous value of the byte during the checking process. CC shows whether the byte was zero, positive, or negative. Based on this instruction, an actual inline implementation of the get permission and free resource are as follows:

<u>GetPermission</u>
```
    TS    x
    BNZ   *-4  //Go back 4 bytes, if not zero
```

<u>FreePermission</u>
```
    MVI  x,'00'
```

Pentium processors use BTS (bit test and set). A bit is moved to CF (carry flag) and the bit is set to one if it is zero. The instructions JC (jump if carry flag is one) and JNC (jump if carry flag is not one) can be used to implement the get permission and free resource operations.

Some Motorola processors have TAS (test and set operand) machine instructions for this purpose.

Test and set lock method is not restricted to two processes, but it also suffers from busy-wait.

Swap (or exchange) method

Yet another method for enforcing mutual exclusion is the **swap method**. A global variable acts as the key for using a shared resource. Whoever gets the key first, takes the resource. The key is available when the variable is zero. It is not available if its value is one. Every process tries to get the key by exchanging the global variable's zero value (accessing the variable when it is zero) with a one value provided by the process, all in one operation (or atomically). If successful, the global variable's value becomes zero. So, every process has a one value ready and continuously tries to exchange its one value with the global variable. If the global variable is one, nothing happens. If it is zero, one process gets the permission to use the shared resource and blocks the other competing processes from getting the resource. Suppose the global variable's name is S and its initial value is set to zero. The following two procedures for getting permission and freeing the resource would be respectively:

```
void GetPermission (void)
{
    int p = 1;
    while (p != false) exchange (p, S);
}
```

```
void FreePermission(void)
{
    S = 0;
}
```

Note that, for this method to work correct, the *exchange* operation must be done atomically (see side box). There are specific machine operations to exchange the contents of two memory locations. For example, **byte swap**, BSWAP, in the Pentium family is for this purpose. Having a machine language operation for this purpose guarantees its atomic execution. In the absence of such machine instruction, the *exchange* operation has to be implemented atomically. One way to do it is to have *exchange* be a kernel routine. There, we can use enable interrupt and disable interrupt instructions to ignore any interrupt which running this reoutine.

> An operation is executed in an *atomic* manner if its execution once started is not interrupted until it is fully completed. As explained earlier, machine instructions are performed in an atomic manner (with very few exceptions). However, special techniques must be used to ensure the atomicity of user-defined operations (operations that are done by more than one machine instruction or roughly speaking, procedure). In database environments, the definition of atomicity is slightly different. There, the execution of an atomic operation can be interrupted. However, we are interested in its effect on the database. This must be either equal to the effect of not executing the operation or fully executing the operation. In other words, partial execution of an operation that is supposed to be atomic is not acceptable.

The **exchange method** is applicable in the single-processor or multiprocessor environment. It is applicable for IPC implementation for two or more processes. This is a robust method, especially when there is a machine instruction for the *exchange* operation. Its one weakness is busy-wait. Worth mentioning in multiprogramming, which runs many programs "simultaneously", only those processes that are executing their busy-wait loop waste the processor's time. All others use the processor's time in perhaps a more productive way.

Busy-wait-based methods may sometimes cause **priority inversion**. With a priority-based scheduler, a low priority process is executed if there is no higher priority process in the ready queue. Suppose, in the absence of a higher priority process, a low priority process starts (or restarts) and enters a critical region to use a resource. Now, suppose a higher priority process enters the ready queue. Therefore, it will force the scheduler to switch immediately (or after the current time quantum is finished) from the low priority process to the higher priority one. If the critical region of the low priority process is not completed and the higher priority process tries to enter its critical region to use the same resource it will enter a busy-wait state. On the other hand, the scheduler is not allowed to schedule the low priority process to complete its critical region and free the resource. In this situation, neither of the processes will progress.

8.2.3 Semaphore-Based IPC

The most technical way to think of **semaphore** is to imagine it being an **Abstract Data Type** (ADT); see the side box. An abstract data type, for our discussion, is composed of one or more data and zero or more operations that are all packaged together. A realization of a semaphore ADT has a variable

> An *abstract data type* is user-defined (as oppose to programming language-defined). It includes data objects and operations on these data objects. The whole entity is encapsulated. This is to prevent manipulation of the data objects by any operation except for the operations defined on the data object within the abstract data type.

of a type limited po-sitive integer upon which ope-rations **wait** and **signal** are applicable. The variable is supposed to be private and can be manipulated only by *wait* and *signal* operations (all of which are encapsulated). The ADT concept has evolved into the "class" concept in object-oriented programming languages. The ADT gives us a better understanding of what a semaphore is, but the concept is not exactly implemented for semaphores. Operating system implementers define a semaphore as an integer variable usually called a *counter*. The *wait* and *signal* operations are implicitly available to manipulate this variable. The variable is not protected against manipulation by regular operations such as addition and subtraction. With the ADT concept in mind, we will follow the implementer's steps in our examples. Operations *wait* and *signal* are, in some systems, called **down** and **up**, respectively. *Wait* and *signal* are atomic non-interruptible operations. A technique like a "disabling interrupt" can be used to implement these operations within the operating system kernel. In the UNIX operating system, the operations *wait* and *signal* are defined as follows. In other operating systems, they may be defined a little bit differently.

> **Down** (or **wait**). Checks the content of the semaphore variable; if it is grater than zero decrements the counter by one and continues (in other words, the permission to enter the critical region is granted). Otherwise, puts the process in the queue of processes waiting for this semaphore and suspends the execution of the process, or putting it to sleep.

> **Up** (or **signal**). Increments the content of semaphore variable by one; if there is any process waiting for this semaphore wakes one up to continue its execution. The process that has just wakened up must do the *down* operation again.

We can talk of two kinds of semaphores: binary and integer. A **binary semaphore** can only take one of the values, either zero or one. An **integer semaphore**, on the other hand, can take any integer greater than or equal to zero. However, it must be bounded to a predefined value. Often the initial value of an integer semaphore is the maximum value that the semaphore can take.

Producer-consumer problem

A classic IPC problem that is analyzed and designed using semaphores in almost all operating system books is the **produces-consumer problem**. In operating system terms, it can be used for queue management which was mentioned at the beginning of this chapter in the discussion about race. Processes that run in a multiprogramming or parallel manner are producers of say output files to be printed. The printing process or processes, in case there is more than one printer, are consumers. The print-queue which has a limited number of slots is the shared resource. The implementation that is given below could be used for many similar problems. Like the print-queue problem, *producer* and *consumer* are general names for certain types of communicating processes. Producer process(es) produce entities and put them in the shared queue. Consumer(s) take entities from the shared queue and use them for whatever purpose they are designed to do.

To design the system, we start by listing the constraints and assigning a semaphore to each constraint that a semaphore can enforce. As you will see, semaphores are not only used to enforce mutual exclusion but also to enforce other constraints.

1. Enforce mutual exclusion in using the entity-buffer
2. Make sure not to put new entities in a full buffer

3. Make sure not to remove articles from an empty buffer

The mutual exclusion enforcing semaphore is considered to be m*utex,* a common name which is used for binary semaphores. The variable *available* shows the current number of available slots in the buffer. It is also used to check whether or not the buffer is empty. The variable *occupied* indicates how many slots of the buffer are occupied at any given time. It is also used to check whether or not the buffer is full. A semaphore is explicitly defined as an integer variable and operations *wait* and *signal* are implicit applicable operations for it.

An important issue that must be carefully handled is the initial value assignment to semaphores. For our case study, the initial value of the *available* semaphore is the size of the buffer which is expressed in terms of slots. This makes sense as it represents the number of available buffer slots at the start-up of the producer-consumer processes. Similarly, the initial value of the *occupied* semaphore is zero. Related statements are globally defined. The **semaphore-based** solution of the producer-consumer problem follows.

```
#define true  1
#define BC 1000              // Buffer capacity
typedef int semaphore;       //Defines the keyword semaphore
semaphore available = BC;    //All buffer slots are available
semaphore occupied = 0;      //Buffer is empty
semaphore mutex =1;          //Shared Resource is not in use
```

The following is the producer procedure.

```
void producer (void)
{
   struct buffer_slot  entity;
   while (true) {
      produce_an_entity(&entity);
      wait (&available);           //Wait for a free slot
      wait (&mutex);               //Get permission
      insert_the_entity(&entity);  //Put entity in queue
      signal (&mutex);             //Free resource
      signal (&occupied);          //One slot is filled
   }
}
```

Look at the *producer* procedure. The shared buffer is grabbed after the entity is produced and is ready to be inserted in the buffer. Also, right after the entity is finished with the buffer; it is freed to be used by others. Deciding to keep a shared resource for a longer time span forces other processes that also need the resource to wait for a longer time. A good solution must always make sure not to keep a shared resource longer than necessary.

In the *producer* procedure, every *signal* primitive corresponds to its nearest *wait* primitive, from the inner most block outward. When a procedure is designed with this property, its correctness analysis becomes straightforward. However, if we have to force this property all the times, we may not be able to design all IPC problems. Now, let's see the consumer procedure.

```
void consumer (void)
{
  struct buf_slot entity;
  while (true) {
    wait (&occupied);                 //Wait until there is an entity
    wait (&mutex);
    remove_the_entity(&entity);
    signal (&mutex);
    signal (&available);
    consume_the_entity(&entity);
  }
}
```

We have learned from *producer-consumer* that when a process sleeps, other processes have to wake it up. Although there are examples, it is usually not possible for a process to wake itself up, after having fallen asleep. In the statement *wait(&available)*, a producer goes to sleep when the buffer is full. A consumer wakes up the sleeping producer with the statement *signal(&available)*. A reverse situation occurs when a consumer goes to sleep and a producer wakes it up.

Producer and consumer are two procedures that can perform predefined operations indefinitely. Two processes (or threads) have to be generated and each must be assigned to run one of these procedures in order to start the produce-consume process. The following is the main program for this purpose.

```
void main (void)
{
  int pid;
  pid = fork();
  if (pid != 0)  producer();
  else consumer();
}
```

Dijkstra's P and V

The semaphore was first introduced by Dijkstra. The following is the original implementation of *GetPermission* and *FreeResource*, which was called P and V, respectively. The semaphore name is *s* and P and V have to be implemented atomically.

<u>**P(s)**</u>
s = s-1;
if s < 0 wait (s);

<u>**V(s)**</u>
s = s+1;
if s ≤ 0 signal(s);

    In this implementation, *wait* puts the process, that is, the same process that executes the *wait* primitive, to sleep on the specified semaphore. The *signal* wakes one of the sleeping processes from the queue of processes that are sleeping on the corresponding semaphore. Here, when a semaphore value is zero or less than zero, new processes that execute the P operation will cause the semaphore value to decrement. In other words, the semaphore value could go lower than zero. If a semaphore value is, for example -5, it means there are 5 processes waiting on this semaphore. That is, if a semaphore value is negative, the same numbers of processes as the absolute value of the semaphore value are waiting on the semaphore. On the other hand, if a semaphore value is positive, the same number of processes as the semaphore value can pass the P-barrier and continue their execution.

    The semaphore method provides an almost perfect way of implementing IPC problems. It does not suffer from busy-wait. It is not restricted to two processes. It can be used in multiprocessor environments. The only weakness of this method is said to be its difficulty of understanding and properly solving IPC problems. Within the operating system, this weakness is not crucial because operating system implementers are highly skilled professionals. To overcome the complexity of using semaphores to enforce mutual exclusion in application programs (or even within operating systems), another concept called *monitor* has been introduced by Per Brinch Hansen. We will discuss this concept next.

8.2.4 Monitor-Based IPC

The inspiration behind the **monitor** concept is simplifying the implementation of mutual exclusion. The monitor concept is not usable for constraints other than mutual exclusion. For example, to make sure a new entity has not been inserted into a queue which is full, other tools must be used. The goal is to design a structure which includes all routines for working on a given critical resource. The structure will make sure only one routine at any given time can be used by only one process (or thread). This is what mutual exclusion actually means. Within a monitor, a process which is executing one of the routines may need to execute a *wait* primitive. *Wait* and *signal* primitives are methods, or routines, of the semaphore ADT. Semaphores may be combined with monitors to enforce mutual exclusion and other constraints at the same time. Variables upon which *wait* and signal may be executed inside a monitor (i.e., semaphores) are distinguished from other variables by a syntax called *condition*. Further discussion is presently postponed until a **monitor-based IPC** implementation of producer-consumer is presented.

```
class insert_remove : public monitor
{
  private:
  condition available, occupied;
  int count;
  public:

  insert (struct buffer_slot &entity);
  {
    if (count == BC) wait (&available);
    insert_entity(&entity);
    count = count +1;
    if (count ==1) signal(&occupied)
  }

  remove (struct buffer_slot  &entity)
  {
    if (count == 0) wait (&cooupied);
    remove_entity(&entity);
    count = count - 1;
    if (count = BC-1) signal(&available);
  }
  Insert_remove (condition available=BC, condition occupied=0,
                 int count=0);
}
insert_remove   IR;

class producer_consumer
{
  private:
  struct buffer_slot   entity;
  public:
  producer()
  {
    while (true)  {
```

```
            produce_entity (&entity);
            IR.insert (&entity)
        }
    }

    consumer()
    {
        while (true) {
            IR.remove(&entity);
            consume_entity(&entity);
        }
    }
    producer_consumer (struct buffer_slot entity ="");
}
```

To activate two processes to start producing and consuming, the following main program is used.

```
void main (void)
{
    int pid;
    producer_consumer    PC;
    pid = fork();
    if (pid != 0)  PC.producer;
    else PC.consumer;
}
```

8.2.5 Message-Based IPC

Message is a concept which is mainly used for information interchange between different processes in a distributed system environment. A message is a data structure composed of many fields such as sender's address, receiver's address, data load, error correcting data etc. One process in one computer sends a message, which one or more processes in one or more computers are supposed to receive. The concept of message is extended to non-distributed system (i.e., standalone multiprocessor or single-processor computers). Message can also be used to transfer information between processes within a standalone computer. All contemporary operating systems support message passing techniques. As a matter of fact, message-based information transfer is so essential that primitive procedures for implementation of the message concept are realized in the kernel of every operating system.

Two of the most important primitive procedures are called as:

```
send (source, destination, message) ;
receive (source, destination, message) ;
```

In these statements, *source* is the sender process, *destination* is the receiver process, and message is the data load to be transferred. This syntax may change from one operating system to another and the number of arguments may vary. It is to be understood that these primitives are called from the upper layers of the operating system. The designer of the kernel defines how the primitives to be called. It is the responsibility of the kernel to pass every message to its destination(s). Before sending a message towards its destination, the kernel supplies complementary fields like error correcting bits according to the message-passing protocol used. Similar to the regular paper mail, there are different message-passing protocols. Although full synchronization of the sender and receiver of a message is not always necessary, every party is

> A *communication protocol* (or protocol, for short) is a set of rules for connecting computers (and other digital devices) and enabling them to communicate with each other. A protocol is designed to provide a standard means for connecting digital devices and letting them interchange information by using the (software) facilities that are provided by the protocol. Protocols make information interchange easy, reliable, fast, and most important of all, collision-free.

usually aware of the other party's intention concerning messages. This implies some degree of synchronization between the sender and receiver(s). To simplify the matter we clarify those aspects that are essential for our discussion. Sending or receiving a message could be blocking or non-blocking.

Blocking send: In blocking send, the sender process is blocked, that is, its execution is suspended, until the message is delivered and the receiver informs the sender of the matter.

Nonblocking send: The sender, in this method, executes the *send* primitive and relies on the local kernel to deliver its message. It does not wait until the message is delivered and continues to execute the next statements. The sender will not become aware of whether or not the message was actually delivered.

Blocking receive: The receiver(s) of a message executes a *receive* primitive and waits until the message is fully received, before proceeding to execute the next instructions.

Non-blocking receive: The receiver of a message executes a *receive* primitive and continues to execute the next instructions. If the message has already arrived it is received. Otherwise, when the message is received the kernel will take care of it and perhaps will send an interrupt to the corresponding receiver process.

Two methods of sending and two methods of receiving make four combination methods.

How do we use messages to enforce mutual exclusion? Suppose there is a common **mailbox** with one message in it. Whichever process grabs the message first is allowed to execute its critical region or use the critical resource. After the execution of its critical section is completed, the process sends back the message, which is a similar message to what it had received, to the mailbox. Proper *send* and *receive* statements for this purpose would be:

```
receive (mailbox, message) ;
send (mailbox, message);
```

A very common practical system that uses this idea to enforce mutual exclusion is the **token-ring network.** The bus that connects all computers in this network is the critical resource. A token (i.e., a special short message) moves from one computer to another in a circular manner. The computer which owns the token is allowed to use the communication media, or the shared bus. When this computer sends all its pending messages, the token is passed to the next computer. Using the **message-based IPC** method, the producer-consumer problem is implemented in the following:

> A *token-ring network* is a local area network based on a closed ring wiring concentrators called Multistation Access Unit (MSAU). This network was developed by IBM. Up to eight workstations can form a star-shape cluster which is connected to an MSAU. The network follows the IEEE 802.5 protocol. It can support up to 72 devices using standard telephone wiring. With Shielded Twisted Pair (STP) up to 256 devices can be connected.

```
#define true  1
#define BC 1000     // Buffer capacity

void producer (void)
{
    struct buffer_slot  entity;
    message msg1, msg2;
    while (true) {
        produce_an_entity(&entity);
        receive (consumer, producer, &msg1);//Wait for consumer's message
        receive (mailbox,&msg2);     //Get permission to use the entity-queue
        insert_the_entity(&entity);          //Put entity in queue
        send (mailbox, &msg2);            //Free the resource, i.e., queue
        send (producer, consumer,&msg1);    //One slot is filled
    }
}
```

```
void consumer (void)
{
    struct buffer_slot entity;
    message msg1, msg2;
    for (i=0; i<BC; i++) send (consumer, producer, &msg1); //BC slots are free
    while (true) {
        receive (producer, consumer, &msg1);    //Wait until there is an entity
        receive (mailbox, &msg2);
        remove_the_entity(&entity);
        send (maibox, msg2);
        send (consumer, producer,msg1);
        consume_the_entity(&entity);
    }
}

void main (void)
{
    int pid;
    message msg2;
    send (mailbox, &msg2);
    pid = fork();
    if (pid != 0)  producer();
    else consumer();
}
```

For semaphore, its initial value was very important. It is the same for message-based IPC. Here, Initial value is the number of messages that have to be sent at the beginning. In order to make sure not more than one object can use the shared buffer, only one initial message was sent to the mailbox. Similarly, to show the number of available slots in the buffer in the beginning, as many as the buffer capacity messages were sent. Each one of these messages is a permission for a producer to put one item into the buffer.

8.3 Summary

If the allowable number of processes simultaneously using a resource is lower than the number of processes that have attempted to use the resource, then the uncontrolled attempts by concurrently running processes (or threads) to use a shared resource causes a collision of processes over the shared resource. This collision causes a race condition and thus the processes that are participating in the race condition may produce incorrect results. There is numerous hardware and software shared resources within every multiprogramming operating system. These resources have to be used in a collision-free manner for the operating system and application processes to work properly. In this chapter, many methods were introduced that are effective under different circumstances to guarantee mutual exclusive (race-free) resource usage. The disabling interrupt method works well for single processor systems. This can only run in a protected mode because the corresponding machine instruction is privileged. A strict alternation method is for synchronizing two processes. Processes have had to alternate when using a shared resource. Peterson and Dekker methods remove the restriction of alternate shared resource usage by processes. The test-and-set-lock method accomplishes the same thing but with the help of a machine instruction provided only for this purpose. Yet another similar method is the swap method. This tries to obtain the permission to use a shared resource by swapping the value of a local variable with the value of a global variable (that acts as the permission). This is done by running an atomic routine called *swap*. Some processors have a machine instruction that can swap the contents of two memory locations in one machine instruction. These methods (except the disable interrupt) all suffer from busy-wait consumption of CPU time. A semaphore-based method is a busy-wait free form of guaranteeing mutual exclusion. Due to its generality and efficiency, it is used by many operating systems. The concept of monitor complements semaphore through the simpler implementation of multi-constraint synchronization problems. The message-based method is borrowed from distributed operating systems, but it works on centralized systems, as well.

8.4 Problems

1. For the processor of your personal computer see whether or not there is a machine instruction that performs operations that is similar to the test and set lock concept. Note that, it must do two actions; (1) test (or load) the content of a memory location and (2) set its value to one, all in one machine instruction. If there is, name this instruction and explain what it does, exactly.

2. Express the reasons for insisting on doing these two actions: (1) test (or load) the content of a memory location and (2) set its value to one, using one machine instruction, in order for this instruction to be useful in implementing mutual exclusion.

3. For the processor of your personal computer, check whether or not there is a machine instruction that exchanges the contents of two memory locations. If there is, name this instruction.

4. Show that if Peterson's method is correctly used to enter and leave a critical region, then only one process at a time can be in its critical region.

5. Suppose Peterson's method is modified so that, instead of using the global variable *turn* a random number generator is called upon to return one of the zero or one values. Comment on this solution.

```
void GetPermission (int  process)
{
  int other;
  other = 1-process;
  desire [process] = true;
  while (desire[process] && desire [other] &&rand(0,1)!=process) ;
}

 void FreePermission (int process)
{
  desire [process] = false;
}
```

6. Suppose that we replace the *turn=process* to *turn=other* in Peterson's solution to mutual exclusion. Will the new solution work well all the time? If not, what will go wrong?

7. See the following program. This is suggested by Hyman [Hym66] as a method for guaranteeing mutual exclusion. Although published by Communications of the ACM, it is incorrect. Show that, this program does not work right all the time. This exercise shows how difficult it is to verify and prove the correctness of mutual exclusion solutions.

```
#define true 1
#define false 0
int blocked[2];
int turn;
void main(void)
{   int pid;
     blocked[0]=false;
     blocked[1]=false;
     turn=0;
     pid=fork();   // Suppose that a child process is successfully created
     if (pid==0) p(0);
     else p(1);
}
void p(int id)
{
   while (true)
   {
     blocked[id]=true;
     while (turn != id)
     {
        while (blocked[1-id]) turn=id;
     }
      // Critical section
```

```
        blocked[id] = false;
        // Other computation
    }
}
```

8. In the semaphore-based solution of the producer-consumer problem, what are the consequences of interchanging the two statements *wait(&available)* and *wait(&mutex)* in the producer procedure?

9. The following two processes are running concurrently. These two processes use two global variables x and y. Assume that the execution of each assignment statement is atomic (that is when started, it continues until completion without being interrupted).

> a. If the values of x and y are 1 and 3 respectively before the processes start, list all the possible values of x and y after the two processes finish.

> b. List all possible values of x and y, if the assumption of the atomicity of the assignment statements is removed. Hint: it is better to first translate the body of each process to assembly language.

```
Void proc1(void)                     void proc2(void)
{                                    {
    x = x + 5;                           x = x + 7;
    y = y + 23;                          y = y + 31;
}                                    }
```

10. A single-processor system is running ten processes concurrently. Two of these processes do nothing but mutual exclusively using a shared resource. A busy-wait method is used to possess the resource. If the CPU scheduler is round robin what percent of the CPU time is wasted due to busy-wait?

11. Four processes are going to use a common buffer the size of 1500 bytes. The following table shows the allocated and the maximum requirements of the first three processes. A process cannot finish unless its complete requirements are allocated.

Process	Total required space	Allocated space
P1	700 bytes	450 bytes
P2	600 bytes	400 bytes
P3	600 bytes	150 bytes

a. If the fourth process enters with a total requirement of 600 bytes and it immediately requests 250 bytes, is this request safe (with respect to deadlock)?

b. If the fourth process enters with a total requirement of 600 bytes and it immediately requests 350 bytes, is this request safe?

12. Two processes, A and B, are being executed in a multiprogramming (or multiprocessing) manner. Process A has only one instruction, $a=1$, and process B has two instructions, $b=a$ and $c=a$, respectively. List all possible sets of final values for a, b, and c. Variables a, b, and c are global and the initial value of a is zero.

13. Initial values of semaphores x and y are 0 and 1, respectively. What is the typical output that is generated by processes P1 and P2 when executing concurrently?

P1
```
...
while(1){
        P(x);
          print ("A");
          V(y);
}
...
```

P2
```
...
while(1){
        P(y);
          print("B");
          V(x);
}
...
```

14. Three processes P1, P2, and P3 are concurrently running. To use shared resources, these processes execute the following set of *down* and *up* primitives

on semaphore *s* in the same sequence that is shown in the following table. At the end, what is the state of every process?

P1	P2	P3	P2	P1	P3	P2	P2	P3	P1
down(&s)	down(&s)	up(&s)	down(&s)	up(&s)	up(&s)	down(&s)	down(&s)	up(&s)	down(&s)

15. The Initial values of semaphores *x*, *y*, and *z* are 1, 5, and 10, respectively. At the most, how many processes may be awaiting each of these semaphores, with respect to the following pseudo code?

```
...
down(&z);
    down(&y);
        down(&x);
        ...
    up(&x);
    up(&y);
up(&z);
...
```

Recommended References

The formalization of many concepts in interprocess communication and synchronization is due to E. W. Dijkstra. For two-process mutual exclusion see [Dij65]. Dijkstra [Dij65] is responsible for the semaphore concept. For a general discussion concerning the mutual exclusion concept, refer to [Lam86]. The critical region concept is presented by Hoare [Hoa72] and Brinch-Hansen [Han72]. For the monitor concept see [Han73]. For a general discussion concerning concurrent programming refer to [Ben06] by Ben-Ari.

Lamport presents a solution to the n-process mutual exclusion problem in [Lam74]. As the name suggests, Peterson's mutual-exclusion algorithm is credited to G. L. Peterson [Pet81]. Dekker presented another solution for the two-process mutual exclusion problem [Dij68b]. For the details of locking mechanisms used in Solaris, refer to [Mau01] by Mauro and McDougal

Chapter 9

Deadlock and Starvation

Methods for enforcing mutual exclusion were discussed in the previous chapter. As explained, enforcing mutual exclusion prevents race condition. That is, processes will not produce incorrect results due to uncontrolled use of shared resources. However, some processes, in the first palace, may never terminate to produce correct results. In the following sections, undesirable standstill situations that might occur to processes are discussed, plus methods for preventing or curing this.

9.1 Deadlock

Imagine a situation in which every person needs one chair and one desk in order to do an assignment, whatever it might be. There is only one chair and one desk available that are long-term shared critical resources that people have to use in a short term exclusive manner. A mutual exclusion-free solution will guarantee that no more than one person will ever sit on the chair at any given time. Similarly, no more than one person will ever use the desk at any given time. However, what if one person gets a hold of the chair and another person grabs the desk. Neither of these people would be able to do their assignment nor, by the method that guarantees mutual exclusion, would they be able to let go of what they have taken in order to break the standstill. This standstill is called a deadlock. Therefore, **deadlock** is a situation in which two or more processes are unable to proceed with their execution because of each process is waiting for something from another process and a closed wait cycle is formed. Without an external intervention this waiting situation will not end.

9.1.1 Deadlock Conditions and Modeling

A single process cannot cause a deadlock by itself. A process may be stuck in a situation in which it needs a resource which is not ready right now and it will not become ready in the future. For example, a printer may be off and the system has posted a warning for the user to turn the printer on, even though the user is not planning to do so. Although this process will wait indefinitely, this situation does not match the definition of deadlock.

In context of deadlock, there is no difference between a hard resource such as a printer, processor, main memory, etc. and a soft resource such as a message, a datum, a procedure, etc. Suppose a set of processes are dependent and for example, communicate with each other by sending messages, then each one of the processes may simultaneously need a message from another so that these needs form a cycle. This situation leads to a deadlock if the message-passing protocol is of receive-blocking type.

The possibility of a deadlock exists only if the following three conditions are simultaneously present in an environment.

1. **Mutual exclusion:** There are resources in the system for which mutual exclusion is enforced to prevent race condition. However, if such resources exist but mutual exclusion is not enforced, there will not be any deadlocks. That is, we may prevent deadlocks at the price of letting race condition occur. By doing so, the overall results are unreliable and the integrity of the system is questionable.

2. **Hold and wait:** This refers to a situation in which a process is holding one or more resources and is also waiting for one or more other resources that are not available for the time being. In the case of independent processes, when a system accepts a process only if it can supply all its resources upon creation, a hold and wait cannot occur. That is, whenever the system cannot supply all its resources the process is not accepted.

3. **Non-preemptable resources:** A non-preemptable resource is a resource that cannot be forcibly taken away from the process that is holding it. The existence of such resources in a system points to a deadlock condition. A device such as a scanner is a non-preemptable resource. A process is not able to scan part of a page and give the scanner to another process and get back the scanner and do the other part of the page. Operating systems are designed so that when a scanner is given to a process, the process keeps it until its scanning job is completed. On the other hand, with page-based virtual memory management a page frame that is owned by a process can be taken away from the process whenever the page replacement algorithm wants to. Page frames of main memory, in this context, are preemptable resources.

The three conditions discussed above fulfill the necessary requirements, i.e., necessary conditions, for deadlocks to occur. In almost all contemporary environments, these three conditions are always met, unless the operating system's designer intentionally removed one of these from the system to make sure deadlock will not occur. If the following condition also exists, in addition to the three previously mentioned conditions, a deadlock has occurred and it is too late to keep it from happening.

4. **Circular wait:** A set of two or more processes form a closed chain in which each process needs a resource that is held by the next process in the chain. This closed chain is said to form a **circular wait** chain. In our previous example of one chair and one desk, if one person takes the chair and another takes the table, nobody can do his assignment. Each person is waiting for the other to let go of what he has taken. Depending on the generosity of these persons the situation creates a circular waiting chain. In fact, the heart of a deadlock is the circular wait; when this happens, we know that a deadlock has occurred. This means that the other three conditions definitely hold, as a circular wait could not occur otherwise. The definition of circular wait matches that of a deadlock. As a matter of fact, if there is a circular-wait, then there is a deadlock and vice versa. Recall that, in a circular-wait, the other three conditions unquestionably hold, too. In fact, condition four is a sufficient condition for deadlock.

To show a pictorial representation of a deadlock, Holt suggested using the symbols in Figure 9.1:

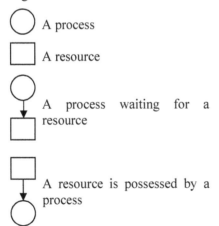

Figure 9.1: Deadlock modelling symbols

Suppose there are two processes, A and B. A holds the CD drive and waits to get the scanner. B holds the scanner and waits to get the CD drive. This circular wait is depicted in Figure 9.2.

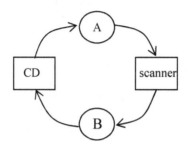

Figure 9.2: A process-resource circular wait graph

Figure 9.2 represents a **process-resource wait-for graph**, or a **wait-for graph**, for short. Sometimes resources are removed from this type of figures and only processes are used to show a circular wait graph.

As the system continues giving and getting back resources to processes, the last action that closes a wait chain is always a request that is made by one of the processes to use a resource which is possessed by another process. This request reflects the need of the requesting process to continue its execution. Presumably, the requesting process cannot ignore its need for the resource.

Solutions to the deadlock problem are categorized into four classes.
1. Ignoring Deadlock
2. Deadlock Prevention
3. Deadlock Avoidance
4. Deadlock Detection and Recovery

9.1.2 Ignoring Deadlock

Although we are aware of the possibility of a deadlock, we may intentionally ignore it altogether. There are reasons for doing so. Some environments are not very sensitive to minor malfunctions of a system. For example, in an educational environment, where students program just to learn, if two or more processes are trapped in a circular wait, the user will notice it. He or she will probably go to task manager window and terminate it and try to catch up with what he was doing, without incurring any serious harm to fatal information or apparatus. On the other hand, the cost of preventing deadlock or recovering from deadlock may be very high and the operating system designers, for some versions of the operating system, may decide to ignore the possibility of deadlock.

By **ignoring deadlock**, we are not actually suggesting a solution, but rather erasing a problem statement. It is possible that deadlock may occur and the computer user has no option but to terminate some jobs, turn the computer off, or to reset it. In some environments, the side effects of such an action could be very harmful. For example, if a process is supposed to transfer a large sum of money from one bank account to another. What will happen if a deadlock occurs when the money is withdrawn from the first account but not yet deposited into the second account? It is, therefore, not wise to ignore deadlock in sensitive environments.

9.1.3 Deadlock Prevention

For deadlock to be possible, all three necessary deadlock conditions must be simultaneously met. Besides, to achieve an actual deadlock, the fourth condition must also exist. Therefore, for **deadlock prevention**, we can arrange that at least one of the necessary conditions is not satisfied. If we cannot ensure this, then circular wait, the fourth condition, can be prevented. The three conditions necessary for the possibility of deadlock are always satisfied in contemporary operating system environments. Removing one of these conditions greatly reduces the performance of the system. It is, thus, not recommended to remove one of these conditions. However, in some rare cases, for which these solutions are acceptable, we shall discuss the methods used.

Removing the mutual exclusion condition

By not enforcing mutual exclusion, we allow race conditions to occur. It follows that, as a consequence of race condition, processes may produce unacceptable results. It is obvious that this is not acceptable by any computer user. One environment that does not require mutual exclusion is the single-programming single-processing environment. Not more than one active program (i.e., process or thread) runs at any given time and this process does not have any resource competitor for its whole life time. There are also rare resources for which we do not have to enforce mutual exclusion. As this is a property of the resource, we do not actually do anything to prevent a deadlock. For example, a block of main memory may have fatal operating system data that is needed by many processes to read. However, only one process of the operating system is allowed to modify it. This block of main memory can be used by many reading processes simultaneously, without violating any constraint. Therefore, mutual exclusion is not necessary to impose on this resource. For reading processes, a circular wait will not occur when this resource is involved. Once again, we have not done a specific action to prevent deadlock, but, rather, the property of the resource is such that it excludes deadlock.

Removing the hold-and-wait condition

Another necessary condition for deadlock is hold-and-wait. To prevent deadlock, we may prevent hold and wait situation. In other word, a process should not be allowed to request a new resource, which is possessed by another process, while holding other resources (preemptable resources are exempted). Therefore to prevent hold and wait, there are two suggestions:

1. Partition all the devices into collections of disjoint set of resources. Make sure no process needs more than one set of resources simultaneously, a restriction that the system has to enforce. This suggestion is almost impossible and very rare processes satisfy this condition. Enforcing this condition will prevent many processes from being executed.

2. Allocate all the needed resources of each process right after its generation or else do not accept it at that time. The process may be regenerated in the future when there are enough resources available. By doing so, the hold and wait situation will not occur because no process will request a new resource during its execution. This method has many disadvantages. Every process must list its complete resource requirement, including hard and soft resources, before its execution. This is almost impossible for contemporary processes with their vast dynamic resource requirements. Some resources may not be needed at the beginning of the execution or they may be needed at the end of execution. However, the system will assign these resources long before being used. It is clear that the resource utilization will be very low. In order to return a resource when it is no longer needed, the process has to make sure it will not require the resource in the future. This will force an overhead on the system. Although this is possible, it is not practical.

Removing the non-preemptability condition

The third necessary condition for deadlock is the existence of non-preemptable resources. If all resources are preemptable, then this condition is not met and there will be no deadlock in the system. However, if some resources are non-preemptable, i.e., the system cannot forcefully and safely regain the resource from the process which owns it for the time being, this condition has met and deadlock possibility depends on other conditions. Preemptability, here, is an attribute of resources and cannot be overruled. We cannot force processes not to use non-preemptable resources either.

Removing the circular-wait condition

What is left for preventing deadlocks is to prevent circular wait. Note that if a circular wait has occurred, we are faced with a deadlock and it is too late to prevent it. To prevent deadlock, we must propose methods that prove a circular wait will not develop. One method is to use **resource ordering.** All (non-preemptable) computer resources are clustered into n ordered classes. If a process is given a resource from class i, it can only request resources from classes of a higher order, i.e., $i+1$, $i+2$, ..., n. A simultaneous request for more than one resource from one class is acceptable as long as it does not contradict the assignment ordering with respect to previously allocated resources to this process. Resources possessed by a process must be returned in a descending order. This method is applicable without clustering resources thus ordering resources, directly.

To show that this method prevents deadlock, consider two processes that have respected these rules and yet a circular wait occurred; see Figure 9.3.

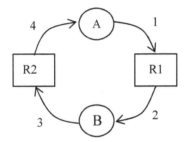

Figure 9.3: Two processes with a circular wait situation

From (4) and (1) in Figure 9.3, we conclude that A possesses R2 and has requested R1; thus R1>R2. From (2) and (3) in Figure 9.3, we conclude that B possesses R1 and has requested R2; thus R2>R1. These two results contradict each other and so the circular wait assumption is impossible. Although this is not a complete proof, it gives a feeling of what could go wrong if we assume there can be a circular wait for this method. The disadvantage of this method is that sometimes we are forced to assign a resource which will be needed much later. For example, if a process needs a resource from class 5 and it will later request a resource from class 3, we have to assign the resource from class 3 before assigning the resource from class 5. Such circumstances reduce the utilization of the resources and the overall efficiency of the system.

An example of removing the circular wait condition is given in the following.

Example 9.1: Suppose every resource forms a class by itself and classes are ordered and each class is given a unique number. Process A will be executed and it will need resources 5, 18, 13, 20, 22, 28, 32, and 45 during its execution. The order of requests and releases are defined in the following. To understand how deadlock prevention works, next to each request or release statement we have shown what the operating system will do.

...

1- Resource number 13 is requested // OS will allocate resources 5, 8, and 13

...

2- Resource number 22 is requested // OS will allocate resources 20 and 22

...

3- Resource number 22 is released // OS will take back this resource

...

4- Resource number 45 is requested // OS will allocate resources 22, 28, 32, and 45. Remember that we are not sure that when the process returned resource number 22 it meant the process will not need it again

..

5- Resource number 28 is released // OS will not take back this resource because the process still possesses resources 32 and 45

...

6- Resources number 32 and 45 are released // OS will take back resource numbers 45, 32, and 28

...

7- Resource number 22 is released // OS will take back this resource

...

To clarify the algorithm, we have included important situations that might happen, in Example 9.1.

9.1.4 Deadlock Avoidance

Similar to deadlock prevention, deadlock avoidance ensures that deadlock will not occur. To make it clear, out of the four deadlock handling strategies, deadlock prevention and deadlock avoidance guarantee that deadlock will not occur. However, in ignoring deadlock and deadlock detection and recovery, deadlock may occur. The term "deadlock avoidance" appears to be very close to "deadlock prevention" in a linguistic context, but they are very much different in the context of deadlock handling. As we saw in the previous section, deadlock prevention does not require examining what will happen in the future if a request for a resource is accepted and the resource is allocated. Some deadlock detection methods do not even need to know in advance the total resource requirements of every process. With available information at the time of a request, the system can decide whether or not to allocate the requested resource.

Deadline avoidance is based on careful analysis of every request by examining what will happen in the future if the requested resource is allocated.

The resource is allocated if the system is safe and will not be allocated otherwise. If not allocated, the requesting process withdraws its request and resubmits it at a later time.

One of the most respected deadline avoidance methods is the **banker's algorithm**. Think of a bank branch that has certain amount of capital in the form of cash. Its capital will not increase for the purpose of our discussion. The bank manager (i.e., banker) grants credit to customers who need to invest in their respected businesses. He knows that the probability of all customers requesting all their credit simultaneously is very low. If that happens, he can postpone lending to some customer for a later time. Therefore, the total sum of all credits can be greater than the bank's capital. A customer may start to pay back a loan having received all his credit. Customers may claim all their credit at one time or this can be done in a number of installments. The banker is not allowed to forcibly collect the money from a customer. In other words, the money resource is not preemptable. The banker carefully checks every request from every customer to make sure that, by lending the requested amount to the customer the banker will not encounter deadlock. A deadlock will occur when lending a requested amount leads to a situation in which there is no way to complete total needs of all customers, no matter what the future ordering of the requests would be. This can be avoided if the total need of every customer is known in advance. The Banker's Algorithm was formalized by Dijkstra.

In the context of an operating system, a process is a customer and all hardware/software resources of a specific type, say all printers, correspond to the capital to be lent. Every process has to declare all its resource needs, at the start time. A process is accepted by the system if its total needs do not exceed the total number of resources. For every resource request, the banker's algorithm executes the steps in the following algorithm. All actions concerning the assignment or the taking back resources in this algorithm are artificial and no actual resource assignment and take back is performed. The algorithm's output will tell whether the assignment is safe or not.

Banker's algorithm for one resource type:

1. *If the number of requested resources is greater than the number of available resources the request is not valid; return from this algorithm; otherwise continue with the next step*
2. *Suppose that the required resources are given to the process (it is not actually given)*
3. *See if there is a process that can complete its job with the available resources; if there is one, mark it as completed; suppose that all of its resources are taken back and are added to available resources; repeat this step for unmarked processes until there are no more unmarked*

processes or there is no process left that can complete its job with the available resources

4. *If all processes are marked, it is safe to allocate the requested resources to the process; otherwise declare that the allocation is unsafe and return.*

In the Banker's algorithm, if the request is unsafe or invalid no resource is given to the process; the process has to resubmit its request (or the system may automatically reevaluate it if some resources are returned) at a later time in the hopes that some resources will be freed and that there will be enough resources available.

If we start with a **safe state**, the above explained algorithm guarantees that there will be no deadlock with respect to the controlled resource type. A safe state is a system condition in which all processes, in some order, can receive their needed resources from the resource type that is being controlled and that they can complete their jobs with the resource. A process that has completed its work is supposed to return all of the resources it possesses of all resource types. To check for the safety of a state, Step 3 of the Banker's Algorithm is executed and all processes must be marked at the end. Sometimes, checking for the safety of a state is called **deadlock detection**, although deadlock detection is usually used when we talk about the detection and recovery method. If the current state of the system is unsafe not all the processes can complete their execution with the remaining resources; this means there will definitely be a deadlock. However, this deadlock may not include all processes.

A scenario of the Banker's Algorithm used to avoid deadlock is presented as follows. Although the controlled resource type is usually considered to be printers, tapes, or scanners, in our scenario it is "opened files". You have probably been faced with a restriction on the number of opened files in your computer's operating system. Perhaps, you have encountered illogical behavior of your operating system in cases where the number of opened files exceeds the limit. If the Banker's Algorithm is used, the system's behavior can become more predictable. The example follows.

Example 9.2: Suppose the number of simultaneously opened files is restricted to 128 and there are four processes in the system that need to simultaneously open, in the worst case, 55, 95, 10, and 80 files, respectively. Neither of the processes will need to have more than 128 open files (which is the maximum number of possible opened files), simultaneously. Thus all four processes are accepted for execution. The sum of all worst case needs is 55+95+10+80=240 which is more than the total number possible simultaneous open files. Therefore, banker's algorithm should be used. Each process may open one or more files in every step. When a file is opened by a process, it will remain open to the end of process execution, although it may be closed when it is no longer needed. The sequence of requests to open files follows. This sequence corresponds to the order in which requests are submitted to the system. A request that arrives earlier is listed before a request that arrives later.

1. Process p1 needs to open 20 files
2. Process p3 needs to open 2 files
3. Process p1 needs to open 15 files
4. Process p4 needs to open 25 files
5. Process p3 needs to open 3 files
6. Process p2 needs to open 47 files
7. Process p4 needs to open 7 files
8. Process p3 needs to open 5 files
9. Process p2 needs to open 33 files
10. Process p1 needs to open 20 files
11. Process p4 needs to open 30 files
12. Process p4 needs to open 18 files
13 Process p2 needs to open 15 files

Table 9.1 summarizes the state of the system after every request is generated and the safety is checked. It is after the safety checking process that, if it is safe, the resource is actually allocated. Step 0 is the initial state when the system has just started and no request has arrived yet. The table is developed until Step 7 when the state of the system becomes unsafe. Therefore, the request from p4 in Step 7 is not safe and the system will not give the required resources to that process. The process may regenerate its request at a later time. The system will continue its operation ignoring process four's recent request. An intelligent system will recheck every outstanding request whenever some resources are returned.

Table 9.1: Banker's algorithm applied to a four-process system.

Step no.	Process	Request	Given, so far	Will need in the future	Available, overall	Safety
0					128	Safe
1	P1	20	0	35	128	Safe
2	p3	2	0	8	108	Safe
3	p1	15	20	20	106	Safe
4	p4	25	0	55	91	Safe
5	p3	3	2	5	66	Safe
6	p2	47	0	48	63	Safe
7	p4	7	25	48	16	Unsafe

In Step 1, if 20 files are opened for Process 1, 108 options will remain. With these, Process 1 can complete its job and then return all its resources, making the number of resources 128. With 128 resources, Process 2 can complete its job and return all its resources. Similarly, Processes 3 and 4 can complete their jobs one after the other. Thus, the assignment is safe and the system can allocate 20 resources to Process 1, meaning Process 1 can open 20 files. In Step 6, for example, if 47 resources are given to Process 2, 16 resources will remain. With that, Process 3 can complete its job and return all its resources. The number of available resources then becomes 21. Now, Process 1 can complete its job and return all its resources. We will have 51 resources and, at this time, Process 2 can complete its job and return all its resources. With 98 available resources Process 4 can complete its job, too. Therefore, the assignment is safe and Process 2 is allowed to open 47 files. In Step 7 if 7, resources are given to Process 4; the remaining number of resources will be 9. With that, Process 3 can complete its job and return all its resources. We will have 14 resources now and no other process can complete their jobs. Thus the assignment is unsafe and this request is not accepted. Process 4 may regenerate its request at a later time.

The Banker's Algorithm for deadlock avoidance can be used for multiple types of resources. The algorithm steps that are designed for a single type of resource have to be modified, a little bit, so as to be applicable for multiple resource types. This will better resemble a computing system. See the following algorithm.

Similar to single resource case, every process has to declare all its resource needs at the start time and a process is accepted if its total needs do not exceed the total number of resources in the system.

Banker's algorithm for multiple resource types:

1. *If the number of requested resources from each type is greater than the number of available resources of the corresponding type the request is not valid return from this algorithm; otherwise continue with the next step*
2. *Suppose that all the requested resources are given to the process (it is not actually given)*
3. *See if there is a process that can complete its job with the available resources; if there is one, mark it as completed; suppose that all of its resources are taken back and are added to available resources; repeat this step for unmarked processes until there are no more unmarked processes or there is no process left that can complete its job with the available resources*
4. *If all processes are marked it is safe to allocate the requested resources to the process; otherwise declare that the allocation is unsafe and return.*

A process is not created if the number of simultaneously needed resources of at least one resource type is greater than that resource type's total number of resources in the system. Every process can simultaneously request one or more resources from one or more resource types. The request is either accepted as a whole or it is rejected. In the following, we present a short scenario of a system with two types of resources and three processes. There are eight CD drives in the system and, at the most, 20 files can be opened simultaneously. The maximum number of simultaneously required resources of every type for each process has to be declared at the process creation time. In this case, Process 1 will need to open 6 files and use 4 CD drives. Process 2 will need to open 8 files and use 4 CD drives, and Process 3 will need to open 5 files and use 3 CD drives. The following is the actual list of requests in the order of their arrival. The total requirements of processes are summarized in Table 9.2.

Table 9.2: Total requirements of processes

Process ID	Number of open files	Number of CDs
P1	6	4
P2	8	4
P3	5	3

1. Process p1 needs to open 2 files and use 3 CD drives
2. Process p2 needs to open 4 files and use 2 CD drives
3. Process p1 needs to open 3 files
4. Process p3 needs to open 5 files
5. Process p3 needs to use 2 CD drives
6. Process p2 needs to open 4 files and 1 CD drives
7. Process p1 needs to open 1 file and use 1 CD drives
8. Process p2 needs to use 1 CD drive
9. Process p3 needs to use 1 CD drive

The following table shows the status of the system right after each request is made but before the required resources is given away. There are 8 CD drives in the system and not more than 20 files can be opened simultaneously at any given time.

Table 9.3: Banker's algorithm applied to a multiple resource system.

Step no.	Process	Request	Given, so far	Will need in the future	Available, overall	Safety
0					20 files 8 CDs	Safe
1	p1	2 files 3 CDs	0 0	4 files 1 CD	20 files 8 CDs	Safe
2	p2	4 files 2 CDs	0 0	4 files 2 CDs	18 files 5 CDs	Safe
3	p1	3 files	2 files 3 CDs	1 file 1 CD	14 files 3 CDs	Safe
4	p3	5 files	0	3 CDs	11 files 3 CDs	Safe
5	p3	2 CDs	5 files	1 CD	6 files 3 CDs	Safe
6	p2	4 files 1 CD	4 files 2 CD	1 CD	6 files 1 CD	Unsafe

Steps 1 through 5 are all safe. For example, to analyze Step 5 we assume that two CDs are given to Process p3. The system is left with 6 files and one CD. With that, p1 can complete and return 2 files and 3 CDs. The system will have 8 files and 4 CDs. With that, Process p2 can complete its job and return 4 files and 2 CDs, which brings the total available resources to 12 files and 6 CDs. Process p3 can also complete its job because it needs one more CD drive. Therefore, the allocation is safe and 2 CDs are allocated to Process p3. Step 6 is not safe because, if the resources are allocated, the system will end up with 2 files and no CDs. However, each of the processes needs one more CD to complete. Therefore, the allocation is not safe. The system has to ignore this request and process other requests. Process p2 has to wait to regenerate its requests. We can continue examining Steps 7, 8 and 9.

Deadlock avoidance methods guarantee that no deadlock will take place in the system, but the price of this assurance is very high. Every process makes tens of requests and there are tens of simultaneous processes in a multi-user system at any given time. For every request, a time-consuming process of checking whether or not the system would be safe if the requested resource(s) is assigned takes a tremendous amount of time which increases the overall system overhead. This, in turn, increases the **average waiting time** of the computer users. An alternative solution to deadlock detection and deadlock avoidance is deadlock detection and recovery. This policy allows a deadlock to happen, but tries to detect it and recover from the situation.

9.1.5 Deadlock Detection and Recovery

In this policy, we allow deadlocks to occur, but a deadlock monitoring process, called deadlock detection process, will recognize the occurrence of every deadlock and notify the system whenever such an event occurs. The system recovers from this situation by killing a process, or rolling back one of the transactions, which is in the **process-resource wait cycle**. At the beginning of deadlock section in this chapter, we clarified that three conditions are necessary for a deadlock to occur: mutual exclusion, hold and wait, and non-preemptable resources. The existence of the fourth condition, circular wait, is sufficient alone for occurrence of a deadlock. If one of the three necessary conditions is not present, we do not have to worry about deadlock. Unfortunately, in almost all circumstances, for contemporary computers, these conditions are present. Therefore, a method for detecting

> *Transaction* is an essential concept in operating systems and database management systems. A transaction is a piece of work that has to be done either completely or not at all. Therefore, the incomplete execution of a transaction is not acceptable. The underlying system must guarantee that transactions are executed correctly. For example, if a person issues a banking query to transfer $1,000 dollars from his checking account to his savings account, this piece of work is indivisible and must be done as a whole. If, after the execution of part of this query, a deadlock occurs and the process is killed, the $1,000 may have been withdrawn from his checking account but not deposited to his savings account. As a result, this person has lost his money, for the time being.

deadlocks must concentrate on detecting a **circular wait**, i.e., the sufficient condition. If a circular wait is detected we have a deadlock. After a deadlock has occurred, there is no choice but to cure the system. We will concentrate, in this section, on describing methods to detect circular wait. By implementing these methods, actual deadlocks can be detected. Deadlock recovery is not fully covered in this section. This requires careful examinations of all processes that are participating in the circular wait. This must be done to find out which process to kill in order to break the circular wait.

When a request arrives and the required resource is already assigned to one of the processes in the chain, a process-resource wait chain may close and turns into a circular process-resource wait cycle. Therefore, to check for a deadlock, a circular-wait finding algorithm must be executed, for every request to use a non-preemptable resource. The algorithm is simple and does not consume a lot of processor time compared to what is done in deadlock avoidance case. The graphical representation of the process-resource cycle is beneficial to us, but it is not applicable within the computer. A simple and efficient method of implementation must be used.

Circular-wait detection method

The method that is presented here uses existing data structures with minor additions to detect deadlock. In Chapter 4 we talked about the **process table**, PT. It is a table that directly or indirectly stores information that is necessary to identify and control all processes in the system. For the purpose of circular wait detection, a column called "waiting for" is added to this table. This field is filled for the purpose of circular wait detection. Similarly, a **resource table**, RT, is used to identify and control the resources in the system. A field called "possessing process" is added to the resource table to show what process (if any) is currently holding this resource. Values are assigned to this field during the execution of the circular wait detection process. The "waiting for" field of all processes in the process table, PT, and the "possessing process" field of all resources in the resource table, RT, must be initialized to become null, during the system start or restart. The addition of a process to the process table and the introduction of a new resource to the system require the initialization of the corresponding fields. When a resource is released by a process, the resource table must be updated so that this resource becomes available again.

The following is the detection algorithm. This algorithm is executed every time a resource is requested by a process.

Circular-wait detection algorithm

Suppose that a process, whose ID is p, has requested the possession of a resource whose ID is r. The following steps are executed to update PT and RT and to detect a possible deadlock.

Step 1. If the resource r is available, allocate it to Process p and place p in the possessing field of this resource in the resource table. A circular-wait cannot occur when the required resource is available. Return from this algorithm; otherwise continue

Step 2. Place r in the "waiting for" field of Process p in the process table.

Step 3. Assign p to $p1$ and r to $r1$.

Step 4. Look at the resource table and assign the process that possesses resource $r1$ to $p2$. If $p2$ is the same as p, a circular wait has occurred. Announce *this and return from this algorithm; otherwise go to the process table; if process p2 is not waiting for a resource, a circular wait does not exist; return from this algorithm; Otherwise assign the resource for which p2 is waiting for, to r2.*

Step 5. *Replace p1 by p2 and r1 by r2; repeat from Step 4 on.*

Since a long example will consume too much space to explain the details of computations, a very short example can serve the purpose of understanding how the circular-wait detection algorithm works. See Example 9.3.

Example 9.3: Consider a multiprogramming or multiprocessing system that runs two processes. Each process will require one CD drive and one set of speakers to complete its job. There is only one CD drive and one set of speakers in the system. For simplicity, process IDs are 1 and 2, respectively. The sequence of requests is:

1. Process 1   requests   CD drive
2. Process 2   requests   speaker set
3. Process 1   requests   speaker set
4. Process 2   requests   CD drive

The detail of actions taken for the detection of circular-wait is as follows. Once again, the process IDs of Process 1 and Process 2 are 1 and 2, respectively,

1. Process 1   requests the CD drive
   Step 1: The CD drive is assigned to Process 1.

Process table, PT

Process ID	Waiting for	Other attributes
1		
2		

Resource table, RT

Resource ID	Possessing process	Other attributes
1	CD drive	
2		

2. Process 2   requests the speaker set
   Step 1: The speaker set is assigned to Process 2.

Process ID	Waiting for	Other attributes
1		
2		

Resource ID	Possessing process	Other attributes
1	CD drive	
2	speaker set	

3. Process 1 requests the speaker set
  Step 1: No action.
  Step 2: Process 1 waits for speaker set.
  Step 3: $p1=1$, and $r1=$speaker set.
  Step 4: $p2=2$, but process 2 is not waiting for a resource, so there is no circular wait.

Process ID	Waiting for	Other attributes
1	speaker set	
2		

Resource ID	Possessing process	Other attributes
1	CD drive	
2	speaker set	

4. Process 2 requests the CD drive
  Step 1: No action.
  Step 2: Process 2 waits for CD drive.
  Step 3: $p1=2$, and $r1=$CD drive.
  Step 4: $p2=1$, $r2=$speaker set.
  Step 5: $p1=1$, $r1=$speaker set.
  Step 4: $p2=2$, now $p2$ becomes equal to p, thus a circular-wait exists, which means a deadlock has occurred. The identity of the processes that are involved in the circular-wait can be saved during the execution of the algorithm.

Process ID	Waiting for	Other attributes
1	speaker set	
2	CD drive	

Resource ID	Possessing process	Other attributes
1	CD drive	
2	speaker set	

  The circular-wait detection algorithm works well when there is one resource of each type. Minor considerations must be taken into account when, for some resource types, there is more than one resource. First, if there is more than one resource available, a process that is requesting a resource from a resource type can possess any of the available resources of that type. Second, if a process has to wait for a resource of a resource type, it should not matter which resource it waits for. Therefore, in the process of detecting a circular-wait, whenever a process has to wait for a resource type, we have to exhaustively check to see whether there exits a resource of this type so that if the process waits for, a circular-wait will not occur. If such a resource does not exist, circular-wait is inevitable and, thus, a deadlock has occurred. Otherwise, we may have a cycle of processes and resource types but not a circular wait chain. Figure 9.4 shows a cycle of processes and resource types which does not represent a deadlock.

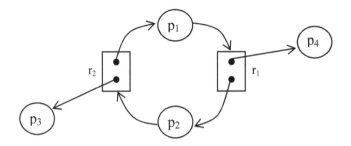

Figure 9.4: A cycle which does not represent a deadlock

Figure 9.5 depicts a sample scenario of a process-resource wait-for graph with one resource type, which includes two resources and two other resource types, each with one resource. This demonstrates a real deadlock. Whichever resource of type one that Process p_2 waits for, leads to a cycle. Therefore, a circular-wait has occurred and a deadlock is present. In this case, two cycles p_2--r_1--p_3--r_2--p_2 and p_2--r_1--p_1--r_3--p_3--r_2--p_2 are necessary to form a deadlock.

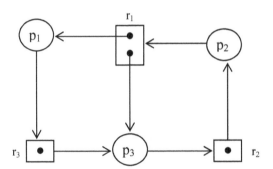

Figure 9.5: As p_2 requests a resource of type one a deadlock occurs

9.2 Starvation

In a multiprogramming and/or multiprocessing system, processes or threads have to compete for resources. The constant competition of processes may force a process to indefinitely wait without being able to possess its requested resource(s). **Starvation** is the condition in which a process requires some resources but will not ever receive it. The process is not in the wait state but its execution does not **progress**. Starvation is a possibility not a true fact because we cannot wait until infinity to see what will happen. Besides, the future is usually impossible to foretell. How can we know how many new user requests we will have in the next two hours?

In a priority-based system, the scheduler always picks the task with the highest priority to be executed next. Therefore, the execution of a low priority task may be delayed indefinitely, if new higher priority tasks keep arriving at a rate that gives no chance to the lower priority task to execute. In this situation, the possibility of starvation for the low priority task exists. The possibility of starvation is not restricted to scheduling algorithms, or processor allocation algorithms. It can occur to almost all resource allocation algorithms, if they are not designed to be starvation-proof. Memory allocation, device allocation, and communication link allocation are some examples. **InterProcess Communication** (IPC) solutions are sensitive to both deadlock and starvation. They must be carefully checked in order to detect deadlocks and, thus remove the possibility of starvation. In the following a classic example of a hypothetical problem is defined, which many researchers have carefully studied and presented deadlock and starvation free solutions for. The comical nature of the problem is an advantaging attraction for students to think about the possible ways to analyze this problem and, by doing so, experience the difficulty of providing correct, or deadlock and starvation free, solutions.

9.3 A Classic Example of IPC

The dining philosopher problem was first made up by Dijkstra, though comical and unreal, it is one of the simplest problems that best conveys the difficulty of designing deadlock and starvation-free solutions to the complex problems in modern operating system to correctly and efficiently share resources.

A round table with five chairs, five spaghetti plates, and five forks is set. Each fork is located between two spaghetti plates, and vice versa. Five philosophers sit at the table while each has his/her own spaghetti plate automatically refilled as the spaghetti is eaten. A philosopher's life is simplified into two states: think and eat. Every philosopher indefinitely repeats these states. A philosopher cannot continuously eat or think and must change his/her state every once in a while. The case becomes complicated when the rule that every philosopher has to use two forks to eat spaghetti must be observed. In order for a philosopher to eat, she or he must seize the two forks at the right and left side of his/her spaghetti plate.

If each philosopher is compared to a computer process, the forks become the shared resources. In the absence of shared resources, when there are enough forks, the processes are independent and there is no need for **interprocess communication/synchronization**. Every process, or philosopher, can go about its business, thinking and eating whenever he or she wishes. Figure 9.6 shows the table setup for the five philosophers.

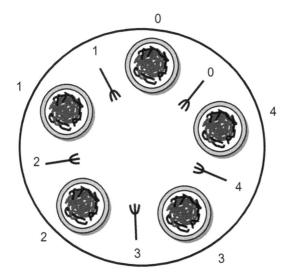

Figure 9.6: The philosophers' dining-table model

In Figure 9.6, plates are numbered in a counter clockwise direction from 0 to 4 and philosopher i, i=0, 1, ..., and 4, is sitting at the table so as to use plate number i. Forks are numbered so that fork number i, i=0, 1, ..., 4, is next to philosopher i at his/her left side. For most of our discussion the number of philosophers is of no importance, so, sometimes we may talk about n, n>2, philosophers, instead of 5. The following is the first attempted solution.

Attempt 1

The first solution that comes to mind is to let every philosopher take his/her forks one at a time and start eating. That is, if two forks are successfully grabbed. When through eating, the philosopher puts down the forks one at a time. It does not really matter which fork is taken first by a philosopher, so, we will assume the fork on his/her heft hand side is grabbed first. Let's suppose two primitives *grab(int fork_no)* and *put (int fork_no)* are available for grabbing and putting down the nominated fork, respectively. Proper care is taken, in writing these procedures, to avoid race conditions when grabbing or putting down a fork. Therefore, these procedures are atomic and, hence, **race free**. The following procedure is executed by each philosopher.

```
void philosopher (int  i)  // i =0,1,...,n-1, is the philosopher number
{
    while (1) {                      // Do this loop forever
```

```
        think;                  // Think for a while
        grab_fork(i);           // Grab left fork
        grab_fork((i+1)%n);     // Grab right fork
        eat;                    // Eat as you like for a limited time
        put_fork(i);            // Put left fork
        put_fork((i+1)%n);      // Put right fork
    }
}
```

In a multiprogramming and/or multiprocessing environment, it is possible that all philosopher processes get to the point where each one has taken the left fork and tries to take the right fork, executing *grab_fork((i+1)%n)*. In such circumstances, no fork is available and all philosophers will enter a wait state. This will result in a circular-wait condition which in turn indicates a **deadlock**. In another scenario, Processes 0 and 3, on the one hand, and 2 and 4, on the other hand, are so synchronized that whenever 0 and 3 are eating, 2 and 4 are thinking and as soon as 0 and 3 put down their forks, 2 and 4 grab their forks immediately and start eating. Also, whenever 2 and 4 put down their forks, 0 and 3 grab them immediately and start eating. If this cycle repeats forever, Philosopher 1 will starve to death and, thus, a **starvation** state is possible.

Attempt 2

In this attempt, we will focus on removing the possibility of deadlock from the Attempt 1's solution. In order to do so, one way is to remove the possibility of a hold-and-wait situation. If a philosopher gets either both forks, when he or she wants to eat, or gets neither of them, then the possibility of hold-and wait is removed. This complies with complete allocation of resources before starting any process. Suppose we prepare a new race-free procedure, called *grab_forks(int philosopher_no)*, to grab both forks at one time, whenever possible. The resulting algorithm is:

```
void philosopher (int i)  // i =0,1,...,n-1, is the philosopher number
{
    while (1) {             // Do this loop forever
        think;              // Think for a while
        grab_forks(i);      // Grab both forks
        eat;                // Eat as you like
        put_fork(i);        // Put left fork down
        put_fork((i+1)%n);  // Put right fork down
    }
}
```

This algorithm removes the possibility of a hold-and-wait situation. Hence, it is deadlock free. However, if *put_fork(i)* simply puts a fork down, the starvation possibility persists, similar to Attempt 1.

The Dining philosopher's solution

In the following algorithm, in order for a philosopher to access any fork, a *down(&mutex)* is first executed. As soon as the access is completed, an *up(&mutex)* is executed. The critical section of accessing forks is kept as short as possible in order to make sure that the effective degree of concurrent execution by philosophers is not reduced. *Mutex* is a binary variable semaphore whose initial value is set to 1 to allow the first attempt to access to be successful. The proper use of *down(&mutex)* and *up(&mutex)* ensures that no more than one philosopher will try to simultaneously grab forks or put down forks. A philosopher may have to wait because either or both forks next to him/her are being used by a neighbor(s). To provide for this possibility, an array of n, (the number of philosophers in our solution) semaphores, called *available,* is supplied. When a philosopher decides to eat he or she has to make sure that the two forks next to him/her are available. If they are, the philosopher can go ahead and start eating. Otherwise, he or she has to wait for the corresponding semaphore. Each philosopher's neighbor has to signal to the philosopher when he or she puts down a fork. Upon receiving a signal from a neighbor, the philosopher is allowed to eat. Note that before signaling, the philosopher putting down his/her forks will make sure that his/her neighbor can eat.

```
#define n  5
semaphore   mutex=1;
semaphore   available[n]={0};  // All elements of available are set to zero
int forks[n] ;
int waiting[n];          // Is the philosopher waiting?

void main (void)
{
    int pid;
    for (int i=0; i<n; i++)
        forks[i] = 1;
    for (int i=0; i<n; i++)
    {
        pid = fork();           // Create one philosopher process
        if (pid==0)philosopher(i);  // This is the created philosopher
    }
}
```

```
void philosopher (int  i)  // i =0,1,...,n-1, is the philosopher number
{
    while (1) {         // Do this loop forever
      think;            // Think for a while
      grab_forks(i);    // Grab both forks
      eat;              // Eat as you like
      put_forkL(i);     // Put left fork down
      put_forkR(i);     // Put right fork down
    }
}

void grab_forks (int i)
{
      int success = 0;         // To be set to one if both forks are available
      down (&mutex);           // Forks are protected
      waiting[i]=0;      // To be set to one if philosopher has to wait
      if (fork[i] && fork[(i+1)%n] {    // If both forks are available
         fork[i] = 0;                   // Grab left fork
         fork[(i+1)%n] = 0;             // Grab right fork
         success = 1;
      }
      else waiting[i]=1;       // The philosopher has to wait
      up (&mutex);             // Leave forks critical region
      if (!success) down (&available[i]);   // The philosopher has to await forks
}

void put_forkL (int i)
{
    down (&mutex)     // Forks are protected
    if (waiting[(i-1)%n] && fork[(i-1)%n])
    {
       fork[(i-1)%n]=0;
       waiting[(i-1)%n]=0;
       up(&available[(i-1)%n]);
    }
    else   fork[i] = 1;    // Return this fork
    up (&mutex);           // Leave forks critical region
}

void put_forkR (int i)
{
    down (&mutex)     // Forks are protected
    if (waiting[(i+1)%n] && fork[(i+2)%n])
    {
       fork[(i+2)%n]=0;
       waiting[(i+1)%n] = 0;
```

```
        up(&available[(i+1)%n]);
    }
    else  fork[(i+1)%n] = 1;      // Return this fork
    up (&mutex);       // Leave forks critical region
}
```

The final solution to the dining philosopher, that is presented here, is deadlock and starvation free. Deadlock is prevented by grabbing both forks, when available, at one time and preventing a hold-and-wait condition. The starvation freeness is guaranteed by the way the waiting neighbor(s) are alerted when a philosopher puts down his/her forks. This is accomplished by checking whether or not both forks of the neighboring philosophers are available whenever a philosopher puts down forks. In any case, in terms of simplicity and efficiency, this seems to be a good solution, compared to other deadlock and starvation free solutions.

9.4 Summary

The controlled usage of shared resources, by guaranteeing mutual exclusion to prevent race condition, causes two undesirable side effects called deadlock and starvation. There are four different policies for attacking deadlocks: ignoring deadlock, deadlock prevention, deadlock avoidance, and deadlock detection and recovery. The first policy erases the problem statement altogether. The second and third policy forestall deadlock from happening, even though the system usually pays a high price for this. The last method monitors the system. If a deadlock occurs it is detected and, in response, the operating system can take proper actions. Starvation was another concept which was discussed and using the dining philosopher problem example a solution was provided.

9.5 Problems

1. Three processes are running concurrently. There are four types of resources in the system. The current status of the system is as follows: The "available" vector shows the number of available resources of each type. The "request" matrix shows the total number of resource types that will be simultaneously needed by each process. Row *i*, *i=1, 2, and 3,* of this matrix is for process *i*. The "allocated" matrix shows the number of resources of types that are already allocated to each process; similarly, row *i*, *i=1, 2, and 3,* of this matrix is for process *i*. Is the current state of the system safe, that is, without deadlock? If the system is unsafe, can we tell which processes are deadlocked? Explain your answer.

Available = [0 0 1 1]

$$\text{Request} = \begin{bmatrix} 3 & 1 & 0 & 2 \\ 1 & 0 & 2 & 1 \\ 1 & 2 & 3 & 1 \end{bmatrix} \qquad \text{Allocated} = \begin{bmatrix} 1 & 1 & 0 & 1 \\ 1 & 0 & 1 & 1 \\ 1 & 1 & 2 & 1 \end{bmatrix}$$

2. What are the circumstances under which priority inversion occurs? Which process is in a busy-wait situation? Why does busy-wait cause this situation?

3. The following procedures are proposed to obtain permission for entering and leaving critical sections. If used properly, is mutual exclusion guaranteed? Can it cause starvation? Array *desire* is global and all its components are initially zero.

```
void enter-region(int process)
{
    int other;
L: desire[process]=0;
    if (desire[other] != 0) goto L;
    desire[process] = 1;
    if (desire[other] !=0) goto L;
}

leave-region(int process)
{
    desire[process] = 0;
}
```

4. Four processes are concurrently running. These processes compete for two reusable resources of the same type. Each process needs two resources to complete, but it can request the resources one at a time. In how many different ways can deadlock occur?

5. [Hol71] Three processes are competing for four reusable resources. Each process needs two resources to complete, but it can request and release resources one at a time. Is there a possibility of deadlock? Why or why not?

6. [Hol71] n processes are competing for m reusable resources. Each process needs, at the most, m resources to complete, but it can request and release the resources one at a time. The sum of the maximum need of all processes is less than $m+n$. Show that a deadlock cannot occur.

7. A system is running m processes. It consists of n shared resources of the same type. If every process needs two resources to complete and it can request

resources one at a time, what is the minimum number of resources to avoid deadlock?

8. A barber shop can be modeled as a barber, a barber chair, n customer waiting chairs, and customers who come to cut their hair. If there is no customer the barber goes to sleep. If a customer comes and all chairs are occupied (including the barber chair), the customer leaves the shop. If the barber chair is occupied but there is at least one unoccupied customer-waiting chair, the customer sits in one of the available chairs. If the barber is asleep, the customer wakes up the barber. Write a synchronization algorithm for the **sleeping-barber problem**.

9. With the Test-and-Set-Lock (tsl) mechanism of guaranteeing mutual exclusion, if five processes repeatedly need a shared resource is there a possibility of starvation?

10. Three processes are concurrently running. There are three type R1 resources, two type R2 resources, and two type R3 resources. These processes are currently holding one R1, two R2, and one R1 resources, respectively. If the following requests arrived in the order below, would the system be safe?

P1 requests one R2
P2 requests one R1 and one R3
P3 requests one R1.

11. In a multiprogramming system, the average CPU wait fraction is 0.8. Five processes will run in the system with the properties given in the table. There are five CD-drives in the system and every process will simultaneously need two CD-drives to complete its execution. For every process, the first CD-drive is needed at creation. If the CD-drive is not available, the process has to remain in *created* state, similar to what UNIX does in such cases. Each process will request its second CD-drive when it has exactly used 50% of its required CPU time. If it is not safe to obtain the required CD-drive, the process will go to the *wait* state. In any case, CD drives are given to processes if it is safe to do so according to the banker's algorithm. The two CD-drives of a process are taken back when the process is completed. When one or more CD-drives are freed, the system will assign them to as many processes as it is safe to do so in a FIFO manner. Round-robin is used for process scheduling. Compute the average turnaround time of the system.

Process	Arrival time	CPU burst
P1	6.0	4
P2	7.0	5
P3	8.0	3
P4	9.0	1
P5	10.0	4

12. The following is a proposed solution to the dining philosopher. It assumed that all forks are placed in the middle of the dining table. Whenever there are enough forks, any philosopher can take any two forks and start eating. *mutex1* and *philo* are two semaphores. For implementation of each semaphore, a FIFO list (queue) is utilized. There exist five philosophers. Comment on the following questions.

   (a) Is mutual exclusion guaranteed? Hint: Mutual exclusion is guaranteed if not more than one philosopher is in his/her critical region at any given time.
   (b) Is there any possibility of deadlock? Explain.
   (c) Is there any possibility of starvation? Explain.
   (d) What is the biggest misconception regarding this solution?

```
semaphore   mutex1=1; philo=0;
int forks = 5;
int philo = 0;
void philosopher(int i)
{
   while (1) {
      think();
      down (&mutex1);
      forks = forks - 2;
      if (forks < 0) down(&philo);
      up (&mutex1);
      eat ();
      down (&mutex1);
      forks= forks + 2;
      if (forks <= 0) up(&philo);
      up (&mutex1);
   }
}
```

13. [Han73] suppose that we have a synchronization primitive called *await* which delays a process executing the primitive until a Boolean expression becomes true. For example, *await B* delays the process executing this primitive until *B* becomes true. Of course, another concurrently executing process has to manipulate *B;* otherwise the waiting process will wait indefinitely. Design a solution for the producer-consumer problem using the *await* construction.

14. Highlight the exact differences between deadlock avoidance and deadlock prevention.

Recommended References

Deadlock modeling notations can be found in [Hol72]. He also discussed starvation in the same paper. For deadlock prevention and avoidance algorithms consult [Hav68, Hab69]. For the resource ordering method, see [Hav68]. Reading the paper by Coffman et al for deadlock detection methods [Cof71] is recommended. The sleeping barber problem is introduced in [Dij65] by Dijkstra. The dinning philosopher was first discussed by Dijkstra in [Dij71].

Chapter 10

Information Management

In a computer, there are many types of memory and storage for storing and retrieving information. We have already become familiar with some, such as register, cache memory, associative memory, read-only memory, and main memory. Main memory along with many efficient memory management techniques, were thoroughly explored in detail. Except for read-only memory, all the other types of memory mentioned are of a **volatile** nature. That is, if the electric current to any such memory is cut off, all of its contents will be lost. Although nonvolatile, a read-only memory (ROM) has a small capacity and hence cannot store heaps of information. Besides, replacing ROM information requires a time consuming procedure. It is usually the case that its whole content must be cleared before new information can be written. Read only memory is often used to store the Basic Input/Output System (BIOS) program (refer to Chapter 2) which contains, among its other contents, a small program for execution as soon as the system is started or restarted. There are other types of memory that can retain their contents even after the computer is turned off. For example, a Complementary Metal Oxide Semiconductor (CMOS) memory is a Read/Write (RW) memory which can retain its information for extensive periods via a durable battery that provides its necessary electric current. CMOS memory is also very limited as it can hold only very few kilo bytes of information. Other types of memory are needed to store vast amounts of **persistent information**. Software programs, the data and results of applications, picture albums, and electronic mails are examples of persistent information.

There are various different kinds of devices in which information can be stored persistently. Flash memory, hard disks, Compact Disks (CD), and Digital Video Disks (DVD) are some of these devices. The organization of information on such devices is the topic of this chapter. The organization of information is attained by designing and implementing a **file system**. There are plenty of file systems for numerous types of devices. A file system, or what is also called an

information management subsystem, is an essential part of any operating system. The investigation of all file systems is well beyond the scope of a chapter of a book. For this reason, our study is restricted to the most common devices, i.e., those on which information is stored along common center circular **tracks**. All tracks of a surface have the same capacity regardless of their circumference size (see Chapter 6).

Every track of these devices is divided into an integer number of fixed size portion called **sectors**. The size of a sector is 512 bytes, for the time being. Floppy and hard disks comply with these properties. Therefore, the organization of information on hard and floppy disks is studied in this chapter.

A floppy disk can be considered as a special kind of hard disk, in which the number of plates, information on is stored, is one. Thus, in the rest of this chapter, file systems for hard disks (or disks, for short) will be focused on. To simplify matters, we can assume a disk is a long string of m tracks, with each track composed of n sectors. Using this simplification, Figure 10.1 presents a model of a disk.

Figure 10.1: The model of physical organization of a disk

A disk usually contains the following types of information:

- The information related to the disk characteristics and its file system attributes
- The boot strap program which helps in picking the operating system to be used, whenever there is more than one operating system available on the disk, and/or the program to start the process of loading one of the operating systems
- The information showing where different directories and files are stored
- The actual data of files and directories

To find out the capacity, number of partitions, number of stored operating systems, type of file system, size of sectors, size of blocks, and much other **metadata** of a disk, we must refer to the disk itself. It is like hiding the treasure map with the treasure.

> Metadata is information about the data in question. For example, a file's content is called data; the location of this data on the disk is the metadata of the file.

Everything starts by reading the first sector of track zero of the disk by BIOS (see Chapter 2). This sector contains valuable metadata, such as whether the disk is bootable, the number of partitions, the size and location of partitions, the total size of the disk, and the bootstrap program which is either a system picker (whenever there is more than one operating system installed on this disk) or a starter program for loading the operating system. Let's assume the more general case in which there is more than one partition on the disk. Figure 10.2 presents the structure of a disk having more than one partition.

Figure 10.2: The structure of a partitioned disk

The actual structure of each partition depends on the file system used for that partition. There are tens of different file systems, each having many versions. FAT, NTFS, UFS, NFS, and EXT are a few of the well-known ones. In considering the purpose and desired length of this book, we are obviously unable to present the design and implementation details of all these file systems. Instead, two file systems, the UNIX File System (UFS) and the New Technology File System (NTFS) for Windows are discussed. These, follow two completely different designs. Linux, another very popular operating system, has its own file system called EXT which is very similar to the USF file system.

Before starting with a specific file system, some topics common to all file systems will be presented.

10.1 Storage allocation

There are three approaches for the allocation of storage areas to a file or directory data.
1. Contiguous allocation
2. Chained allocation
3. Indexed allocation

Contiguous allocation

In this approach, a file (or directory) is considered a chunk of data that must be stored in a contiguous data area of the storage device. For every disk, the smallest possible **allocation unit**, which we will call a **block**, is defined and is always respected. If, for example, this unit is one kilo byte and the size of a file is 1025 bytes, the system will allocate two consecutive blocks to this file. With this approach in mind, Figure 10.3 depicts the storage of i files on consecutive locations of a disk.

| Disk attributes, metadata, ... | File 1 | File 2 | ... | File i | Unallocated area |

Figure 10.3: Contiguous allocation of *i* files

Contiguous allocation has two important advantages. First, address calculation is very simple and efficient. If the start location of the stored area of a file is known, the address of any location of the file, with respect to its displacement to the beginning of the file, is immediately computable. In reality, addresses are expressed in block number. Therefore, if the starting block number of a file is known, the block number of any address of the file can be easily calculated. Second, if a file is to be accessed sequentially, it is possible to pre-fetch what will be needed in the future. In the best case, a whole file can be read with only one seek.

The disadvantages of contiguous allocation outweigh its nice advantages. These disadvantages emerge when some files are deleted and others are added and/or when some files are updated resulting in their size being changed. As we have learned from dynamic partition memory management, which is very similar to this kind of space allocation but with the one difference that in contiguous allocation, disk area is managed rather than main memory area, is that such methods cause external fragmentation. To reduce storage waste, the system must frequently run a defragmenting program. Considering the large size of secondary storage and the slow relocation process, defragmentation will take an unacceptable amount of time and, hence, contiguous allocation is not recommended.

Chained allocation

In the **chained allocation** method, a file is broken down into blocks of the same size and each block can be stored in each empty block of the data area of the disk (or partition if there is more than one partition on the disk). To preserve the integrity of the file, these blocks are chained together. A pointer will point to the first stored block of the file and, from this block, a link will point to a storage block in which the second block of the file is stored and so on. The pointer which points to the first stored block of the file is the file access handle. Figure 10.4 shows a stored file with its stored blocks linked together in order of appearance. The dark areas represent previously allocated areas during space allocation of this file.

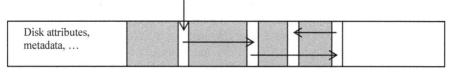

Figure 10.4: A chained allocation sample

With this method, it would seem that reading a file sequentially is simple and efficient. Unfortunately, there are some minor problems. The unit of allocation is a block which is 2^iK, i.e., 1K, 2K, 4K ... Suppose the block taken is 4K or 4096 bytes. With this method, the first four bytes of each block is used to point to the next data block of the file. Therefore, the usable size of every block is 4092 bytes which is not a power of the two sectors, thus making address calculation cumbersome and time consuming. If logical location of the data is known with respect to the beginning of the file, it is not possible to easily calculate the physical location of the data on the disk. In addition, in chained allocation, reading a file randomly is not easy, especially when the file is large and the portions to be read are located close to the end of the file. The system has to start from the first stored block of the file and follow the link to read the next block and so on until the desired block is reached. Due to seek time, the average disk access time is high and so results in a slow process. Despite these problems, there is one major advantage to this method. As opposed to contiguous allocation, chained allocation does not produce external fragmentation.

Indexed allocation

Based on the **indexed allocation** method, the data area of the disk (or partition) is split into equal size blocks (i.e., block frames). The size of a block (or **cluster**) is a power of two of the sector size. Therefore, 512 bytes, 1K, 2K ..., are acceptable sizes. Usually, if the size of a partition is larger, the size of the block is larger too and vice versa. Files and directories are also split into equal size blocks. Blocks of files and disks are the same size. Each block of a file (or directory) can be stored in each available block frame of the disk. A table, called **index table**, will make note of which block is stored where and uses disk block numbers instead of the physical address of the block. Knowing the block number the file system can compute the actual address of a block by knowing the beginning address of the data area and the size of each block. However, address is expressed by the sector numbers.

Two different approaches are used in indexed allocation. In the first approach, there is a different index table for each file (or directory). Each table is a one dimensional array in which the row number corresponds to the file's block number in which is stored the disk block number holding that block. Figure 10.5 is a sample index table which belongs to a file that is four blocks long. Block number zero is stored in block number four of the disk partition; block number one of the file is stored in block number seven of the partition, block number two in three, and block number three in nine. **UNIX** adopts this approach in its **UFS File System**.

4
7
3
9

Figure 10.5: An index table for a file of four blocks

In the second approach, one large table represents the disk partition's status. All information about all files storage location is stored within this table. The partition's block number that holds the first block number of each file is externally identifiable by the file system. From there, other location information is found within the table. Information concerning the storage location of a file is linked together producing a liked list within the partition's status array. This approach is adopted by **FAT16** and **FAT32** of the Windows operating system. Figure 10.6 presents a very small version of such an index table. In this table, the storage information of the file discussed earlier is shown. The pointer points to block number four which holds the first block of the file; row four points to row seven which holds the second block of the file and so on. The partition has 10 blocks. if there are say *n* files (and directories) on this partition there would be *n* lists organized within the table. Each block has its own head and termination.

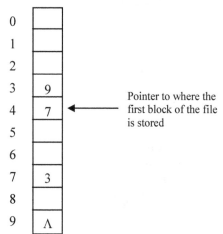

Figure 10.6: Partition's block table with one file's linked list

Indexed allocation is the most common method because of its advantages. There is no external fragmentation. There is no need for defragmentation unless an increase in efficiency of the file system is desired with respect to average access time. The index table is, at least, partially, kept in the main memory thus rendering both sequential and random access to files and directories efficient.

To store a file or directory, the available locations of the destination device must be known. Efficient management of free disk space greatly affects the overall efficiency of the device. The next topic addresses the investigation and presentation of free space management methods.

10.2 Free space management

To allocate storage space to files and directories, first one must know if there is adequate available space. Second, the exact locations of the required space must be identified. Following is a discussion of some general **free space management** approaches. Of course, not all approaches are applicable to all file systems. For each file system, usually one of the free space management approaches is appropriate.

Chained free pieces

With the **chained free pieces** approach, a linked list of free pieces is made and kept updated to reflect the current state of the storage device. The size of each piece is an integer multiple of the block size. A pointer will point to the beginning of the list. The list is formed either within the free pieces or outside of the pieces. In the former, the list pointer will point to the first piece of free space. The first two locations of this free space will represent the size of the piece and the pointer to the next free piece. The next free piece represents similar information. The pointer of the last free piece is null. In the latter technique, a linked list is formed outside the free pieces. Here, the pointer points to the first node. Within each node there are three fields. The first field provides the beginning address of the corresponding piece of free storage. The second field is the size of this piece and the third is a pointer to the next node of the list. An addition and deletion from the list starts from where the pointer points and continues until a qualified piece is found or until the list is completely scanned.

This method is general and can be used in almost all space allocation approaches. In storage allocation methods in which free pieces are not the same size, there is a disadvantage to this approach in that the pieces at the beginning part of the list gradually become small. In the future, this will require more time to be spent in finding a qualified pieces.

Bitmap

The **bitmap** approach to free space management relies on block size, which is the logical unit of reading and writing secondary storage data and each file or directory occupies an integer number of blocks. The size of blocks of a partition is the same. Each device is an ordered set of blocks. A bitmap is an array of bits of length n, where n is the total number of blocks of the device. Each bit represents the status of its corresponding block. If a block is free the corresponding bit is zero. Otherwise, it is one. The advantage of this approach is that the total size of a bitmap is small and, hence, it can be kept completely in the main memory. For example, if the partition size is 2^{32} blocks and every block is 64K, then the total capacity of the partition is $2^6 * 2^{10} * 2^{32} = 2^{48}$ bytes, which adds up to 256 tera bytes. For this size of partition, a bitmap of size $2^{32}/2^3 = 2^{29}$ bytes, or 512 mega bytes, is sufficient. With this approach we can look for both free blocks and also different size pieces of free storage. In the latter, the system searches for multiple adjacent free blocks, i.e., multiple adjacent zeros in the bitmap array.

Index table

With the **index table** approach, information about free pieces of storage is kept in a table. The information for each piece of free space occupies one row of the table. The size of this table can vary to reflect the current number of free pieces. Although, in theory, the size of this table can be very large, in practice, it is usually small and manageable.

10.3 Bad block management

A hard disk is accessed billions of times during its life time. Considering both mechanical movements and electronic actions, it is unreasonable to assume that no faults will occur during this time. Although some faults might render a disk unusable, most faults are tolerable. Bad sectors, when recognized, can be put aside and no longer used in the future. Actually, a block with a bad sector can be set aside. In this section, different approaches for handling bad sectors are discussed.

Substitute sectors

There are some reserved sectors for each track of a disk. During disk production, if bad sectors are recognized, they are substituted by reserved sectors. Reserved sectors are placed in different cylinders and tracks to make the substitution efficient. In a sector substitution table, the disk controller will make a note of the substitutions made. Substitution can also take place during disk operations. The controller is independent of the file system but, in disk operations, the substitution decision is made in concert with the operating system. It is clear that, if a sector has been fault-free but has become faulty, it may not be possible to properly recover its contents, thus resulting in loss of information. Therefore, the system pays more attention to recovering the file system after a fault occurs than to recovering a file. Consequently, when there are too many bad sectors on a disk, the disk will be deemed unusable.

File of bad blocks

A file occupies some blocks of secondary storage. The file system guarantees these blocks will not be assigned to any other directory or file. Therefore, the system may make a file of bad blocks. This file does not have any usable information but encompasses all bad blocks of the disk (or partition). The size of this file is dynamic and may grow as time passes. Recognition of bad sectors, and, hence, bad blocks, is performed in close collaboration with hardware and the operating system. One disadvantage of this approach is that the file of bad blocks must be hidden from all software applications, especially ones dedicated to the backup operations. This may make matters a little complicated.

With this approach however, the possibility of bad sectors existing during disk manufacturing cannot be ruled out. Therefore, substitute sectors and the file of bad blocks do not exclude each other.

10.4 Directory tree

It is usually the case that the contents of a book are organized and presented in the table of contents located at the beginning of the book. A table of contents outlines what subjects are covered and in what sections. Using the table of contents, it is easy to find the page number of where certain subjects are covered. Similarly, there is a tree structure for files and directories stored in a disk (partition or **volume**). A tree has a root and some sub-trees. Figure 10.7 shows a directory tree of a volume. This tree presents how the eight directories, Root, A, B, C, X, W, S, and R and five files D, P, Q, L, and K are logically organized in the volume. The root of the tree is usually represented by "/" or "\". However, the root does not have any stored name in the file system for itself.

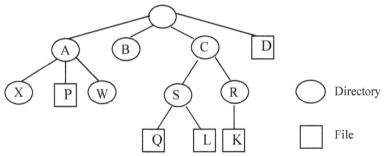

Figure 10.7: A tree of directories and files of a volume

It is clear that the tree in Figure 10.7 is not a single directory, but rather a directory tree composed of eight directories and five files. The visual representation of a directory tree is sufficient for us to grasp the organization. However, it is not suitable for implementation by an operating system. Therefore, it is better to observe the way file systems implement directories by investigating actual case studies.

Three types of information are noteworthy for files: (1) file name, (2) file attributes, and (3) file data. It is obvious that every file has to have a name. The name acts as the identity of the file and obviously distinguishes different objects from each other. Naming requires regulations. Although it is not discussed here, this does not mean they do not exist. Regulations not only vary from file system to file system but they also vary from version to version. For example, one regulation may be that the length of a file name cannot be greater than 255.

The creation date of a file, its current size, the date it was last modified, etc. are the file's attributes. These attributes have to be stored somewhere as part of the file system. If a file is, for example, a letter to a friend, then the contents of the file is what is written in the letter (i.e., sentences and punctuations). The name and attributes of a file are collectively called the file's **metadata**. Therefore, a file is composed of data and metadata. What can we say about directories? Similar to a file, a directory (or **folder**) has a creation date, a current size, and the date it was last modified. Except for the root directory, directories also have names. This information is the metadata of a directory. Traditionally, the root directory does not have a name. Instead, its storage location is known by the file system and so there is some way of identifying the root directory. A directory has data, too. The data show what files and subdirectories (subfolders) are within a given directory. For example, in Figure 10.7, subdirectories S and R are in Directory C. These are the data of Directory C. However, what is in Directories S and R is the concern of those directories not the concern of Directory C.

In order to make the discussion shorter, there are many topics related to file systems that will not be covered here. These topics are less technical and can be found in other texts. They include file types, file naming, access methods, file operations, directory operations, file sharing, information consistency, reliability, security, and protection. The rest of this chapter studies the design and implementation of two major file systems.

10.5 UNIX File System

The UNIX operating system is, on the one hand, expertly designed but, on the other hand, it is also very practical. From the historical point of view, it can be considered one of the oldest operating systems. Historically, it ranks after the **THE operating system** and the **Multics operating system**. UNIX has been the foundation of many contemporary operating systems especially because of its professional design and its earlier versions being open source. UNIX, itself, has evolved through the years and today it has many versions. However, the differences among their file systems are not fundamental. An attempt will be made to present the core of the **UNIX File System** design and implementation which are common to all versions. Later, two of UNIX's improvements will be discussed. Under UNIX in each disk partition, there are four logical areas, as shown in Figure 10.8.

Boot block	Superblock	i-node list	Data blocks

Figure 10.8: Four different logical areas of a disk partition

The first area is for the boot block, and the second area is dedicated to the partition's metadata. In the second area, information such as partition's size, block size, the number of i-nodes, total number of free blocks, and the pointer to the list of free blocks is stored. Block size is a power of two times 512 bytes which is assumed to be 1K for the rest of this section. Indexed allocation is used to allocate available blocks to file and directory data. Every file or directory has its own index table. The index table is a special one called index-node (or i-node for short). The third logical area is for all i-nodes. The length of all i-nodes is the same, usually 64 bytes and the total number of i-nodes is fixed for a given partition. This number is the upper bound for the total number of directories and files that can be stored in this partition. If we assume this limit is 1024, then the space requirement for this area is 64*1024 bytes or 64 kilo bytes. Starting from the beginning of this area, i-nodes are numbered from 1 to k, where k is the total number of i-nodes in this partition.

I-node number 1 is the index node of the root directory. As soon as the computer is turned on the first partition of the main disk is active and its root directory becomes the current directory. In other words, the main partition's root directory is moved to the main memory. A brief list of information that is kept in each i-node is given in Table 10.1.

Table 10.1: List of information stored in each i-node

File mode	Flags for file type, execution, owner permissions, Group permissions, and other permissions
Link count	Number of links to this i-node
OwnerID	ID of the owner
GroupID	ID of the group of the owner of this file
File size	File size in bytes
Last accessed	Time of last access
Last modified	Time of last modification
Inode modified	Time of last i-node modification

Direct addresses	Ten direct addresses
Single indirect addresses	Pointer to a block of addresses
Double indirect addresses	Pointer to a block of addresses
Triple indirect addresses	Pointer to a block of addresses

There are two sets of metadata in Table 10.1. The first set is file or directory attributes, except for, its name and i-node number. These attributes are: 16 access related flags, the number of pointers to this i-node, the owner's identification, the owner group's identification, the file size in bytes, the time last accessed, the time last modified, and the time the i-node was last modified. The second set of metadata in the i-node consists of thirteen direct and indirect pointers to data locations. There are 10 direct pointers (that are actually 10 block numbers) to the first 10 blocks of file's data location.

There is one indirect pointer to a block of pointers. This block will contain 256 four-byte long pointers to actual data storage blocks. The location of this block of pointers is not within the i-node but it is taken from the data area of the partition. It contains parts of file's metadata, i.e., these 256 pointers are metadata. The single indirect pointer will be used if the size of the file is more than 10 blocks, i.e., when the ten direct pointers do not suffice.

The next pointer is a double indirect pointer. The contents of this pointer are valid if the size of the file is more than $10+256=266$ blocks. If so, it points to a block of 256 pointers. Each pointer in this block points to a block of 256 new pointers. Each of the final pointers points to a data block.

The next pointer is a triple indirect pointer. The contents of this pointer are valid if the size of the file is more than $10+256+256*256=65802$ blocks. If so, it points to a block of 256 pointers. Each pointer in this block points to a block of 256 pointers. Each pointer in these blocks points to a block of 256 pointers. Each of the final pointers points to a data block.

The length of each of the thirteen pointers within an i-node, i.e., ten direct pointers, the single indirect pointer, the double indirect pointer, and the triple indirect pointer, is three bytes for the i-node of size 64 bytes. The length of pointers in pointer blocks is for bytes each.

With this way of addressing data blocks, a file or directory can be at the most $10+256+256*256+256*256*256=16843018$ blocks. This maximum size calculates to 16Giga+64Mega+266K bytes. It is worth reminding that, here, block size is taken to be one kilo byte. For a bigger block size, this method can handle higher capacity disks.

In Figure 10.9, the structure of the i-node and pointer blocks of a very large file is shown. Depending on the size of the file, some parts of this structure may not be used. For example, if the size of a file is up to 10K bytes, neither of the indirect pointers will be used. However, if the size of a file is 11K, the first indirect pointer will be used. It will point to a block of 256 pointers out of which only the first pointer will be used. It will point to a data block which is used to store the eleventh block of data of the file.

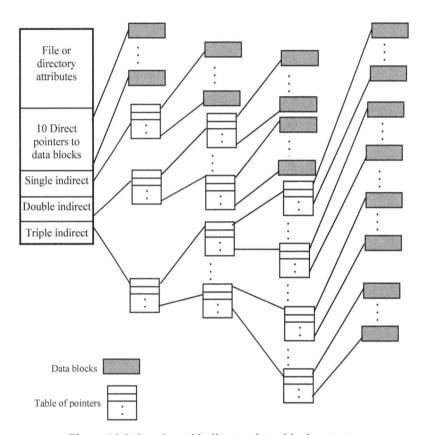

Figure 10.9: I-node and indirect pointer blocks structure

We now turn our attention to a different subject. What is the data of a directory?

A directory's data is the names of files and subdirectories within this directory. A folder can contain other folders and files. The contents of these folders and files are not of interest here, only their names. Another noteworthy piece of information is the i-node number of each of these files and directories. The i-node number is the key to finding a file's or directory's attribute, storage location, and its data. The third and last piece of information amongst a directory's data is the i-node number of this directory's father (i.e., its super-directory) and this directory's i-node number. These are useful for the implementation of some directory operations, such as the make directory and the remove directory. This way of implementing directories reflects a special tree structure of a partition's files and directories in which both father-son and son-father relations are materialized. The root directory is the only directory without any ancestor, instead of its father's i-node number the root directory's own i-node number is used. See Figure 10.10.

1	.
1	..
5	A
8	B
6	C
4	D

(a) **Root directory's data of Figure 10.7**

6	.
1	..
12	S
9	R

(b) **Directory C's data of Figure 10.7**

Figure 10.10: Structure and data of directories

In the following discussion, the question of how to locate the data of a file or directory is answered.

Based on Figure 10.7, we can ask how can the file Q's data storage location be found? Knowing what its current directory and i-node are, the operating system goes to this i-node and locates Q and its i-node number. Thus, the key to file Q's data is found. Suppose file Q's i-node must be located, it is not in the current directory but its absolute path is given: /C/S/Q. The file system will access i-node number 1, which is the root directory's i-node, and search for the root's data location. Using this data (Figure 10.10a) the file system looks for C and its i-node number which is six. Using i-node number six the file system looks for directory C's data block. In this databblock (Figure 10.10b) the file system looks for S and its i-node number and it continues this process until Q's i-node number is found. Then, from this i-node number the file system searches for Q's data storage blocks.

It is worth mentioning that contemporary **Graphic User Interfaces** (GUI) are user friendly and directory operations are performed by few clicks of the mouse. However, what is actually done by the file system is the same whether the requests are made via a graphic user interface or a **Command-based User Interface** (CUI). For example, the file system performs the same action by either double clicking a folder in a GUI environment or by typing "dir" and pressing the enter key in a CUI environment.

10.5.1 UNIX file system improvements

Two attempts for improving UNIX file system performance has resulted in two improved versions, the Berkeley **Fast File System** (FFS) and the **UNIX File System 2** (UFS2). We will briefly introduce these improvements.

Fast file system

In the Berkeley's Fast File System (FFS) block size is larger. Thus accessing a directory's or file's data is faster because the number of seek times is usually less than that of the original file system. Of course, this method increases internal fragmentation. **Internal fragmentation** is due to file or directory sizes not being integer multiples of the block size. Therefore, the last block of a file or directory may not be completely filled, hence, causing internal fragmentation. In FFS, to decrease internal fragmentation, a data block is divided into a number of equal size fragments (often eight). These fragments can be independently assigned to files and directories. Usually, not all the fragments are assigned to one file or directory. Since UNIX frequently has many small files and directories, most of the time these are placed in the fragments left over by larger directories and files. It is worth mentioning that only the last block of each file or directory may be broken into fragments. In order to know which of the fragments of the last data block assigned to a file or directory are used by them, in the file's or directory's i-node eight bits are reserved for this purpose. If a bit is set to one, the corresponding fragment is used by the file or directory, otherwise, it is not. Since internal fragmentation takes place when the last data block is not completely used, this approach uses the leftovers of the last data block of files and directories, hence decreases internal fragmentation.

> The Linux file system, called EXT, is designed based on the Berkeley Fast File System (FFS). However, it is not exactly the same as FFS. One of the interesting points about the Linux operating system is that its source is open, which makes modifications possible. Therefore, the Linux file system has different versions.
>
> Linux supports many other file systems. During installation, a different file system may be introduced. The system will be generated to be able to use the specified file system.

A second innovative feature of FFS is its enhancement of access time through better organization of i-nodes. Data blocks of a file or directory are stored in cylinders that are placed as close as possible to each other. A number of adjacent cylinders are called a cylinder group. The i-node of a file or directory, i.e., blocks of pointers, is stored in the same cylinder group. Using this technique, disk head movements are reduced thus raising overall performance. Beside this, data blocks of directories are distributed across the whole disk's data area so that a directory's data blocks are close to its files data blocks. Furthermore, a file's and directory's i-node, i.e., blocks of pointers, is stored as close as possible to the file's or directory's data blocks.

A third improvement, for recovery purposes, is that the Berkeley FFS has two superblocks instead of one. If one of the superblocks becomes faulty the system immediately switches to the other and commences to a new superblock to replace the faulty one. Superblock is an important part of a UNIX file system and contains fatal metadata such as partition size, the current number of free blocks, the list of free blocks, and different flags and pointers.

Another FFS enhancement is the increase in the file name's length. In UNIX, the maximum length of a file (or directory) is 14. The length of an i-node number is two bytes. Therefore, the length of each row of a directory's data table is 16 bytes. With its longer length, the name of a file or directory can be up to 255 characters.

The last FFS improvement of note is its two different block sizes, for example, 4K and 8K. These sizes are stored in the superblock. For small size files (or directories), the first block size is used and for large size files there is the second block size.

It should be understood that FFS improvements dramatically increase the complexity of the file system implementation.

The Fast File System can be used with both the UNIX File System and UNIX File System 2. The latter is discussed next.

UNIX File System 2

UNIX File System 2 (UFS2) is an improved version of UFS1, i.e., UFS. The differences between the two are highlighted here.

Pointers to USF2 data blocks are eight bytes long. In USF1 its thirteen direct pointers within the i-node are each three bytes long and the other pointers are each four bytes long. With the eight-byte (64 bits) length of UFS2's pointers a one tera byte file can be stored.

In UFS2, the size of each i-node is 256 bytes which is four times the size of each i-node in UFS1. With such large i-node, USF2 can store more file or directory attributes.

Another improvement of UFS2 is its assignment of free blocks to files and directories. In allocating these free blocks, usually a few bunch of consecutive blocks are assigned, simultaneously. For example, for a 100K-size file a bunch of eight consecutive blocks, a bunch of ten consecutive blocks, a bunch of consisting one block, and a bunch of six consecutive blocks may all be assigned. If the size of a block is 4K, the total space that is assigned to this file is 100K. For this file, instead of having 25 pointers each pointing to the file's one block of data, in USF2 four pointers would be sufficient. Each pointer points to the first block of a bunch of blocks. For every pointer, there is another field which specifies the size of the bunch expressed by the number of its consecutive blocks in the bunch.

10.6 NTFS File System

Another popular file system is the **New Technology File System** (NTFS) which was developed by the Microsoft Corporation. This file system is commonly used in Windows operating systems. NTFS offers new capabilities that are not found in previous generations of Microsoft file systems such as FAT16 and FAT32. With vast capabilities comes more complexity. However, since not all aspects of this file system can be covered here its significant design and implementation techniques will be presented instead, starting with a brief description of its capabilities.

10.6.1 NTFS objectives and properties

NTFS is a new generation file system which is designed for the age of information technology and the following objectives.

Supporting a wide range of systems

NTFS has many versions each installable on different computing systems such as powerful servers, workstations, and personal computers. NTFS is capable of simultaneously handling numerous different requests by different users and programs. It can also manage a large volume of storage.

Recoverability

File system recovery is an action that has to be taken after a fault or failure occurs. Recoverability is another objective of NTFS. In very complex systems such as a server, since fault and failure of either a transient or a permanent nature is inevitable the system must be armed to cope with such situations. The goal is to recover without losing any persistent information existing prior to the fault or failure. File system information is much more critical than a file's or directory's information. Loosing a file system means loosing all files and directories. Therefore, the system must be able to recover from any fault or failure occurred in the file system. A file system without this ability should not be used in any sensitive application.

Transaction is a central issue in any recovery system. A transaction is a unit of work which either must be executed to the end or does not have any effect on the file system, files, or directories. If a system has the capability of recovery, any changes made to the file system (including its files and directories) are considered a transaction. Although, the transaction concept appears simple, from the implementation point of view transaction poses a new complex issue. Redundant data storage, events logging, and file system modification logging are all essential for the recovery subsystem.

Security and protection

Authentication, **security**, and **protection** are all important issues dealt with by NTFS. In NTFS, everything such as directories, files, metadata, and bitmaps are considered as files and every file is considered an object. To access an object, one must have the required rights.

One method of finding other people's critical information such as username, password, and salary is to perform a blind search into storage areas that are assigned based upon an authorized user request. If the assigned storage areas are not cleared beforehand, valuable information belonging to the previous user may be divulged. NTFS clears all allocated clusters before handing them over to the new user. There are many issues like this that must be considered in a secure system. Windows security is based on the Department of Defense Orange Book which is designed for military environments.

One way for preventing a user from accessing other user's information is encryption. Windows provides the capability to encrypt file information upon the user's request. For this purpose, it uses a well known method called the Data Encryption Standard (DES). Based on DES, only a user with a private key is able to decrypt enciphered information and observe the plain information.

Very large files

With NTFS, disk addresses are 64 bits long. Theoretically, a file can be as large as 2^{64} bytes, which is around one million tera bytes. In the previous Windows file system, FAT32, addresses are 32 bits, thus, a file can be as large as two tera bytes. In the calculation of the maximum size, the address of sectors on the disk, i.e., sector number, is at the most 32 bits long. Therefore, $2^{32}*2^9=2^{41}=2$ tera bytes. In the FAT16 file system, addresses are 16 bits, bringing the maximum size of a file to 2^{16} blocks or 2 giga bytes, for the block of size 32K. Here, the restricting parameter is block size not sector number.

10.6.2 NTFS general design

Before investigating the design of the NTFS file system a few concepts and terms should be defined.

Cluster

In NTFS, the cluster is the secondary storage allocation unit. A **cluster** is a power of two sectors. The smallest size of a cluster is one sector (i.e., 512 bytes) and the largest size cluster is 128 sectors (i.e., 64 kilo bytes). The actual size of a cluster is a function of the size of the partition (actually, the size of a volume to be defined later.) A cluster is the corresponding term to a block in UNIX. Table 10.2 shows the size of a cluster with respect to the size of a volume.

Table 10.2: The size of cluster based on the size of a volume

Volume size	Cluster size
Volume size $\leq$ 512M bytes	512 bytes
512M bytes < Volume size $\leq$ 1G bytes	1K
1G bytes < Volume size $\leq$ 2G bytes	2K
2G bytes < Volume size $\leq$ 4G bytes	4K
4G bytes < Volume size $\leq$ 8G bytes	8K
8G bytes < Volume size $\leq$ 16G bytes	16K
16G bytes < Volume size $\leq$ 32G sbyte	32K
32G bytes < Volume size	64K

Volume

A collection of clusters for which a file system is used is called a **volume**. Volume can be considered the file system unit. A volume can be part of a disk, a complete disk, or a set of parts of many disks. The maximum size of a volume is 2^{64} bytes. From a logical point of view, four general sections are identified in a volume. See Figure 10.11.

Boot sector	Master file table	Recovery data	Attributes and data blocks

Figure 10.11: Four logical sections of a NTFS volume

Similar to UNIX File System, NTFS implements directories and files the same way. Therefore, in this discussion, file may mean a file or directory. Every file consists of a name, attributes, and data. However, in NTFS, name, attributes, and data are all called attributes. In order to be consistent with other parts of this book, these distinctions will be recognized and should not create conflicts in this presentation. Some general background on boot sectors, attributes, and data clusters are included. With respect to previous information provided, this background will be sufficient for understanding these structures. To thoroughly explain recovery, a whole new chapter would be needed. However, for this book's purpose, the types of information needed for recovery will be presented. We will focus on the **Master File Table** (MFT).

Boot sector

In every volume, one operating system can be installed and each operating system requires a boot sector. The first section of a volume is dedicated to the boot sector. The size of this section is one sector or 512 bytes. This sector is mainly a small machine language program. The rest of the space is occupied by some very essential metadata of the volume like, the number of bytes per sector, the number of sectors per cluster, disk type (floppy, hard), the number of sectors per record, the location of master file tables, disk identification, and whether the volume is bootable or not. The first part of a volume is sometimes called the Master Boot Record (MBR) in 32-bit computers or the GUID (Globally Unique Identifier) Partition Table (GPT) in 64-bit computers.

Master file table

Master file table is a stored table of information on how to find files and directories attributes and data. It serves the same purpose as i-node does for UNIX operating system. In a master file table, there is at least one record for each file (or directory) of the volume. Thus, this table is of variable size. MFT is itself a record-based file with each record holding exactly one kilo byte. These records store the file's metadata. A file's entire metadata may not fit in one record. In such case, extra records, called extended records, are allocated. The first MFT record of each file is the base record. A pointer from the base record points to the extended record, if there is one.

A file's metadata includes the file name (which is maximum 255 characters), file attributes, and the file's data location. Therefore, if a file is large, its metadata will require many MFT records. The metadata of a file can occupy at least one MFT record and, at the most, 2^{48} records.

The name of some file's attributes are: file name, security descriptor, attribute list (the list of other MFT records used to store a file's metadata), volume name, volume information, and file data locations. Note that not all attribute names are applicable to all kinds of files.

The first sixteen records of the master file table (records 0 to 15) are reserved for sixteen essential file system files. The contents of these files are the metadata of the file system itself that did not fit in the boot sector of the volume. The name of each of these files starts with character $, the fist one being $Mft. This file belongs to the master file table itself. For example, the fifth file is for the legal attribute names of files and directories and the sixth file is for the root directory of the volume. Once again, root directory does not have a name instead, its location is fixed within the MFT. In Figure 10.12, the names and short descriptions of the first thirteen system files are given.

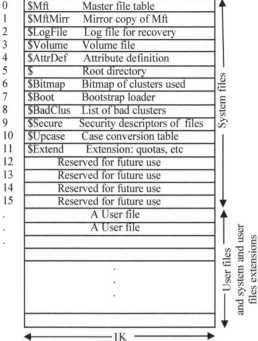

0	$Mft	Master file table
1	$MftMirr	Mirror copy of Mft
2	$LogFile	Log file for recovery
3	$Volume	Volume file
4	$AttrDef	Attribute definition
5	$	Root directory
6	$Bitmap	Bitmap of clusters used
7	$Boot	Bootstrap loader
8	$BadClus	List of bad clusters
9	$Secure	Security descriptors of files
10	$Upcase	Case conversion table
11	$Extend	Extension: quotas, etc
12	Reserved for future use	
13	Reserved for future use	
14	Reserved for future use	
15	Reserved for future use	

Figure 10.12: MFT records with the emphasis on the system files

As briefly mentioned, not all attributes of all files and directories are the same. For example, volume name is only applicable in the $volume file. Therefore, before giving an attribute value, the name of the attribute must be mentioned.

In Figure 10.12, the first record of the metadata of each file is given. Each file may occupy up to 2^{48} records of this table depending on the size of its metadata and data. Record numbers are located at the left side of the table.

Figure 10.13 provides the general sections of a MFT file.

Some metadata	Other MFT records for this file	File data clusters	Unused

Figure 10.13: Different sections of a MFT record

Shown in Figure 10.13 is the MFT base record's logical structure. Other records (i.e., extended records) have different structures. Generally speaking, the base record and all extended records of a file act like the i-node and extended data blocks of pointers of a file in the UNIX File System. There, if the i-node number is known, the file's attributes and data are accessible. In NTFS, if the record number of the base record of a file is known the file or directory, i.e., MFT record number, is accessible.

Recovery data

This section's information applies when a fault or failure has occurred and some metadata needed to access files of directories are lost. The reconstruction of this metadata is possible by using **recovery data.** The most important recovery data is the copy of the master file table. Some sample recovery information is copies of records 0, 1, and 2 of MFT, the bitmap of occupied clusters of the volume's data location, the table of attribute types, and recovery log file records showing the actions taken against the file system information. This last piece of information enables the redoing or undoing actions in order to bring the system back to a consistent state, after a fault has occured.

Data clusters

This section presents the collection of all clusters that are used to store file or directory data. Clusters are the same size and its common size can be calculated using Table 10.2. For example, if the total size of the volume is 20 giga bytes, then the size of a cluster is 32 kilo bytes.

10.6.3 Detailed design of NTFS

In this section, the method that is used to record all data clusters which are used to store file or directory information in base or extended MFT file records is discussed.

Base and extended MFT records of a file

Suppose that a file's data is stored in cluster numbers 501, 502, 503, 585, 586, 587, 588, 589, 621, 622, 623, 624, 625, 674, 675, 676, 677, 678, 690, and 691. The question posed is how this information is stored in the file's base and extended MFT records. If each set of adjacent clusters is called a bunch, then this file's clusters will form five bunches: 501 to 503, 585 to 589, 621 to 625, 674 to 678, and 690 to 691. To introduce a more complex situation, suppose that two MFT records are needed to save the attributes of this file. The first record is the base record with record number 125 and the second one is an extended record with record number 482. Roughly speaking, the information shown in Figure 10.14a is stored in the base record of this file and the information in Figure 10.14b is stored in the extended record of this file.

Headers and file attributes	Header	482	Header	501	3	583	5	621	5

(a) Record number 125 of the MFT file

Headers	674	4	690	2	Free space

(b) Record number 482 of the MFT file

Figure 10.14: A files attributes and storage clusters

As shown in Figure 10.14, besides the name, different headers are added by the system to distinguish different information classes within the file's base MFT record and to also facilitate fast access to the file's data storage locations. After this, MFT record numbers that are used as the file's extended MFT records are stored. Following MFT record numbers, another header is stored and then the information of all pairs of data cluster bunches are stored. For example, the pair 501, 3 indicates a bunch of three clusters which starts with cluster number 501. The remaining pairs are stored in the extended record. If one extended record is not enough, then extra records are allocated. The record numbers of all extended records have to be stored in the base record (or its extensions) before the actual data location pairs.

Accessing a file and its data

In order to discuss the details of how to reach a file's data locations, suppose Figure 10.7 is the structure of the files and directories of the specific volume in which file K's data is to be located. The absolute path of the file is /C/R/K. The root directory of this volume is stored in record number 5 of MFT. This record is read and it is noted that root's data are stored in say cluster number 950 of the volume. Cluster number 950 is accessed. The information stored in this cluster is the names and base MFT records of the root directory's files and directories. From amongst the files and directories, C is located. Since there usually are many files and directories within a given

A B+ tree is a method for organizing information so it can be accesses by fast searches. The actual information is stored in the leaf nodes of the B+ tree. The root node and other nodes from the root to a leaf are all indexes to guide the search algorithm to the desired information. In contrast to binary trees whose node can have, at the most, two subtrees, a B+ tree's node can have a maximum of m subtrees. The larger m, the smaller the depth of the tree will be. The search time is proportional to the length of the path from the root to the required information, which is, at the most, equal to the depth of the tree. With the B+ tree structure, insert and delete operations are performed efficiently.

directory, a sequential search to find a file or a directory is not recommended as it may take a long time. Instead, a B+ search is performed. In order to facilitate this, the names of large directories have to be organized as a B+ tree. However, for small directories a linear list of names is used. Suppose then that C has been found and its base MFT record is 125. This record is accessed. Just as C was searched for, so R is looked for. Remember that record 5 is replaced by 125 and C is replaced by R. Now assume that record number 85 is the base MFT record for R. Now, K must be found. Suppose this is done and the base MFT record 94 is extracted for file K. From this base record and its extensions, all metadata and data of file K can be located.

10.7 Summary

Caches and main memories lose their contents as soon as the computer is turned off. We must store persistent information on persistent devices. The well thought out organization of information in secondary storage, especially in light of its vastness, is extremely crucial. This responsibility lies with what is usually called the file system. Many file systems have been developed to address this task. In this chapter, the design foundation of file systems was studied. The design details of two major file systems, the UNIX File System, and the New Technology File System, were thoroughly investigated. Other aspects of file system such as recovery and encryption were not of our interest. Interested readers could follow these subjects in specific books of related file systems.

10.8 Problems

1. In a file system similar to the UNIX File System, the block size is 4 kilo bytes and i-node size is 64 bytes which includes file or directory attributes, seven direct addresses, one single indirect address, one double indirect address, and one triple indirect address. Block numbers are 4 bytes long. For the time being, the partition includes only the root directory with only one file and no subdirectory. However, the whole area of the data blocks is occupied. If the total capacity of the data block area is 128 giga bytes, what is the actual data size of the file?

2. What would your answer to Question One be if the NTFS File System is used? Use the actual NTFS file system properties for any information you might need.

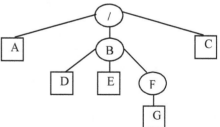

3. Under the UNIX operating system, the following directory tree is

given. The i-node numbers for the root, A, B, C, D, E, F, and G are 1, 2, 3, 4, 5, 6, 7, and 8, respectively. The size of every i-node is 64 bytes. Block size is one kilo byte which is also the disk read/write unit. The root is the current directory. We would like to read the whole file G which is 20 blocks large. How many disk reads must be performed? Suppose there can be at the most ten direct addresses in each i-node.

4. Solve Question Three for the NTFS File System. Use actual NTFS File System properties for any information you might need.

5. In a version of the UNIX File System, files, directories, bad blocks, free blocks, and other similar objects are implemented using i-nodes. In this file system somehow the i-node of free blocks is lost. Assuming that all else is fine, write an algorithm to rebuild this i-node. Provide a clear explanation of how free blocks are recognized.

6. In a certain UNIX File System, an i-node stores much information including: ten direct pointers, one single indirect pointer, one double indirect pointer, and one triple indirect pointer

   a. What other information is stored in an i-node?

   b. Explain why the name of all files and subdirectories of a directory should not be stored within the i-node of that directory and they have to be stored in data blocks?

   c. If the block size is 512 bytes what is the maximum size of the file? Write out your assumptions.

6. In other textbooks, look for the algorithm for finding and fixing **inconsistencies** in the UNIX File System. Afterwards write your opinions about it.

8. Suppose that the total capacity of a partition is 1480 kilo bytes. In the UNIX File System, one kilo byte would be used for the boot sector and its copy and the maximum number of i-nodes would be 128. In addition, each i-node would be 64 bytes and the disk allocation unit (i.e., block size) would be one kilo byte. The following tree shows the current state of the directory, with the size of all three files a, b, and c being equal:

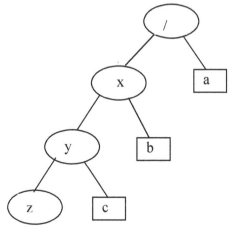

    a.   What is the maximum possible size of each of the files a, b, and c?

    b.   If files a, b, and c use up their maximum space, how much the external fragmentation would be?

    c.   If files a, b, and c use up the whole disk space, how much the internal fragmentation would be?

9. Solve Problem Eight for the NTFS File System. Use actual NTFS File System properties for any information you might need.

10. In a version of the UNIX File System, files, directories, bad blocks, free blocks, and other similar object are implemented using an i-node. In this system, somehow the whole superblock is lost. Assuming that all else is fine, write an algorithm to rebuild it. The information in the superblock is the size of a data block and the size of the partition. Assume the maximum number of i-nodes is fixed and the size of each i-node is 256 bytes.

11. Find out the differences between UNIX file system and Linux file system.

Recommended References

Basic knowledge about designing file systems can be found in [Har88, Gro86]. For complementary information on the UNIX File System, look in [Tho78]. The foundations of the Berkeley Fast File System is discussed in [McK84]. References [Naga97, Cus94] are usefull for the contemporary Windows File Systems. For security issues of file systems, see [Bel73].

Chapter 11

Operating System Categories

This chapter is dedicated to reviewing some concepts that are explained in previous chapters and some new concepts in the area of operating system categorization. We will try to mention ongoing research activities in newer fields of operating systems. This chapter will be kept short. Readers that are interested in the areas touched upon in this chapter are urged to refer to other specialized documents, some of which are listed in the "Recommended References" section of the chapter.

11.1 Software Technology and Operating Systems

Software development technology has advanced tremendously, especially during the last two decades. The development of the operating system, which is a gigantic and complex piece of software, has benefited very much from these advances. The operating system has changed from a monolithic nonstructural hard-to-follow source into a well structured modular software system. This trend is roughly described in the following pages.

11.1.1 Monolithic Operating Systems

A small noncomplex application can perhaps be developed in the form of one main program, or a main program and a collection of procedures. Each procedure can be called from the main program, and/or other procedures, without any structural limitations. Such a method of application development corresponds to the state of the art techniques in system development of the 1950s, before the structured programming era. Even now, one may decide to develop small applications using monolithic guidelines but not an application that is composed of millions of instructions as in contemporary operating systems. The operating systems of the early days were unstructured and thus were called **Monolithic**

Operating Systems. The advantages and disadvantages of monolithic operating systems compared to **structured operating systems** are similar to those of unstructured programs versus structured programs having in mind that oprating system is gigantic. In short, a monolithic operating system is difficult to debug, difficult to modify, difficult to substitute parts with new program sections, difficult to document, difficult to implement because of not being able to use many programming teams, etc. When applicable, however, monolithic kernels are efficient and fast. Any procedure can be called from anywhere within the kernel, without the need to observe any structure and/or hierarchy.

11.1.2 Structured Operating Systems

Writing huge software like operating system demands an organized mind and a well structured technique to analyze, design, and implement. The structured implementation of such software requires a structured programming language. Structured programming languages are designed to eliminate the difficulties in writing and supporting applications using spaghetti logic, or unstructured control, programming languages. A structured programming language is based on the philosophy of creating applications consisting of a number of modules interconnected in a manner to form a hierarchy of modules. Each low level module is recognized so that it performs one independent task. In order to prevent undesirable modification of these variables, a module is supposed to use local data and avoid using global data. Code reusability is achieved, to a certain degree, by the proper identification of modules for use in many other processes. Of interest are the many benefits of structured programming among which is the possibility of individually testing every module, of easily replacing every module, and of using well defined modules in many applications. Another more important benefit of structured programming is the capability of defining the interface of a module and assigning the development of the module to another programmer or group of programmers. This capability is very efficient in the development of huge programs like the operating system. In contrast to a monolithic operating system, a **Structured Operating Systems** has the aforementioned advantages. It is much easier to maintain and extend a structured operating system than a monolithic operating system. Operating systems are very frequently revised. It is usually the case that just after releasing a new version, or even before that, the work on the next version has already started.

11.1.3 Object-Oriented Operating Systems

Compared with structured programming, object-orientation is one step forward in the direction of program structuring and abstraction. In structured programming, little attention is paid to structuring data similar to that of structuring the control of the application. There, we emphasize that every module (or block) better rely on its local data and try not to use global data. In object-oriented programming, an object is composed of public data, private data, methods for manipulating data to perform proper functions, and implicit mechanisms for protecting private data from being manipulated by methods other than those within the object. The hiding of information is another aspect of object-oriented application development. By this we mean, the internal representation of data and algorithms that methods follow to perform the required functions which are not exposed to the application user. Objects better represent entities of the real world. Implementation of real applications becomes more natural. Objects can be used in many applications that deal with their corresponding real world entities. Therefore, code reusability, or object reusability, is extending. Objects modules are much more suitable for re-use in other applications than the modules of structured programming. Other benefits of **Object-Oriented Programming** (OOP) are the reduction of correctness verification efforts, the robustness of the application that is developed and the improved extensibility of the application. An **Object-Oriented Operating System** is designed and developed with object-orientation in mind and by using object-oriented programming tools and languages. As a result, object modification and replacement is simplified and better maintained. Presumably, the machine language translation of such an operating system will include all the necessary codes for private data protection and information hiding, all of which will make the code a little slower.

11.1.4 Agent-Oriented Operating Systems

Agent-Oriented Programming (AOP) is a new programming technique in which the concept "agent" plays a fundamental role. Let's suppose an agent is an encapsulated entity of code, data, and execution context that can be extended with the abilities to migrate autonomously, follow an aim to reach a goal, interact with other agents, react sophisticatedly to external events, autonomously decide what to do in response to changes in the environment, etc. Although agents are natural successors of objects in object-oriented programming, they are not direct extensions of objects. For example, the inheritance property of objects is not defined for an agent. Agent-oriented programming reveals new horizons for building a piece of software that is proactive and need not be activated by another process to do certain work. A set of agents can collectively cooperate to tackle a problem.

Agents have been used in operating systems since the UNIX operating system made use of a concept called **daemon**. A daemon is a process that listens to a communication port. When a request is received, the daemon processes it and performs the proper action. For example a daemon may be used to take care of telnet or ftp, i.e. file transfer protocol, file requests. Daemons are clearly reactive since they listen to communication ports to see whether something has arrived that they can react to. Daemons are autonomous because they do their tasks without the supervision of other processes. Some can be even social and communicate with the requester to clarify any confusion in the request.

There are other properties of agents, such as collaboration, intelligence, etc. The degree of agents varies from one entity to another depending on the type and number of properties that each one has. We could definitely say that an agent is a fuzzy term rather than a crisp one. In an **Agent-Oriented Operating System**, the system is designed using agent technology via an agent programming language. Such a system will have all the advantages and disadvantages of agent programming.

11.2 Acting Entities and Operating Systems

A **program** is a set of instructions that is prepared to do a specific job, if executed. The software entity that runs a program, by using a processor, may be a process, a thread, or an agent. This software entity has many properties like a location counter, stack pointers, current contents of registers, current status, etc. these are all properties of the acting entity, or the entity that runs a program. Note that we are not talking about a hardware entity, like a processor, but rather a software entity.

11.2.1 Process-Based Operating Systems

In a structured operating system, subsystems, modules, and procedures are interconnected so that the whole superstructure is capable of performing the duty of the operating system. Whatever superstructure is used during the analysis or the design of an operating system, a layered structure is usually used to extend the capabilities of the operating system, going from the lowest level, that is, the layer closest to the hardware, to the highest level, or the application level. In layered operating systems, higher layers are independent modules, each capable of performing a major managerial function. A well defined boundary separates the inner layers of the operating systems, where privileged instructions are allowed from the outer layers, where privileged instructions are forbidden. The inner layers are collectively called the kernel. The **kernel** may be a giant monolithic program or it could be a collection of modules each capable of performing one managerial function, plus a set of primitives that are used by many kernel modules, higher layer modules and, perhaps, user processes. The monolithic structuring of the kernel is a thing of the past and is no longer an acceptable method of kernel design. Therefore, for modern operating systems modules can be executed by "processes," "threads," or "agents."

A **process-based operating system** is an operating system in which the kernel is composed of a collection of processes, a collection of procedures, and a collection of primitives. Procedures and primitives are passive entities. However, every process or active entity, in such a system, is given a unique responsibility. This concept should not mean that, in a process-based operating system we cannot create threads. Rather, it clarifies the way we look at the operating system, for the purposes of design and implementation. In a process-based operating system the centre of attention is the process. We try to provide managerial rules and regulations for processes, process synchronization methods, process scheduling, process communication protocols, and so on.

11.2.2 Thread-Based Operating Systems

A **thread-base operating system** is an operating system in which kernel activities are performed by a set of threads. Each thread belongs to a process with a given responsibility. A single process may produce many threads to do similar or even different tasks. A kernel can still have many primitives with very low level functionalities. Every primitive could become part of many threads. By doing so, code reusability is achieved and kernel size is reduced. Threads are not only the active entities of the kernel, but they are also the only active entities of the outer parts of the operating system. The concept extends to application programs, too. When a new process or child process, is created, a primary thread is immediately created to do the job, or run the program, using one or more processors and other devices.

In a thread-based operating system, although a process is not an active entity, but it persists to exist. A process plays the role of a house where all threads, that are created based on the process, live within it. Since a primary thread is created right after a process is created, there are no empty houses, that is, processes with no thread. A hierarchy of parent-child processes is perfectly acceptable by thread-based operating systems and each process in this hierarchy can have one or more threads of its own. If there is no parent-child relation within the threads of a process, then all threads of that process are called **sibling threads**. Although there may be a parent-child relation between some threads of a process, some thread-based operating systems do not recognize this structure and treat all threads of a process as siblings.

All contemporary operating systems support the thread methodology and technique. It is the thinking backbone of the operating system's designer which makes an operating system process-based or thread-based. In a thread-based operating system, the thread is the only active object and the process is just the container for its threads. Procedures, routines, primitives, etc. are all a passive collection of instructions that are only useful when they become part of a threads and are executed with the thread execution. To summarize, for an operating system to be classified as a thread-based, the thread methodology must be well respected within the kernel. Newer Windows operating systems and its descendents are the most widely-used near thread-based operating systems.

11.2.3 Agent-Based Operating Systems

Agents have many exciting properties that can be utilized in **agent-based operating systems**. Think of an operating system whose essential duties are performed by a set of agents. The overall control of the operating system is distributed among these agents and there is no need for a central control module. Every agent does its duty without the need for another entity to tell it when and how to do it. An agent is intelligent in the sense that it can make proper decisions in response to new events that are sensed, or received, from the environment. Larger tasks are collectively carried out by many agents. To do so, they can intelligently communicate and decide how to perform such tasks. If it feels it is necessary, an agent is able to move from one computer to another. These abilities and many more make an agent an ideal acting entity for the implementation of operating systems. One disadvantage is the facilitation of every one of these properties as a substantial amount of source codes must be produced. Too many codes lead to the low overall performance of the system.

The inner part of the operating system, the kernel, is composed of a set of agents, in **Agent-Based Operating Systems** (ABOS). Procedures and primitives within the kernel are passive entities. Much ongoing research is in progress to efficiently develop agent-based operating systems. Similar to process-based and thread-based operating systems, we expect that an agent-based operating system to produce agents to run user programs. That is, when a user double clicks on a program icon, this kind of operating system will generate an agent to run the program. However, in current (experimental) agent-based operating systems process is generated instead. Even though agent-based operating systems are not currently popular, in the future these kind of operating systems will dominate and will take the responsibility of computer management.

11.3 Kernel Types of Operating Systems

In this section, kernels are categorized into three classes: macro-kernel (or simply, kernel), microkernel, and extensible kernel. Most general-purpose operating systems rely on regular kernels, that is, the macro-kernel. However, this trend may change in the near future to microkernels or even extensible kernels. Microkernels are being used in multiprocessor computers and/or distributed systems. A brief introduction of kernel types follows.

11.3.1 Macro-kernel Operating Systems

Although in some literature the phrases "macro-kernel" and "monolithic kernel" are used interchangeably, I would like to distinguish between the magnitude and the structure of operating system kernels. In regards to this viewpoint, when we talk about the **macro-kernel** we are focusing on its size and how much code and functionality it is composed of. Most functions of the operating system are implemented within the kernel, in a macrokernel operating system. The layer above the kernel is usually a shell, which receives the commands, interprets them, interacts with users if necessary, and passes the command to the kernel for processing. Linux is a macro-kernel operating system. All essential managers, including the process manager, memory manager, scheduler, information manager (file system), communication manager, etc. are parts of the Linux kernel. The ability to use all machine instructions including privileged ones within the kernel can be an advantage when implementing an efficient kernel. The macro-kernel is not usable in multiprocessor systems in which the management of only local resources, like cache and read/write memory, is performed locally. It is not possible to install a gigantic-size kernel in every processor's local memory because most kernel functions will not be usable.

Most embedded systems require a minimal operating system and the main functionality is achieved through special-purpose software. Airplane control systems, medical digital systems, and robot control systems are some of the systems with an embedded computer-based system. For these kinds of systems, a macro-kernel operating system is not appropriate. Large central computers, which are either single processor or multiprocessor with minimal local resources, are best suitable for macro-kernel operating systems.

11.3.2 Microkernel Operating Systems

Some special purpose computers may run without an operating system. As soon as this kind of computer starts or restarts, it begins running a stored program in its read-only memory. As there is no operating system in this kind of computer, there is no kernel either. On the other hand, in some commercial computers, the operating system may be huge with extensive functionality and ease of use. If the kernel of such a computer encompasses most of the functionality of the operating system, it will be huge in size. The kernel size of an operating system can vary from zero to the overall size of the operating system. In the previous subsection, we talked about macro-kernels, or large size kernels. In this section, we discuss the microkernel, or small size kernels.

The **microkernel** philosophy aims at defining a thin abstraction layer on top of the computer hardware. This layer consists of a set of primitives, a set of procedures and a set of processes, or threads, depending on whether the operating system is process-based or thread-based. Some essential tasks are not possible to move out of the kernel area. We keep these tasks within the kernel, for example, guaranteeing the atomic execution of some program sections in order to achieve mutual exclusion and using the disable interrupt/enable interrupt possibility. These must be done within the kernel. Recall that the disable interrupt instruction is a privileged instruction and cannot be executed outside the kernel area. Actually, we can define a kernel based on privileged instructions. A kernel is that part of operating system within which we, as operating system designers, may use all instructions including privileged instructions. System calls (or kernel services) are procedures that are implemented within the kernel. Once again, in the implementation of most of these services, privileged instructions are used. A kernel service is usable (sometimes indirectly) by all upper layers of the operating system and even by any application program. It is the responsibility of the kernel to transfer messages among different concurrently running processes or threads of one computer or different computers.

A process that wants to send a message to another process will pass the message to the kernel. The kernel will do all the address resolutions (finding the physical destination) and will then pass the message to the receiver's kernel. The microkernel, being an abstract thin layer, is the best place to perform address resolutions. Communication protocols, such as **TCP/IP**, become part of the kernel address space after they are installed. Low-level thread or process management, low-level memory management, cache management, etc. must be part of the kernel. In the microkernel philosophy, we try to move as much functionality out of the kernel as possible and leave as little code as possible with the kernel. Only essential functionalities, like those mentioned above, are left by such kernels.

Mach is one example of microkernel-based distributed operating systems. It was developed at the Carnegie-Mellon University (CMU). Some operating system, such as Linux from GNU (Free Software Foundation) and MacOS (Macintosh Operating System) are developed on top of this microkernel. Mach provides a limited number of basic primitives to support process management, interprocess communication, message passing, memory management, and input/output operations.

11.3.3 Extensible Kernel Operating Systems

Extensible kernel methodology is yet another step towards downsizing kernels. The heart of extensible kernels is limited to protection and resource sharing facilities. Everything else is either moved to upper layers of the operating system or clustered into several libraries, each of which is used as a supplement to the kernel, as needed. It is assumed that computer users are computer professionals who can decide which libraries best match their specific needs. Otherwise they should use professional expert to taylor their operating system to match their needs. Computer users are given the opportunity to directly access computer hardware. The kernel no longer acts as a hardware abstraction layer. Theoretically speaking, an extensible kernel can be extended to become the kernel of the UNIX operating system, or of the Windows operating system or even MacOs operating system. This means that, extensible kernel facilities are so basic that an extensible kernel can grow into the kernel of any operating system, if proper complementary libraries are patched to it. Extensible kernels are built to accept new libraries as part of their internal structure. Similarly, it is possible to replace an existing library with a new one. The idea of the extensible kernel started at universities like MIT, where the **Exokernel** was developed, and Cambridge university. Several prototypes have emerged out of these along with other similar projects and experimental extensible kernel-based applications.

11.4 Hardware Structures and Operating Systems

A particular operating system cannot be used on all types of hardware structures. The efficiency of a system very much depends on the type of operating system being utilized. If an operating system that supports only one processor is installed on a multiprocessor system, the whole system is reduced to a single processor system, thus diminishing system utilization. In the following, four types of hardware structures are discussed and proper operating systems are identified.

11.4.1 Single-Processor Operating Systems

Most personal computers have only one processor which is called the CPU, for the time being. Most operating systems that support one processor are suitable for these computers. Contemporary work stations, mini computers, main frame computers, and supercomputers support more than one processor and, so, a **single-processor operating system** is not suitable for these computers. Even for personal computers, the trend is changing and most current PCs have more than one processor. Newly developed operating systems and even new versions of old operating systems support computers with more than one processor. A single processor operating system runs multiple processes, or threads, in a multiprogramming fashion. It is possible to have concurrently running processes within single-processor operating systems, but this does not mean that more than one process is simultaneously using the CPU. Although, these processes are all living within the computer, they are in different states of life, such as ready, wait, blocked, etc. Some might be printing their output, others might be doing disk I/O and yet others might be waiting for an event to occur. Compared to other types of operating systems, single-processor operating systems are simpler to analyze and implement.

11.4.2 Multiprocessor Operating Systems

It is the new trend for all operating systems, even for personal computer operating systems, to support multiprocessors just as recent personal computer main-boards facilitate having more than one processor. When talking about operating systems for multiprocessor systems, three categories of hardware structures come to mind:

1. **Separate kernel organization**: Every processor has a copy of the operating system kernel. The system is composed of a set of autonomous processors. Processor interactions are at a low level. To use common resources, the system makes use of common variables and memory areas. For example, using a common variable and a swap or exchange operation is a suitable way to guarantee mutual exclusion. The **separate kernel organization** cannot directly support concurrent execution of related tasks. On the positive side, losing one or more processors does not bring down the whole system.

2. **Master-slave organization**: The master processor the only one which has a copy of the operating system kernel. This configuration is called **master-slave organization**. A processor is distinguished and it is given the responsibility of running the operating system. By having only one copy of the operating system, operating system duties are performed in the simplest possible form. Resource sharing, interprocess communication, network communication, etc. are performed very similarly to single-processor multiprogramming systems. There is only one pool of requests and process or thread generation is done by using the master processors. The master processor has the responsibility of assigning processors to processes, or threads, for execution. Besides the operating system, the master processor can execute other processes in a multiprogramming fashion. The disadvantage of master-slave systems is that they are vulnerable to the master processor becoming the bottleneck of the system as it might not be fast enough to take care of all operating system duties in time. In such a case, the whole system efficiency suffers because the operating system is not able to fully utilize computer resources, especially slave processors. The master processor is also the single source of failure of the whole system, but this is less critical as hardware failures are very rare.

3. **Symmetric multiprocessor:** All processors share the same operating system kernel. The most common organization is the **Symmetric Multi-Processor** (SMP) organization. There is only one copy of the operating

system, but every processor is able to run it. The one which is executing the operating system at this time has the power, for example, to assign new tasks to other processors or even pick a task for itself. We can say this processor temporarily acts as the master processor. This organization has all the nice properties of the other two organizations. The failure of one processor cannot bring the whole system down and it is possible to schedule a set of related tasks to run simultaneously in this configuration. The current Windows operating system supports SMP organization with up to 32 processors. Other contemporary PC operating systems have similar capabilities.

11.4.3 Distributed Operating Systems

A distributed organization is a set of computers that are connected together using physical or wireless links. It is not necessary to have all computers locally and they can geographically be far apart. Links are supposed to be fast enough to facilitate efficient information interchange especially between concurrently running processes. The most important goal is to use the power of many computers within the distributed system to run concurrent parts of a complex and time-consuming process, like weather forecasting, in order to provide the required information in time. It may seem more natural to do the same task by using a centralized powerful supercomputer, but there are advantages, and of course disadvantages, in using distributed systems. There are so many computers and personal computers that are connected together via the Internet, but they are not being used all the time. This potential processing power can be used to solve lengthy problems. It is not only the processing power than can be used towards solving a common problem, but rather most of the resources can be used, for this purpose. The main memory of all computers may collectively be used as a common **Distributed Shared Memory** (DSM).

With the advances in computer hardware and communication, distributed organization has become possible. The challenge is in the design of an efficient operating system to utilize such a vast quantity of resources that is spread around the world. The difficulty arises when we wish to design operating systems that perform this complex task without the intervention of computer users and even without managerial activities being noticed by computer users. Extensive research activities are underway to resolve transparency issues, those dealing with operating system activities without the intervention and awareness of users.

11.4.4 Internet Operating Systems

With more than one and a half billion computers connected to the Internet and the growing trend of Internet users, a new technology, called **Internet Operating**

System (IOS), is emerging. Mobile computing has increased the already rapid growth of the number of computers that are potentially accessible through Internet. Not all the computers that are connected to the Internet are always active. Even when they are active, they are not fully utilized. There is an unlimited processing power, main memory capacity, file storage capacity, and resources of all kinds that are available on the Internet and awaiting a capable technology to correctly utilize them.

It is possible to develop an application using the Web services that are available on the Internet. This application may be composed of a vast collection of threads that may be executed concurrently by using many computers around the globe. It may require numerous amounts of resources that are not available locally. During its execution, there should not be any undesired side effects by other applications that are simultaneously running on the same platform. Smooth and fast information interchange between threads of this application during execution is an absolute necessity. It is also necessary for the whole system to be up and active for the duration of the application activity. We also need a programming language that can efficiently interact with the underlying **Internet Operating System** (IOS) to fulfill the requirements of the application during its execution.

There is a lot of ongoing research in the areas of IOS. Establishing efficient methods for resource discovery, especially processor power to run concurrent tasks, is underway. Resource management is a related area of research. We must make sure that an application running on the Internet does not have any unwanted side effects on other applications running simultaneously; applications should be "isolated" from each other. Another area of research is to assure that code and data can easily move from one computer to the other, so that **code and data mobility** is achieved.

Preliminary internet operating system products have been developed. **NetKernel** running on **Java Virtual Machine** (JVM), **REBOL/IOS**, and **Language for Advanced Network Architecture** (Lana) are examples of these products.

11.5 Timeliness and Operating Systems

Most operating systems do not guarantee that a submitted task will be executed by a given deadlock. For example, the objective of an operating system may be to maximize the throughput of the system. In other words, it must maximize the average number of tasks being served in one unit of time. New tasks are continuously being submitted and the system will always pick the task with the shortest execution time to execute next in order to maximize the throughput. A task which requires a long execution time will continuously be delayed in favor of tasks with shorter execution times tasks. Therefore, the longer task may indefinitely be delayed and the system cannot guarantee its execution at a given time. On the other hand, some applications require the system to execute time-critical tasks before a predefined period of time has passed. If we want to forecast the next hour's weather, but the system completes our program two hours later, the execution results are of no use.

11.5.1 Real-Time Operating Systems

In real-time systems, the correct (race-free) execution of processes is not adequate. There are tasks that have to be executed after their request is generated and before certain time span has passed. This is when in-time execution of real time tasks is an essential requirement of the system. In most real-time systems, each software process is set up to monitor/control the behavior of a physical device. For example, a process may be given the responsibility of periodically checking the altitude of an object, say an airplane, processing this data and comparing it to a threshold. If the object is at a low altitude level the process may be responsible for arranging an action or communicating the situation to other processes.

In **hard real-time systems**, failure to execute a process in time may cause a catastrophic situation in which people's lives are lost, for example, when the whole system (for example, a plane) has crashed, and/or capital investments vanish. Therefore, we must make sure that every process is executed in time. To do so, we are forced to use specific scheduling algorithms that are efficient and at the same time, make overrun-freeness analysis possible. A **soft real-time system**, on the other hand, might not crash as a result of a process being unable to execute in time, but there may be other less important side-effects. For example, in an Internet-based teleconference, parts of a conversation may be lost if related voice packets are not delivered in time.

For real-time systems, it is important to provide efficient ways to capture data, process them, and arrange actions. Fast and reliable methods for process communications is also an absolute requirement. The system must respond very quickly to important events. The most important of all is the scheduling of processes, as explained above. Ordinary operating systems are not designed to fulfill the requirements of a real-time system. For example, as explained in Chapter 6, they may distinguish between **real-time processes** and non real-time processes and give higher priority to real-time processes. However, that is not enough. A set of real-time processes may safely execute if a certain scheduling policy is adopted although there might be some process overrun, or failure to execute the process in time, if a different scheduling policy is adopted. **Real-time operating systems** are designed to be fast, efficient, timely, and reliable. At the same time, a real-time system is usually smaller than a regular operating system. Windows CE, QNX, and VxWorks are examples of real-time operating systems.

11.5.2 Non-Real-Time Operating Systems

The most important property of non-real-time operating systems is that there is no guarantee of the system executing requests in time for execution deadlines. Contemporary **Non-real-time operating systems** are designed to accept all kinds of processes with their scheduling policies designed to be "faire" to presumably everybody. Therefore, it is not possible to completely ignore non-real-time requests in favor of real-time requests. Here, rather than executing real-time processes before their deadline, the scheduling goal may be to reduce the average turnaround time while making sure that no request will wait more than a maximum time span.

11.6 Summary

Covering all aspects of all operating systems entails many textbooks with volumes upon volumes of information. A first book on operating system design and implementation of concepts and techniques can only touch upon principle subjects of ordinary contemporary operating systems. It was the goal of this chapter to introduce all categories of operating systems and within each category, present the basic principle topics of investigation. Fortunately, we were able to classify these topics into five major sections. Section one centered on software technologies that are used within the operating system. Monolithic, structured, object-oriented, and agent-oriented technologies fit into this category. Differently acting entities within the operating system, and even within the application programs, were covered in Section Two. Processes, threads, and agents make up these acting entities. Kernel types were the subject of Section Three. Macro-kernel, microkernel, and extensible kernels were talked about in this section. Operating system design is not independent of the hardware upon which it has to run. Single-processor, multiprocessor, distributed and Internet organizations were discussed in Section Four. This chapter ends with the subject of timeliness and operating systems. Real-time and non-real-time operating systems were presented in Section Five.

Recommended References

There are many fine books on the general subject of operating system concepts, methodology, design and implementation [Bac86, Crow96, Dav01, Han73, Mad74, Sil02, Sta11, Tan07, and Vah96]. The general theme of these books is single-processor multiprogramming operating systems. These books collectively cover all aspects such as monolithic, structured, process-based, thread-based, and macro-kernel operating systems. For the object-oriented benefits of software design and implementation, see [Boo07, Jac93]. For the thread concept and its application to operating systems, refer to references by Massalin and Pu [Mas89] and Kogan and Rowson [Kog88]. For an introduction to Mach microkernel see [Tan07] by A. Tanenbaum. For extensible kernels and Exo-kernel, look up [Ber95] by Bershad et al and [Eng94] by Engler et al. The book by Singhal and Shivarati describes distributed and multiprocessor operating system concepts [Sin94]. For real-time topics, study Buttazzo [But10]. Also, see the papers on real-time concepts by Liu and Layland [Liu73], Naghibzadeh and Fathi [Nag01], Naghibzadeh [Nag02], and Naghibzadeh and Kim [Nag03]. Back et al's book is a good reference on the design of the Java Operating System [Bac00].

References

[And89] Andleigh, P. K., UNIX System Architecture, Prentice Hall Inc., 1998.

[Bac86] Bach, M. J., The Design of the UNIX Operating System, Prentice-Hall, Englewood Cliffs, NJ, 1986.

[Bac00] Back, G., P. Tullman, L. Stoller, W. C. Hsieh, and J. Lepreau, Techniques for the Design of Java Operaing System, Proceedings of the USENIX Annual Technical Conference, San Diego, June 2000.

[Bar00] Bar, M., Linux Internals, McGraw-Hill, 2000.

[Bec02] Beck, M., H. Bohme, M. Oziadzka et al, Linux Kernel Programming, Third edition, Addison-Wesley, Reading, MA, 2002.

[Bel66] Belady, L. A., A study of Replacement Algorithms for a Virtual Storage Computer, IBM System Journal, No. 2, 1966.

[Bel69] Belady, L. A., R. A. Nelson, and G. S. Shedler, An Anomaly in Space-Time Characteristics of Certain Programs Running in Paging Environment, CACM, Vol. 12, No. 6., pp349-353, June 1969.

[Ben06] Ben-Ari, M., Principles of concurrent and distributed Programming, Second edition, Prentice-Hall, 2006.

[Ber95] Bershad, B. N., S. Savage, P. Pardyak, E. G. Sirer, M. Fiuczynski, D. Becker, S. Eggers, and C. Chambers, Extensibility, Safety and Performance in the SPIN Operating System. Symposium on Operating Systems Principles (SOSP), Copper Mountain, Colorado, December 1995.

[Bis04] Bishop, M., Introduction to Computer Security, Addison-Wesley Professional, 2004.

[Boo07] Booch, G., Object-Oriented Analysis and Design, Third edition, Addisson-Welsely Publishing Company, Reading, MA, 1994.

[Boy01] Bovet, D. P., and M. Cesati, Understanding the Linux Kernel, O'Reilly and Associates, 2001.

[Bri70] Brinch-Hansen, P., The Nucleus of a Multiprogramming System, Communications of the ACM, Vol 13, Number 4, pp238-241, 1970.

[Bur63] Burks, A. W., H. H. Goldstine, and J. Von Neumann, Preliminary discussion of the logical design of an electronic computing instrument. In Taub, A. H., editor, John Von Neumann Collected Works, The Macmillan Co., New York, Volume V, 34-79, 1963.

[But10] Buttazzo, G. C., Hard Real-Time Computer System: Predictable Scheduling Algorithms and Applications, Springer, Second edition, 2004.

[Cof71] Coffman, E. G., M. J. Elphick, and A. Shoshani, System Deadlocks, Computing Survey, Vol. 3, No. 2, pp67-78, 1971,

[Cro96] Charles Crowley, Operating Systems: A Design-oriented Approach, Irwin, USA, 1996.

[Dav01] Davis, W. S. and T. M. Rajkumar, Operating Systems: A Systematic View, Fifth edition, Addison-Wesley, Reading, Mass., 2001.

[Den68] Denning, P., The Working Set Model for Program Behavior, Communications of the ACM, May 1968.

[Dij65] Dijkstra, E. W., Cooperating Sequential Processes, Technical Report, Technological University, Eindhoven, the Nethrlands, pp43-112, 1965.

[Dij68a] Dijkstra, E. W., The structure of "THE"-Multiprogramming system, Communications of the ACM, Vol. 11, No. 5, p.341-346, May 1968.

[Dij68b] Dijkstra, E. W., Cooperating Sequential Processes, Academic Press, 1968.

[Dij71] Dijkstra, E. W., Hierarchical Ordering of Sequential Processes, Acta Informatica, Vol. 1, No. 2, pp115-138, 1971.

[Eng94] Engler, D., M. F. Kaashoek and J. O'Toole, The Operating Systems Kernel as a Secure Programmable Machine, Proc. of the 6th SIGOPS European Workshop, ACM SIGOPS, Wadern, Germany, Sep. 1994, pp62-67.

[Far03] Farhat, H. A., Digital Design and Computer Organization, CRC press, 2003.

[Gra72] Graham, G. S. and P. J. Denning, "Protection: Principles and Practice, Proc. Of AFIPS Spring joint compute conference, Vol. 40, pp417-429, 1972.

[Hab69] Haberman, A. N., Prevention of system deadlocks, CACM, Vol. 12, NO. 7, pp373-377, 1969.

[Han72] Brinch-Hansen, P., Structured Multiprogramming Systems, Communications of the ACM, Vol. 15, No. 7 pp574-578, 1972.

[Han73] Brinch-Hansen, P., Operaing System Principles, Prentice-Hall, 1973

[Hav68] Havender, J. W., Avoiding deadlock in multitasking Systems, IBM Systems Journal, Vol. 7. No. 2, pp74-84, 1968.

[Hay02] Hayes, J. P., Computer Architecture Organization, McGraw Hill, Third edition, 2002.

[Hoa72] Hoare, C. A. R., Towards a theory of Parallel Programming, in Hoare and Perrot, Operating System techniques, Academic press, NY, pp61-71, 1972.

[Hol71] Holt, R. C., On Deadlock in Computer Systems, Cornell University, Ithaca, NY, 1971.

[Hol72] Holt, R. C., Some Deadlock Properties of Computer Systems, ACM Computing Surveys, 4(3), pp179-196, 1972.

[Hor76] Horning, J. J. and S. Randall, Process Structuring, ACM Computing Survey 5(1), pp5-30, 1976.

[Hsi79] Hsio, D. K., D. S. Kerr, and S. E., Madnick, Computer Security, Academic Press, 1979.

[Hym66] Hyman, H., Comments on a Problem in Concurrent Programming Control, Communications of the ACM, January 1966.

[Jac98] Jacob, B. and T. Mudge, Virtual Memory in Contemporary Microprocessors, IEEE Micro, August 1998.

[Jac93] Jacobson, I., Is Object Technology Software's Industrial Platform?, IEEE Software Magazine, Vol. 10, No. 1, 1993.

[Kog88] Kogan, M. S., F. L, Rawson, The Design of the Operating System/2, IBM Systems Journal, 27(2), 1988.

[Lam74] Lamport, L., A New Solution of Dijkstra's Concurrent Programming Problem, Communications of the ACM, Volume 17, No. 8, pp453-455, 1974.

[Lam86] Lamport, L., The Mutual Exclusion Problem, Communications of the ACM, Vol. 33, No. 2, pp313-348, 1986.

[Lew96] Lewis, B., and D. Berg, thread primer, Prentice Hall, Upper Saddle River, 1996.

[Liu73] Liu, C. L. and J. W. Layland, Scheduling Algorithms for Multiprogramming in a Hard Real-time Environment, Journal of the ACM, 20(1), 1973.

[Los01] Loscocco, P. A. and S. Smalley, Integrating Flexible Support for Security Policies into the Linux Operating System, Proceedings of the FREENIX Track: 2001 USENIX Annual Technical Conference (FREENIX '01), June 2001.

[Mad74] Madnick, S. E. and J. J. Donovan, Operating Systems, McGraw-Hill, 1974.

[Mas89] Massalin, H. and C. Pu, Threads and Input/Output in the Synthesis Kernel, ACM Operating System Review, SIGOPS, Vol. 23, No. 5, 1989.

[Mau01] Mauro, J. and R. McDougall, Solaris Internals: Core Kernel Architecture, Prentice-Hall, 2001.

[Mck96] McKusick, M., K. Bostic, M. Karels, and J. Quartermain, The Design and Implementation of the 4.4BSD UNIX Operating System, Addison-Wesley, Reading, MA, 2000.

[Nag01] Naghibzadeh, M. and M. Fathi, Efficiency Improvement of the Rate-monotonic Scheduling Strategy, Third International Conference on Intelligent processing and Manufacturing of Materials, July 29-August 3, Vancouver, Canada, 2001.

[Nag02] Naghibzadeh, M., A modified Version of Rate-Monotonic Scheduling Algorithm and its efficiency Assessment, Seventh IEEE International

Workshop on Object-Oriented Real-time Dependable Systems, San Diego, USA, January 7-9, 2002.

[Nag03] Naghibzadeh, M. and K. H. Kim, The yielding-first rate-monotonic scheduling approach and its efficiency assessment, International Journal of Computer Systems Science and Engineering, CRL Publishing, Vol. 18 (3), 2003.

[Ogo01] O'gorman, J., Operating Systems with Linux, Palgrave, New York, NY, 2001.

[Pet81] Peterson, G. L., Myths About the Mutual Exclusion Problem, Information Processing Letter, Vol. 12, No. 3, 1981.

[Pfl06] Pfleeger, C., Security in Computing, Prentice Hall, Fourth edition, 2006.

[Pha96] Pham, T., and P. Garg, Multithreaded programming with Windows NT, Prentice Hall, 1996.

[Sil08] Silberschatz, A., P. B. Galvin, and Greg Gagne, Operating Systems Concepts, Eighth edition, Addison-Wesley, 2008.

[Sin94] Singhal, M. and N. G. Shivarati, Distributed, Database and Multiprocessor Operating Systems, Mcgraw-Hill, NY, 1994.

[Sol98] Solomon, D. A., Inside Windows NT, Second edition, Microsoft Press, 1998.

[Sol00] Solomon, David A., M. E. Russinovich, Inside Microsoft Windows 2000, Third edition, Microsoft Press, Redmond, 2000.

[Sta11] Stalling, W., Operating Systems, Seventh edition, Prentice Hall, 2011.

[Sta05] Stalling, W., Computer Organization and Architecture, Prentice Hall, Seventh Edition, 2005.

[Tan07] Tanenbaum, A. S., Modern Operating Systems, Third edition, Prentice Hall, Upper Saddle River, NJ, 2007.

[Vah07] Vahalia, Uresh, UNIX Internals: The New Frontiers, Prentice Hall, 2007.

Index

www.ingramcontent.com/pod-product-compliance
Lightning Source LLC
Chambersburg PA
CBHW051223050326
40689CB00007B/786